Fundamentals of
X Programming

Graphical User Interfaces
and Beyond

PLENUM SERIES IN COMPUTER SCIENCE

Series Editor: **Rami G. Melhem**
University of Pittsburgh
Pittsburgh, Pennsylvania

Fundamentals of
X Programming
Graphical User Interfaces and Beyond

Theo Pavlidis

State University of New York at Stony Brook
Stony Brook, New York

Springer Science+Business Media, LLC

Library of Congress Cataloging in Publication Data

Pavlidis, Theodosios.
    Fundamentals of X programming: graphical user interfaces and beyond / Theo Pavlidis.
        p.   cm.—(Plenum series in computer science)
    Includes bibliographical references.

    1. X Window System (Computer system) 2. Graphical user interfaces (Computer systems)
3. Computer programming. I. Title. II. Series.
QA76.76.W56P387   1999   98-56154
005.2'84—dc21   CIP

ISBN 978-1-4757-8256-1   ISBN 978-0-306-46968-8 (eBook)
DOI 10.1007/978-0-306-46968-8

© 1999 Springer Science+Business Media New York
Originally published by Kluwer Academic / Plenum Publishers in 1999.
Softcover reprint of the hardcover 1st edition 1999

10 9 8 7 6 5 4 3 2 1

A C.I.P. record for this book is available from the Library of Congress.

Preface

This book provides an overview of the X Window System focusing on characteristics that have significant impact on the development of both application programs and widgets. We pay special attention to applications that go beyond graphical user interfaces (GUIs); therefore we discuss issues affecting video games, visualization and imaging programs, and designing widgets with a complex appearance. While the book does not assume previous knowledge of X, it is intended for experienced programmers, especially those who want to write programs that go beyond simple GUIs.

X is the dominant window system under Unix, and X servers are available for Microsoft Windows, thus enabling graphics over a network in the PC world. While Java offers an apparently universal graphics library (the abstract window toolkit), the reality is quite different: For high-quality graphics and image display, we must program on the target platform itself (X or one of Microsoft's APIs) rather than rely on Java peer objects.

X is a vast subject, so it is impossible to provide a complete coverage in a few hundred pages. Thus we selected topics that are fundamental to the system, so that the reader who masters them should be able to read the documentation of the numerous libraries and toolkits. Therefore we provide documentation on the most important Xlib and X toolkit functions only.

Most of the existing X literature and X toolkits (such as *Motif*) focus on GUI applications. This excludes such applications as visualization, imaging, video games, and drawing programs. Such applications may have few windows and a relatively simple layout but the appearance of each window and the user interaction can be quite complex. Usually the applications programmer is left to struggle with the low-level Xlib library or to use an existing toolkit component (widget) for what it was not designed.

If the reader must write an application that cannot be readily assembled from the widgets of an existing toolkit, then it is necessary to understand not only drawing functions, but also such issues as resource definition, selections (for interclient communication), and widget writing. Even if we rely on an existing toolkit, understanding these issues clarifies the functionality of the components and their interactions with each other. Quite often the best solution for a complex application is to write an extension of a toolkit.

In discussing toolkits we tried to avoid limiting our description to a single toolkit, such as *Motif*, to emphasize concepts in contrast to implementation details. A small Starter toolkit is used for rapid prototyping and facilitating drawing operations that normally require low-level Xlib functions. The code of that toolkit as well as code in the examples can be obtained through anonymous ftp as described in Software Installation.

Stony Brook, New York   Theo Pavlidis

Acknowledgments

The text was extensively revised on the basis of comments from its early readers. Kevin Hunter (Ft. Myers) provided significant input on both the organization and coverage. C. J. Smith (Palo Alto) and Thomas G. Lane (Pittsburgh) had many useful comments and suggestions. I am also grateful to my students in the graduate window systems course for their feedback.

Sections 2.2.2, 2.4.1, 3.1.2, and 8.1.3 and Figures 2.1, 2.2, 3.1, 3.2, 3.3, 8.1, and 8.2 are excerpted from, and some other parts of Chapters 2, 8, and 9 are based on, *Interactive Computer Graphics in X* by Theo Pavlidis, © 1996, PWS Publishing, a division of International Thomson, Publishing, Inc. Used by permission.

Contents

Software Installation

Code for examples used in this book can be obtained via anonymous ftp from:

```
ftp.cs.sunysb.edu:/pub/TechReports/pavlidis/Xstart/
Xfund.tar.Z
```

After logging in and changing directory, execute the commands:

```
binary
get Xfund.tar.Z
```

If you are using a web browser you may skip the above steps and, instead, go to:
`ftp://ftp.cs.sunysb.edu/pub/TechReports/pavlidis/Xstart`
and then click on `Xfund.tar.Z`.

To extract the files, execute the two following Unix commands:

```
uncompress Xfund.tar.Z
tar -xvf Xfund.tar
```

Then read the README file for further instructions. There are two directories: `listings` and `starter`. The former contains 12 subdirectories, `ch01–ch12`, each of these contains the files mentioned in the listings of the respective chapter. If a listing does not mention a file name, then there is no file. (This is usually the case for short listings.) *There is no one-to-one correspondence* between files and listings. If many listings mention the same file name (e.g., `sel.c` in Chap. 10), then all the code in the listing is in that file, although not necessarily in the same order. The code of the Starter toolkit is in `starter`. To compile and run various programs, requires Release 4 or later of X.

Introduction

1.1.   OVERVIEW OF X

1.1.1.   Our Goal and Subject   Chapter 1 introduces most aspects of the X Window System. This quick tour of X discussed later in detail provides the context in which each part functions.

Some books use a large application as their central theme, so that by the end of the book, you have written a complete application. This is fine if you are lucky and the application described in the book is similar to the programs you want to write. If not, you are left in the dark because describing a single application may not touch upon aspects of the system that are essential for other applications. For example, graphical user interfaces (GUIs) use only a few colors and books focused on them rarely provide guidance on how to deal with applications such as image displays that need a large palette of colors. In this book we cover all fundamental aspects of X. Therefore you will have all the tools to write not only graphical user interface (GUI) program, but also video games, visualization, and drawing and design programs, which require a deeper understanding of the software platform than simple user interfaces.

Mastering the fundamental material makes it easier to use GUI toolkits because once you understand what such systems are trying to accomplish, you will have to find out only how they achieve their goal.

We assume that you have used a windowing system (not necessarily X), so that you are familiar with screens and such devices as the mouse. Windowing systems rely a lot on *user-driven programs*. Such programs are idle most of the time as they wait for user input or *messages* from other programs. Such actions cause the program to execute a piece of code and then return to the waiting state. Because user actions can be mapped into messages, the usual term for such programs is *message-driven*. The X Window system uses the term message for exchanges in client/server communication, and it uses the term *event* for user actions or messages between applications. Therefore we say that programs in X are *event-driven*. If you are already familiar with programming in another system, such as Microsoft Windows, you may assume that X events are synonymous with windows messages (although this may not be true in all instances). A related term is *interrupt-driven programming*, which is less general than the other terms. While most hardware interrupts are mapped into events (or messages), many events (or messages) do not correspond to interrupts.

1.1.2.   Main Features of the X Window System   The X Window System, developed in the late 1980s, not only enabled Unix workstations to have a GUI, but also made it possible to run applications over a *network*. That is a program running on machine Z can be displayed on and accept input from machine Y. In such a system, instructions that produce a display or describe events must be machine-independent. Machine independence is a major feature of the X Window System.

A system that supports user-driven window programs over a network needs the following parts:

1. Procedures that convert user actions into messages to be transmitted to the appropriate application program
2. Procedures that convert messages from the application program into display instructions.
3. Communications protocol for the messages in A and B.
4. Procedures that coordinate allocation of resources between different applications running on the same machine.

In the X Window System items 1 and 2 are functions of the *server* program. The name is counterintuitive because most people are familiar with *file servers*, machines that are (usually) far from the user and *clients*, machines that are in front of the users. In X the name server is used for both the machine in front of the user and for the program running on that machine that creates displays and converts user actions into events. The application program is called the client, again a counterintuitive term. Figure 1.1 shows a possible machine arrangement, where four client programs use the same server. It is also possible for a single client to use many servers and for a server program to run on another windowing system, for example Microsoft Windows NT.

The rules of communication between client and server are specified by the *X protocol*. Application programmers do not have to deal directly with the protocol

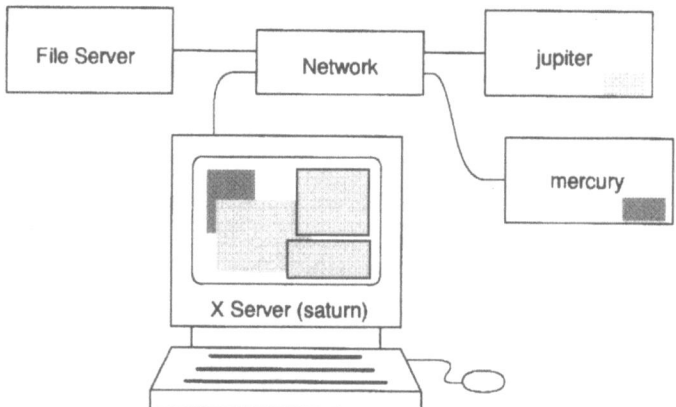

Figure 1.1. A network with four machines. The user is sitting in front of the machine Saturn, which is the X server. There are four open windows, each coded with a shade of gray corresponding to the machine (client) where the application is running. The light gray windows with frames are running on Saturn, which, is also the client for these applications.

because a library, called *Xlib*, of over 600 functions generates and interprets X protocol messages. While there is no one-to-one correspondence between Xlib functions and protocol messages, the connection is very close. Because the X protocol provides only rather primitive messages, Xlib functions are also rather simple in what they do, although rather complex in how they are invoked.

For example to draw a straight line segment, we call the function:

```
XDrawline(Dpy, w, g, x1, y1, x2, y2)
```

where the first three arguments refer to what maybe called the drawing environment and the last four are graphic data. (Dpy is equivalent to a file descriptor referring to the server, w refers to the window where the line will be drawn, and g refers to the *graphics context*, a data structure that contains information about the color, style, thickness, etc., of the segment to be drawn.)

In an interactive program, we must invoke a function that interrogates the server for events. One such Xlib function is

```
XNextEvent(Dpy, result)
```

where Dpy refers to the server and result is a pointer to a structure where the function places information about the first unexamined event from the server. Because the structure must accommodate all possible events, it is actually a union of about 30 structures, most of which have more than 10 members. Thus, even if the call appears simple, a lot more work is needed to find out what happened.

While various toolkits (see Sec. 1.1.3) may conceal the complexity of invoking Xlib functions, they cannot conceal the simplicity of what they do. In particular they (and the protocol) do not allow for definitions of procedures or macros. Thus to display a polygon with 100 vertices in different styles, you must do the scaling in the client, then resend the x, y coordinates of the vertices to the server each time: There is no way of creating high-level parametrizable server objects.

In X a separate application program, *the window manager*, provides the functionality of Item 4; therefore X servers are relatively simple programs. This is one reason for the quick adoption of the system. It is relatively easy for a hardware manufacturer to provide a program that interprets and generates X protocol messages for its devices, since the window manager is just a client (albeit an important one). The window manager is also responsible for supporting windowing system provisions that allow the user to invoke commands by pointing and clicking on a list or an icon.

Communication between the server and client is *asynchronous*: When the program generating the display produces a message, it is usually buffered rather than immediately sent. This delay does not normally pose a problem except in two situations. The first is debugging (discussed in Sec. 1.4.3); the second involves messages from programs that perform lengthy computations or handle large files, such as `Please wait while loading the next frame`. We must flush the buffer explicitly to ensure that the message appears when it is supposed to.

X Releases

There have been seven releases of X. The X directory name usually includes the release number, thus `X11R6` indicates the sixth release. The fourth release had new major contributions to the fundamentals of the system. Later releases dealt with more advanced features, so you should be able to run our example programs on your system if you have Release 4 or later.

1.1.3.   Programming in X   Programming in most windowing systems is laborious because for even a trivial program, we must provide significant code to create a window and handle events or messages. The task is particularly difficult in X because the system was designed as a standard to handle all cases that its designers knew. As a result structures and functions in X involve parameters that do not concern most applications. In this book we start with simple versions of various structures so that concepts become clear, then we gradually move to the real thing. Our goal is to understand the organization of systems and their different parts rather than describe all function calls in detail.

The basic software library of X is Xlib, the primitive functions that deal with protocol messages, as mentioned in Sec. 1.1.2. Because programming with Xlib can be very laborious various toolkits have been developed.

Definition

A *toolkit* is a collection of objects and functions.

Toolkits can be *fundamental*, built directly on top of Xlib, or *derived*, built on top of another toolkit. There are two widely used fundamental toolkits: the X toolkit (abbreviated Xt) and the Tk toolkit. The Tk is related to Tcl, an interpretive language, and it is by far the simplest toolkit for creating GUIs. The Xt, which is part of the X Window System, forms the basis for many other toolkits. It is the fundamental toolkit discussed in this book.

There are three widely used toolkits built on top of Xt: Athena has rather limited facilities, but it is part of the X distribution, which means that it is available on any system running X. Motif, the most common commercial toolkit, is the standard in many environments. The Open Look (OLIT) is still used on many SUN systems, but it seems to be declining in importance.

While there is a `Window` object in X, it is too low a level structure to be useful by itself, therefore applications rely on toolkits to create higher level objects (`widgets`), which are windows with functionality. The latter includes not only the appearance of the window and handling user input but also responding when a message from another program is received. The *Interclient Communication Conventions Manual (ICCCM)* specifies how X programs should communicate with each other, and all X applications are supposed to follow it. Its requirements include support of cut-and-paste operations. If you use Xt (or one derived from it), the task of conforming to ICCCM is greatly simplified.

We often hear the claim that if you program in, say, Motif (or another toolkit) you will not need to use Xlib; unfortunately this is true only for relatively simple GUIs. If you must draw something on a window or display an image, *you must use* Xlib *functions*. For this and other reasons, programming in X remains quite complex even when using one of the major toolkits. Section 1.3 discusses toolkits and software libraries whose main purpose is to deal with either the complexity of X or using X in special applications, such as three-dimensional graphics. There are also many software tools for building X applications interactively; however, that topic is beyond our scope.

Caution

This book is *not* a programming manual. We assume that you have access to manuals for Xlib, the X toolkit, and your favorite toolkit (such as Motif).

1.1.4. Note for Those Familiar with Microsoft Windows Similarities and differences between the X Window System and Microsoft Windows are obscured by inconsistent terminology. We already pointed out the case when a different term is used for similar concepts (event versus message), there are also cases when the same term is used with different meanings. An X window is a much simpler structure than a Microsoft window. The X widgets (see Sec. 1.2.1) come closer to Microsoft windows, but it may be necessary to use more than one widget to create in X an entity whose functionality is comparable to that of a single Microsoft window. Creating new window classes (widget classes) in X is more complex than in Microsoft Windows, so this process should not be undertaken lightly.

The X resources (see Sec. 1.2.2) serve a similar purpose (selecting run-time parameters from a file) as resources in Microsoft Windows, but there are major differences between the two. It is probably best to forget what you know about resources in Microsoft Windows when reading about resources in X.

Drawing functions in Windows are called with a handle to a device context (DC) as their first argument. In Xlib functions that argument is replaced by three. X has a graphics context that is related to, but not the same as, device context. In general drawing parameters are handled more cleanly in X than in Windows because X did not have to worry about backward compatibility.

On the other hand overall program structure is the same: The X event loop is similar to the Windows message loop, and the event-dispatching mechanism has similar (but not identical) functionality to the message-dispatching mechanism. X programs rely a lot on callback procedures as do Windows programs, although the details differ.

In general X allows greater fine tuning of programs than does Microsoft Windows; however, it is much easier to write a fully functional simple program in Microsoft Windows than in X. Roughly speaking the Microsoft Windows API corresponds to Xt functions with only the drawing operations API at the Xlib level.

1.2. HIGHLIGHTS OF THE X TOOLKIT

1.2.1. Simple Program Using the X Toolkit   The X toolkit, discussed in detail in Chaps. 3–7, consists of a library of functions, the *intrinsics*, and a set of structures (objects), the *widgets*, that are helpful in creating windows with particular properties. However since Xt objects are rather rudimentary, we need additional widgets for building an application. This had led to various derived toolkits such as Athena, Motif, or OLIT. Here we provide an example in order to show the flavor of Xt code. Listing 1.1 shows an Xt program (using Athena widgets) that creates a window labeled Hello World. When the user presses the left mouse button, the program exits, closing the window.

There are five function calls:

- XtVaAppInitialize establishes a connection to the server and creates the framework for creating windows with functionality.
- XtVaCreateManagedWidget creates the structure supporting a window that displays a message and has the capacity to respond when the application user presses the left mouse button.
- XtAddCallback specifies what the response to the action should be: When the *left* mouse button is pressed while the pointer (cursor) is in the

Listing 1.1. A Trivial Xt Program

```
/*  A Trivial Xt Toolkit Program (using Athena
widgets)     */
/*  The argument structure is explained in Chapter 4     */
#include <X11/StringDefs.h>
#include <X11/Intrinsic.h>
#include <X11/Xaw/Command.h>
int main (int arc, char **arv)
{
  Widget toplevel, button;
  XtAppContext app;
  extern exit();
  /*  Initialize the Application     */
  toplevel=XtAppInitialize( &app, "Trivial",
    NULL, 0, &arc, arv, NULL, NULL);
  /*  Create a widget structure     */
  button=XtVaCreateManagedWidget ("button",
    CommandWidgetClass, toplevel, XtNlabel, "Hello World",
    XtNwidth, 256, XtNheight, 256, NULL);
  /*  Arrange so that when a mouse button     */
  /*  is pressed the application exits     */
  XtAddCallback (button, XtNcallback, exit, NULL);
  /*  Request that the windows be displayed     */
  XtRealizeWidget (toplevel);
  /*  Enter an Infinite Loop     */
  XtAppMainLoop (app);
  return (0);
}
```

window of the widget, the function exit () is called. (This is *not* a clean design, but it suffices for the trivial program at hand.)

- XtRealize Widget creates windows in the server so these appear on the screen.
- XtAppMainLoop() is a loop that checks for events.

We discuss these functions in detail in later chapters, but it is worth pointing out here some features of the Xt. The first string argument in XtVaCreate-ManagedWidget is used as an internal name, the second argument refers to the class of objects to which the new widget will belong. The intrinsics store widgets in a tree (the *widget tree*), which is used to access the widgets. Thus each new widget must have a parent in the tree, which is the role of the argument `toplevel`, in addition to providing a parent window for the window of the `button` widget.

The remaining arguments are a NULL terminated list of pairs, each consisting of a symbolic string and a value. Symbolic strings are defined in one of the Xt include files, for example:

```
#define XtNlabel  "label"
#define XtNwidth  "width"
#define XtNheight "height"
```

This mechanism makes the order of most arguments in a function unimportant at the expense of having to provide twice as many arguments. Using symbolic names rather than explicit strings guards against misspellings, since if we type `XtNlibel` instead of `XtNlabel`, the compiler will complain

```
XtNLibel undefined
```

However, if we type `"libel"`, the compiler will accept it and Xt ignores the pair, so that we obtain the default label instead.

Symbolic names are also used for user actions, for example we say that the program responds when the user presses the left mouse button but we do not see any reference to such a button in Listing 1.1. However, it is implied by the symbolic string `XtNCallback`, where the term *callback* refers to a function called in response to some event. The X toolkit widget associates specific events with *callback lists* that initially maybe empty. The applications programmer places real functions in that list with calls of the `XtAddCallback()` function.

To compile and link this program, we must find the location of relevant libraries in our system. These usually reside in the same directory as the Xlib functions. Assuming that everything is in the directory `/usr/local/X11R6`, we can use the following makefile:

```
INC_FILE=usr/local/X11R6/include
LIB_FILE=/usr/local/X11R6/lib
CFLAGS=-I$(INC_FILE)
xt: xt.o
    $(CC)-L$(LIB_FILE) xt.o -1Xaw -1Xmu -1Xext -1Xt -1X11
-o xt
```

The flags `-1Xaw -1Xmu -1Xext` are needed to access the Athena toolkit.

1.2.2. Resources and Translations   The Xt uses pairs of arguments for a more important reason than the convenience of passing arguments to functions without worrying about their order: such representations provide run-time parameter values to many programs. When a widget is created the intrinsics look at a *resource* database for values of the widget parameters. The files for such a database may contain such entries as Listing 1.2 shows.

Listing 1.2 also illustrates using the first argument of the function `XtVaCreateManagedWidget()` to identify resources associated with a particular widget.

Because such files can be modified by the user resources allow us to customize of X programs. The Xt defines a structure, `XtResource`, with members that include the name, a default value, a pointer to the memory location where the value will be stored, etc. Try this approach by modifying the program in Listing 1.1 so the `button` widget is created by the statement:

```
button=XtVaCreateManagedWidget ("button",
    commandWidgetClass, toplevel, NULL);
```

Then create a filed called, say, RESOURCE containing the three lines in Listing 1.2 and execute

```
setenv XENVIRONMENT RESOURCE
```

This tells Xt where to look for the resource file for our program. (The X toolkit always looks for resources in certain files so the preceding statement is not always necessary; however, without it we must find those files, then edit them!) When we type xt the window opens with the new dimension and the capitalized label. We continue changing the appearance of the window by editing the RESOURCE file without recompiling the program. We must rerun the program though, since resource values in the environment are checked only when the program starts.

The Xt also allows us to specify events that trigger certain actions, such pairings are defined in resource files by the following lines:

```
xt*canvas.translations: <ButtonPress>: quit()
```

Listing 1.2. Example of Resources

```
xt*button.label: PRESS
xt*button.width: 100
xt*button.height: 100
```

where `translations` is a keyword that takes the place of a resource name (`canvas` is the widget name). The second field is the event that causes the invocation of a function referred to in the third field. However the syntax is misleading: The last entry does not specify a function [parentheses `()` are decorative] but a string that must be matched internally with a function. In other words *the user cannot change the function*, only the event that causes its invocation. For example the following line causes the function *corresponding* to the string `quit` to be invoked when the escape key is pressed

```
xt*canvas.translations: <Key>Escape: quit ()
```

Section 3.2 discusses the use of resources in detail, and Sec. 3.3 discusses the definition of resources.

1.2.3.   Widgets   In X terminology, a window is an area of the screen without functionality, and widgets are windows with functionality. Functionality refers to the appearance of the window (for example a clock) and the response to user actions (for example a window that is a menu).

In X the term widget is used for both what appears on the screen and the internal representation of the object. Code in Listing 1.3 is an example of such an object, tremendously simplified from Xt implementations, hence the term *miniwidget*. This object has eight attributes and two methods. Five of the attributes contain information about the geometry of the window `x`, `y`, `width`, `height`, and `border_width`. Two (`background_color`, and `border_color`) contain information about the color of the main window area and its border. There is also a handle (`window`) to the server structure representing the window itself.

The functionality is provided mainly by two methods: One for creating the appearance of the window and the other for handling mouse events (usually buttonclicks). Note: Objects of Xt widgets are much larger structures. We use simplified versions to focus on key concepts of the system without being burdened

Listing 1.3.   A Widget Object

```
#include <X11/Xlib.h>
typedef struct _mini_widget {
    int     x, y, width, height, border_width ;
    int     background_color, border_color;
    Window  window;
    void    (*paint) ();
    void    (*mouse) ();
} mini_widget;
```

by details. (Incidentally the type `Widget` in Listing 1.1 is a pointer to the widget structure.)

paint () is called whenever the window has to be drawn, either when it is first created or when it becomes visible after being obscured by other windows or after being resized. (X does not guarantee window backup.) The syntax of the call is usually:

```
mini_widget w;
/*...*/
w.paint(&w);
```

Making the drawing function a member of the structure simplifies the program code. In general different window objects require different drawing functions, so if we do not associate a drawing function with each object, we need a loop or switch any time we draw an object.

A method can be provided either by the widget writer or the applications writer. In the former case windows corresponding to that object have a fixed appearance in all applicants that use them. (Although applications may set such parameters, as the dimensions or colors used by the drawing function.) As a rule the drawing function of most widgets is provided by the widget writers; the exception is *canvas* or *drawing area* widgets whose appearance is determined by either the application (in a video game) or the user (in a drawing program). Event handling is almost always implemented by the widget writer. At most applications provide pointers to functions that are called by (the equivalent of) mouse () in response to particular events.

1.3. SIMPLIFYING X

1.3.1. Challenges Two challenges face X programmers: Both Xt and toolkits based on it are heavily oriented to GUIs, so they focus on widgets of pre-defined appearance. While all provide widgets where we can draw, they do not provide support for drawing operations, we must use the Xlib functions for both drawing and event handling. The situation is actually worse: Even widgets intended for drawing *inherit* properties of the general widget set that impose certain restrictions on what can be drawn. Major toolkits (such as Motif) have widgets that *allow* but do not *support* drawing.

The other challenge is the relatively flat nature of function calls in both Xlib and Xt. We need pretty much the same calls to start a trivial application as a complex one. The program Hello World in Listing 1.1 contains 15 lines of code. This situation can be compared to C library output functions for example. There we start with `printf()`, which produces output only at the terminal; output into files comes next with redirection, >; only when it is necessary to write to multiple files do we learn about `fprintf(file_des, ... )`. Even later we learn about `fwrite()` and `fseek()`.

There have been many efforts to address these issues. The Tk toolkit [Ou94] is excellent, particularly in handling the second challenge, but it must be used by itself; it cannot be mixed with Xt code (including Motif). OpenGL [Kr96] is a window system independent library that provides very good functionality for drawing operations, especially for three-dimensional graphics. OpenGL code can be mixed with other Xt code, however, OpenGL does not address the second challenge except to a limited extent through an auxiliary library. In addition the X implementation of OpenGL requires an Xlib extension (GLX) that may not be available on many servers.

Numerous libraries provide simpler interfaces to X, but most of them are self contained. The important issue in meeting the second challenge is to use simple code for a prototype program but then use the full power of X. We may also wish to develop a program with some parts that require sophisticated code, while the rest of the program is simple. This is the case in our examples where we consider a particular feature of X.

For this purpose we developed the *Starter toolkit*, which pays special attention to the needs of drawing programs and the issue of migrating from simple to complex code. This toolkit can be used by itself for simple programs or combined with any toolkit derived from Xt for more complex programs. See Sec. 1.3.2. for an overview of the toolkit and Appendix for a full description.

1.3.2.   Starter Toolkit   The Starter toolkit is based on Xt and *supports* drawing and graphic displays so that it is useful in programs that perform many drawing operations. The toolkit is also designed to facilitate the user's introduction to X and to make it easier to write prototype programs. We use it in this text mainly to create *complete* X programs that need features of the system that we have not yet covered. The Appendix describes how to install and use the Starter toolkit, and it also documents its functions used in examples in this book.

We illustrate the capabilities of the Starter toolkit with a few examples. Listing 1.4 shows a program that displays a single message. The program exits when the user presses any button; thus it has the same functionality as the (much longer and more complex) program in Listing 1.1.

Because the Starter toolkit is built on top of Xt, we can write more complex programs by combining Xlib and Intrinsics calls with Starter toolkit calls. With such programs it is desirable to use a special prefix for Starter toolkit functions. If we include a definition file, `Stdef.h`, we can use function names with the prefix `St_`. The example of Listing 1.5 tests X facilities for automatically *iconifying* (or

Listing 1.4. A Hello World Program

```
void hello()
{
    put_text ("The end of the world is near", 20, 20);
}
main()
{
    vis_window(hello);
}
```

Listing 1.5. A Window that Iconifies Itself

```
#include <X11/StringDefs.h>
#include <X11/Intrinsic.h>
#include <X11/Shell.h>
#include <Stdef.h>
void hello(Widget w)
{
    St_put_text("The end of the world is near", 20, 20);
    St_xflush(); /* to actually display the message */
    sleep (1);
    XtVaSetValues(XtParent(w), XtNiconic, False, NULL);
    XtVaSetValues(XtParent(w), XtNiconic, True, NULL);
}
main()
{
    St_vis_window(hello);
}
```

minimizing) an application that is displaying its window in reduced size, as an icon. It uses the special prefix for the Starter toolkit functions.

XtVaSetValues() is an Intrinsics function that changes the attributes of a widget. In this case its first call requires the widget to be displayed in full size, then to be displayed as a small icon. When the attribute corresponding to the resource XtNiconic changes from False to True, Intrinsics iconifies the widget.

The Starter toolkit supports drawing operations by means of a new widget class, the PaperWidgetClass. Support is achieved in the following ways:

- The widget has its own writable graphics context so that application programmers do not have to create it explicitly; however, they are allowed to modify it by using simple convenience functions.
- The widget has function wrappers for many Xlib functions and a general context function, St_draw_area (), so that we can write such code as:

```
St_draw_area(left_window);
St_put_text("Left", 5, 20);
St_draw_area(right_window);
St_out_text("Right", 5, 20);
```

- The widget has a simplified event structure that provides concise information about events involving the mouse or the keyboard.
- There are no constraints on the widget's use of color, so we can use all available colors to display an image.

1.4.   ODDS AND ENDS

1.4.1.   A Few Words on Display Hardware   A description of computing or display hardware is beyond the scope of this text; however, we provide a very rough outline for future reference.

Most modern display devices center on a piece of memory, called the *frame buffer* or *refresh memory*, whose contents are used to modulate the beams of a television monitor. (Refresh refers to the need to continuously refresh the image displayed on the monitor.) The piece of hardware called the *video look-up table*, translates bit patterns of the refresh memory into the three basic colors—red, green, and blue. Another name for that hardware is *physical colormap*. The table of correspondence between the bit patterns and colors is usually not fixed, so it can be loaded at execution in time. It is called the *colormap* (or *logical colormap* to distinguish it from the device).

The memory unit that determines color and brightness of a single spot on the display screen is called a *pixel* (which usually consists of 8 bits, although 1-bit and 24-bit pixels are also common). The term *plane* refers to the corresponding bits of all pixels. A single plane is also called a *bitmap*, and a set of planes, a *pixmap*. These terms are also used for memory outside the refresh memory, when such memory is equivalent to a part of the refresh memory. For example we may compose an image *off line* in a pixmap, when we finish the composition, we may copy the pixmap to refresh memory for display. See a graphics book for more details on the hardware (for example, sec. 1.2, [Pa96]).

When placing information in the refresh memory, we have various options on how to combine the new information with what exits there. *Replacement* (or *copy*) mode refers to discarding and replacing old information with the new. We may also select any logical or arithmetic operation. The X supports only bitwise logical operations of which the most important is *exclusive OR* (or *XOR*). This mode lets us use the same call for erasing and drawing. Indeed, if *a* and *b* are pixel values, we have

$$(a \text{ XOR } b) \text{ XOR } b = a$$

Other drawing modes include *clear* where each pixel is set to 0 and *set* where each pixel is set to 1.

Most display devices support the concept of *foreground* and *background* colors. Many drawing instructions that write into the refresh memory do not have an explicit argument specifying the color. Instead they use the foreground color for pixels that are set and the background color for pixels that are cleared. This arrangement lets us store drawing information in bitmaps, then present it in different colors just by changing foreground and background values.

X uses the term *screen* to refer to the combination of refresh memory and look-up table, since a particular server may have more than one hardware display. It is also possible to have different logical configurations for the same hardware. In most installations there is only one screen, so in this text we use the terms screen or display screen without further specification. Whenever information about the screen is needed for a program, it is obtained by using a macro returning the display's default screen. X has an additional complication because screens can be referred to either through an integer (the screen number) or by a pointer to a screen structure. The latter specifies a screen by itself, the former only with respect to a particular display. For example to find the bit pattern corresponding to black color, we may use either of the two following macros:

```
BlackPixel(display_pointer, screen_number)
```

or

```
BlackPixelofScreen(screen_pointer)
```

The screen number is obtained using the macro:

```
screen_number=DefaultScreen(display_pointer);
```

The screen pointer using the macro

```
screen_pointer=DefaultScreenOfDisplay(display_pointer);
```

A macro also converts the screen pointer into the screen number:

```
screen_number=XScreenNumberOfScreen(screen_pointer);
```

Chapters 8 and 9 give examples of programs with such macros when we discuss drawing operations in X as well as additional display hardware issues.

1.4.2. A Few Words on Software   Since X makes extensive use of special types, symbolic names, and bit masks, we present a brief review of these concepts. Consider for example the Xlib call that asks a server to keep track of button press events in a window:

```
XSelectInput(Dpy, w, ButtonPressMask);
```

where Dpy is a pointer to a structure that includes a file descriptor used to access a server (an application may use more than one server). w an integer translated by the server into a pointer to a structure, refers to the window. Such integers are commonly called *handles*, and these are widely used in object-oriented programming. X assigns a special type for such handles, *X Identity Number* or XID, which is defined by the statement:

```
typedef unsigned long XID;
```

A special window type is defined as:

```
typedef XID Window;
```

In a program listing the second argument can be declared by the code:

```
Window w;
```

The third argument, ButtonPressMask, is actually one of the constants defined in the file x.h

```
/* ... */
#define ButtonPressMask          (1L<<2)
#define ButtonReleaseMask        (1L<<3)
#define Button1MotionMask        (1L<<8)
/* ... */
```

```
#define ButtonPress        4
#define ButtonRelease      5
/* ... */
#define Button1            1
/* ... */
```

For example to select both button press and button release events we must call

```
XSelectInput(Dpy, w, ButtonPressMask | ButtonReleaseMask);
```

Then the mask value is (in binary notation) 0 ... 0110. Notice that not all symbolic constants can be used as masks.

Masks are quite often used for selecting members of structures. We illustrate that use with a nonX example to keep things simple. Suppose we are dealing with points in the space, where each point has three coordinates and a color:

```
typedef struct {
    int x, y, z;
    unsigned char * c;
} Point;
```

We can create a single routine for copying points and use a flags to determine which coordinates are actually copied, for example:

```
#define Xcoord      1    /* or (1L) */
#define Ycoord      2    /* OR (1L<<1) */
#define Zcoord      4    /* or (1L<<2) */
#define ALLCoord    7    /* or Xcoord | YCoord | Zcoord */
#define Color       8    /* or (1L<<3) */
copy_paint (Paint *src, Paint *dest, long mask)
{
    if (mask & Xcoord) dest ->x=src ->x;
    if (mask & Ycoord) dest ->y=src ->y;
    if (mask & Zcoord) dest ->z=src ->z;
    if (mask & Color)  dest ->c=src ->c:
}
```

Note: The if statements contain the bitwise AND operator (&), not the logical AND operator (&&). In the following code fragment, the first call copies color and the z-coordinate, while the second call copies all coordinates but no color:

```
Point A, B, C;
/* ... */
copy_point(&A, &B, Zcoord|Color);
copy_point(&B, &C, ALLcoord);
```

In some cases it is convenient to include the mask as a member of the structure, especially of operations are not performed between structures of the same kind or if the variables are uninitialized, for example:

```
typedef struct {
    long mask;
    int x, y, z;
    unsigned char * c;
} Point;
Print_Point (Point *pnt)
{
  if (pnt ->mask & Xcoord) printf("x=%d ", pnt ->x);
  if (pnt ->mask & Ycoord) printf("y=%d ", pnt ->y);
  if (pnt ->mask & Zcoord) printf("z=%d ", pnt ->z);
  if (pnt ->mask & Color) printf("Color=%o ", pnt ->c);
  if (pnt ->mask & (ALLcoord|Color) ) printf("\n");
}
```

Using masks reduces the number of necessary functions. If it is desirable, we can hide the masks through such *convenience* functions as:

```
copy_Z_coord(Point *src, Point *dest)
{
    copy_point(src, dest, Zcoord);
}
```

The Xlib contains many such sets: A basic function called with masks and convenience functions that call the former with appropriate mask values.

1.4.3.   Special Issues in Debugging X Programs   Because each X program has two parts, each running as a different process (and possibly on a different machine), debugging can be challenging.

Important Point:

Because of asynchronous communication between client and server, when the server part of the program crashes, the problem cannot be attributed to the last message sent. It may well be the result of an earlier one.

Therefore it is desirable during development to force a synchronous mode. When programming directly with Xlib, we can do so by using the sequence:

```
Dsp = XOpenDisplay( .... );
XSynchronize(Dsp, 1);
```

When we finish development, the XSynchronize () must be removed because it slows down the program execution. Things are a bit easier with the Xt: We need only set a flag at execution time:

```
my_executable   -synchronous
```

Failure in the server produces a diagnostic describing the nature of the error but little else as the following example shows.

```
X  Error of failed request:
   BadDrawable (invalid Pixmap or Window parameter)
   Major opcode of failed request:  53 (X_CreatePixmap)
   Resource id in failed request:  0x1388
   Serial number of failed request:  115
   Current serial number in output stream:  136
```

The first line states the nature of the error, BadDrawable. This suggests that we passed an invalid argument in an Xlib function where a window or pixmap is expected. If our program contains only one such statement, we know where it occurred; otherwise we must look further. The second line refers to the X protocol number and the third to the server memory, which is of help only if we suspect the server to be at fault. The last two lines give the message number. Failure occurred at Message 115, while Message 136 has also been sent. If we ran the same program with the -sync flag, the last two lines would be

```
Serial number of failed request:  226
Current serial number in output stream:  227
```

(or possibly another pair of successive numbers). This is not very helpful either, but in this case we could have used a debugger, such as dbx, to run the application side step by step, so that the failure would have occurred right after the statement with the invalid parameter.

Problems on the application side can be handled with conventional tools with one caveat: If we debug an interactive program that expects input, there may be

contention between the debugger and the program being debugged. This can lock
the screen, so that to continue processes must be killed from another machine.
Therefore we may wish to recompile the program with sufficient diagnostic output,
then run it without the debugger.

1.5. CONCLUSIONS

1.5.1. Other Systems—Simple and Complex Servers

The server–client
model is used by most modern systems that support user-driven programming even
if the separation of the two parts is not so complete as in X. For example the *Win32
API* (Application Program Interface) in Microsoft Windows can be thought of as the
Xlib counterpart in Windows programming. While it is possible to bypass the
`Win32` subsystem, it is not recommended if an application is going to be portable
across various Microsoft Window platforms.

The major issue in all window systems is the functionality of the server. As
pointed out in Sec. 1.1.2, the X server is very simple. The SUN NeWS server is
based on the Postscript language that allows the creation of procedures. The *Blit*
terminal developed at AT&T Bell Labs in the early 1980s was fully programmable
[Pi83]. An application downloaded a customized server module each time it was
executed. While this caused an initial delay, it made for much faster execution later
as the following example indicates.

Consider a pop-up menu. When the user presses the right mouse button, a
small window containing a list of items pops up. As the user moves the mouse (with
the button still pressed), the item under the cursor is highlighted. When the user
releases the button, a selection is made (provided the cursor is still within the menu
window). In X drawing the menu and highlighting items must be done through the
client. The server creates events that the client interprets and issues drawing
instructions. In a server with procedures, we can create a menu selection procedure
so that no message has to be sent to the client until a selection is made.

Rubber band drawing programs offer another example (see for example, sec.
2.4, [Pa96]). As the user moves the mouse, a line joining the cursor with an anchor
point is erased and redrawm in the new position. Thus any time the mouse moves,
an event is placed in the queue, the client reads the queue, receives the mouse
location, then issues two line-drawing instructions, one to erase and another to
redraw the line. It is much faster if all motion events are kept in the server and the
callback for the event is a server procedure.

These issues are important today when personal computers without disc space
and with limited power are used to browse networks. Their programs are stored at
remote sites, then run on remote machines producing output on, and receiving input
from, the local machine. If the local machine is an X server this entails significant

traffic, which may create serious delays. The initial delay in downloading procedures may be preferable to a continuous sluggish response; this is certainly the case with a video game.

1.5.2.   Further Reading about X   Many books describe the basic graphics hardware and software, [Pa96] does so in the context of X. In this book we focus on the concept of X programming, but we do not provide details about the functions of the various libraries, so the user needs the respective manuals: [Ny92] is recommended as a source for Xlib functions; for an in depth coverage of X see [SG92]. For Xt we recommend [AS90]. [Ki95] provides more examples and a documentation of Motif and Athena.

The user also needs a manual of whatever other toolkit is being used: Motif, Athena, or OLIT. O'Reilly and associates publish many books on X, including those completely documenting Motif and Xt. For complete alternatives to X, as discussed in Sec. 1.3.1, see [Ou94] and [Kr96]. A search of the web will reveal many efforts to simplify X programming, especially in educational environments.

1.6.   PROJECTS

1.   Compile and run the program in Listing 1.1. Use suggestions at the end of Sec. 1.2.1 to locate the necessary libraries.
2.   Modify the definition of Listing 1.3 to allow for resources. (You must replace some of the attributes by pairs of strings and values and add methods for changing attribute values.)
3.   Use the Starter toolkit to write a program that reads text from its standard input (or a file) and displays each word in a different color.

2

Fundamentals of the X Window System

2.1.   INTRODUCTION

While most X programming is done through higher level toolkits, a review of low-level structures helps in understanding the capabilities of the system. Furthermore certain applications, such as graphic displays, cannot be written entirely with available toolkits.

We pointed out (Sec. 1.1.2) that applications run on the client machine and send messages to, or receive messages from, the server machine, which does the actual display and receives user input. Message structure, is specified by the X protocol. Messages are generated or interpreted by the functions of Xlib. Chapter 2 focuses on structures used by Xlib as well as functions pertaining to window creation and events. We defer discussion of drawing functions to Chaps. 8 and 9.

2.1.1.   Program Illustrating Basic Concepts   Listing 2.1 shows a program that creates a trivial application using only Xlib calls. The program creates and displays a window that exits when the user presses a mouse button. This program has a functionality similar to that of the program in Listing 1.1 except for the label (which required too much additional code). We use this program to explore some basic Xlib concepts.

The program starts by establishing a connection to the server [the call to XOpenDisplay()], and it ends by closing the connection (the call to XCloseDisplay). The argument of XOpenDisplay() is supposed to be the name of the server, but using the null string makes the program more flexible. When the function is called with an empty string (" ") as an argument, it takes its destination from the Unix shell environment variable DISPLAY. Explicit machine names should be used only in programs that connect to more than one server.

If a connection to the server is established, the function returns a pointer (Dpy) to a Display structure, which contains all information needed for both communicating with the server and creating graphic displays in the server. The function returns NULL otherwise.

The pointer returned by XOpenDisplay() appears as the first argument of all Xlib functions and macros, with different functions using different members of the structure. Most of the functions use the member that is a file descriptor to send messages through the channel to the server. Most macros access some other member of the structure.

In contrast to other windowing systems, it is quite simple to write an X program that uses many servers. All we need is to create an array of Display pointers, then replace each of the individual Xlib calls in Listing 2.1 by a loop. For example if we elect to pass server names as command line arguments, the following code establishes connections to all of them:

```
/* ... */
main (int arc, char **arv)
```

Listing 2.1.   Trivial X Program

```c
/*  A Trivial X Program  */
#include <X11/Xlib.h>
int main ()
{
    Display *Dpy;
    Window w;
    XEvent action;
    /*  Establish a connection to the server. The empty  */
    /*  string argument implies a default server,
        usually */
    /*  the one on the same machine as the client  */
    /*  exit with an error condition if no connection  */
    Dpy = XOpenDisplay ("");
    if (!Dpy) return (-1);
    /*  Allocate a window structure  */
    w = XCreateSimpleWindow( Dpy, DefaultRootWindow (Dpy),
        0, 0, 200, 100, 2,
        BlackPixel (Dpy, DefaultScreen(Dpy),
        WhitePixel (Dpy, DefaultScreen(Dpy) );
    /*  Request that the server informs the application  */
    /*  when a mouse button is pressed  */
    XSelectInput (Dpy, w, ButtonPressMask);
    /*  Request that the window be displayed  */
    XMapWindow (Dpy, w);
    /*  Enter an Infinite Loop  */
    while(1) {
        /*  Wait until an event has been produced at the  */
        /*  server and then place the information about  */
        /*  it in the structure action and return  */
        XNextEvent (Dpy, &action);
        /*  if the event was caused by pressing a mouse  */
        /*  button break from the loop  */
        if (action.type==ButtonPress) break;
    }
    /*  Close the connection to the server and return 0  */
    /*  To indicate successful completion of execution  */
    XCloseDisplay(Dpy);
    return(0);
}
```

```
{
    Display *Dpy[256];
    /* ... */
    for (i=1; i< arc; i++) Dpy[i]=XOpenDisplay(arv[i]);
    /* ... */
}
```

The same process is also available (and easier to use) with the Xt (see Sec. 5.5.3).

2.1.2. Introduction to the Window Data Structure   In X a window is a rectangular area of the screen (refresh memory) represented by the coordinates of its top left corner, its width, and its height. In the server it is represented by a structure that contains two types of data: *attributes* and *properties*.

Attributes refer to parameters that specify internal window features, such as border width, background color, border color, the cursor image to be displayed, etc.

Properties refer to an X mechanism for communication between applications (clients). Properties have a name (a character string) and an associated structure that can contain arbitrary information. These are most commonly used to communicate with the window manager and to contain such information as the window frame label, window position and size, the icon used when the window is iconified (minimized), etc.

If it seems counterintuitive that something as basic as window size is a property rather than an attribute, that is because when an application specifies values for window position and size, these values are mediated by the window manager. In Listing 2.1 a window is created with the call to XCreateSimple-Window (), which has the following prototype:

```
XCreateSimpleWindow( Display * display_pointer,
    Window parent_window,
    int x_hint, int y_hint,
    unsigned int width_hint, unsigned int height_hint,
    unsigned int border_width,
    unsigned long border_color,
    unsigned long background_color);
```

where the first argument specifies the server where the window is created and the second argument specifies the parent window. For the top window of an application, the parent is the server's root (base) window. This window typically encompasses the full screen, and its XID is part of the Display structure. It is retrieved by using macro DefaultRootWindow(). The word default, refers to the default screen. The X supports servers with more than one display screen (a combination of refresh memory and video look-up table), and each of these may have a different root window. We can access the same structure by using two other macros:

```
RootWindow(Dpy, DefaultScreen(Dpy))
```

Of course most servers have only one screen, but X does not let us forget that this is not always the case.

The following four arguments that include `hint` in their name specify coordinates of the top left window corner and its dimensions. However as their name implies, these are only suggestions (hints) to the window manager. Because the window manager is responsible for overall window layout, it may modify requested values. For example if an application is called twice, the window manager may shift their respective positions so that the two versions do not entirely overlap.

The last three arguments are self-explanatory, and these specify values for three attributes of the window to be created. (Attributes values not given here are inherited from the patent window.) In our example we requested: 2-pixel wide black border and white background. Specifying color is not simple: Bit patterns translated by the video look-up table (Sec. 1.4.1) into particular colors are not standard, so we must use macros to extract from the `Display` structure. Note: In this case we must call the `DefaultScreen` explicitly.

When a window is *created* by the call to `XCreateSimpleWindow()`, a structure is created in the server, but there is no fresh memory allocation. The latter is achieved by the call to `XMapWindow()`. A window is *mapped* when a screen area is assigned (though not necessarily allocated) to the window rectangle. However the window does not appear on the screen as yet because messages from the client to the server is buffered. We can force messages sending by calling:

```
XFlush(Dpy);
```

In that case the window *may* appear. Whether it actually appears depends on the window manager. Because a display may have *overlapping* windows, the window manager has its own policy about which windows are displayed. In general mapped windows can be *visible, partially visible,* or *obscured.* Only in the first two cases is a refresh memory allocation made.

Server resource refers to windows and other parts of the server memory, such as color maps or graphics context. Resource is used here generically; server resources have nothing to do with Xt resources described in Sec. 1.1.4.

Normally window creation and mapping are done by Xt functions, so we are not directly concerned with some of the preceding details. On the other hand Xt is constrained by what Xlib functions can do. For example window position and dimensions are always hints to the window manager, no matter how they are specified. We discuss additional window topics in Sec. 2.2.

2.1.3. Introduction to Events   In addition to window creation code, Listing 2.1 contains code to deal with user actions. As explained in Sec. 1.1.1 the server converts user actions into structures called *events*. Events may also be created as a result of other program actions—in particular, by the window manager. For each application the server maintains an *event queue*.

Event-driven programs include an infinite loop, such as the one in Listing 2.1. The function XNextEvent() checks the event queue; if it contains an event, the function copies it into the structure indicated by its second argument (action in our example). If the queue is empty, the function flushes the buffer between client and server. This is essential because the function is *blocking*: the program halts until the queue has events again. Therefore any waiting graphics (or other) instructions must be sent to the server before the program enters the idle state. If an application must perform other computations while waiting for events (for example a video game that keeps an animation going), then a *nonblocking* function must be used to check the event queue.

Applications have some control over the type of events placed in the queue. This is called *event selection*. In general events generated by other programs are always placed in the queue. Events generated by the user (through the mouse and keyboard) must be selected explicitly by a call to XSelectInput(). The relevant statement in Listing 2.1 selects the event caused by pressing a mouse button. This particular program ignores all keyboard input, mouse motion, or events generated when a mouse button is released. Since there events are always selected, we must always check the type of event when the function XNextEvent() returns. In this case the program exists if the type of the event were indeed the one corresponding to pressing a mouse button.

Normally event selection is carried out by the Xt, which also examines the event queue. The correspondence between event types and action is also established indirectly, as in Listing 1.1. However some applications must examine information in addition to event type. For this reason we may have to look at other members from the server return, besides type.

The XEvent type used to store event information is actually a *union* of structures. This arrangement is necessary because the type of information associated with an event depends on the type of event itself. A partial listing of the definition of union follows:

```
typedef union _XEvent {
    int type;
    XAnyEvent xany;
    XDuttonEvent xbutton;
    . . .
    XExposeEvent xexpose;
```

```
    . . .
    XKeyEvent xkey;
    . . .
    XMotionEvent xmotion;
} XEvent;
```

The variable `type` is also the first number of all structures, so the code checking type in Listing 2.1 can safely be used. Once we know the type, we can refer to the appropriate structure; for example in a nontrivial program, we may have the code:

```
switch(action.type) {
case ButtonPress:
    /* access members of action.xbutton */
    break;
case KeyPress:
    /* access members of action.xkey */
    break;
/* ... */
}
```

2.1.4. XEvent Union   After `type` the next four members in all event structures of the union are

```
unsigned    long serial;
Bool        send_event;
Display     *display;
Window      window;
```

Together with `type` these are members of the `XAnyEvent` structure. The last two members refer to the display (server) and the window where the event originated. The member `serial` is the number of the last message sent to the server; it is often used for debugging. The member `send_event` indicates whether another application produced the event rather than originating in the server. Clearly all such information is meaningful regardless of event type, and it is always contained in the structure. The `XAnyEvent` structure is useful for writing a procedure that tries from the client side to find the widget (the client-side window object) where an event occurred. If wp is a pointer to a a window object (such as that in Listing 1.4) and ep is a pointer to a `XAnyEvent` structure, then the following statement forms the heart of an event *dispatch* procedure, which is used in all toolkits.

```
if (wp -> win==ep -> window) return wp;
```

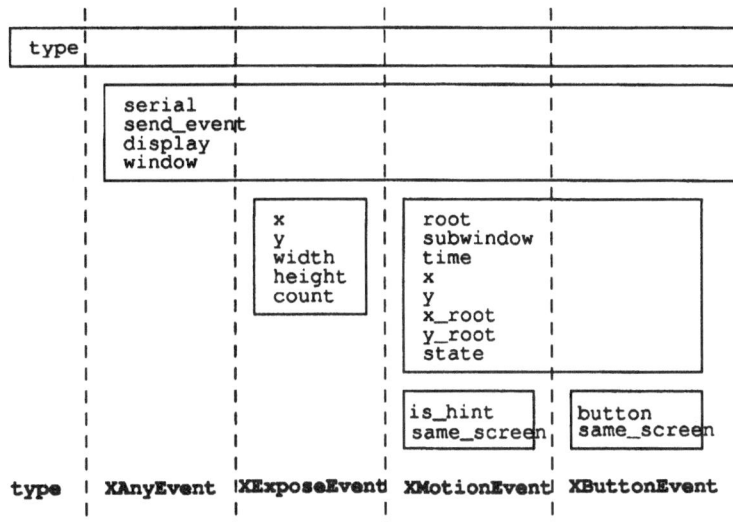

Figure 2.1. Information layout in the XEvent union. The first few individual members of each member of the union are the same. Other members differ depending on the type of event.

Normally after the widget is identified, the appropriate event-handling routines associated with the widget are called. We say that the event is dispatched to the widget.

The event Expose is generated by the window manager when a window becomes visible and must be redrawn (see Sec. 2.2.2). Because a window may be covered by many others, there is a cluster of Expose events when that window is moved in front of the others. It is wasteful to keep redrawing so the XEvent structure for exposures, xexpose, contains a member, count, with the number of remaining exposure events for that window. It is a good idea to wait for that number to become 0 before redrawing. In addition the XExposeEvent structure contains coordinates of the top left corner of the exposed rectangle (x and y) and its dimensions (width and height). Figure 2.1 shows the organization of the structure. Related events (mouse activity and mouse button events) may share additional members.

Aside

Information about the geometry of the exposed rectangle may be used to redraw only the part of the window that needs to be redrawn. However this may differ for each member of the sequence of expose events; therefore besides waiting for count to become 0, we must keep track of this information. For simple displays it is easier to redraw the entire window rather than to keep track of particular areas. To avoid these problems Microsoft Windows handles expose events (called WM_PAINT messages) differently. These are not placed in the main queue, but a flag is set so that if there are not other events in the queue, the program checks the flag, then redraws if necessary.

2.2.   ADVANCED FEATURES OF THE WINDOW OBJECT IN X

2.2.1.   Overview   Several issues concerning windows were either ignored or mentioned only briefly in the overview of Sec. 2.1.2. Each window has attributes and properties. Attributes are members of a structure of type XSetWindowAt-tributes (despite the verb set, this is a type, not a function). Attributes are set by a call to the Xlib function XChangeWindowAttributes(). As arguments this function takes a Display pointer, window XID, *value mask*, and a pointer to an XSetWindowAttributes structure. A value mask is an integer of type unsigned long, whose bits correspond to attributes. If a bit is set to 1, the corresponding attribute is used in XSetWindowAttributes(). See Sec. 2.2.2 for an illustration of attributes in connection with window backup.

We find a window's attributes by using the function XGetWindowAttri-butes(); see Sec. 2.5 for an example of its use.

Properties are strings used for interclient communication. Each property has a name and associated data. Because different applications may run on different machines, the only reliable way of passing data between machines is through their respective windows. Despite the term a property need not pertain to a particular window; for example a property can be the name of the machine on which the application is running. Sections 2.2.3–2.2.5 discusses properties in detail.

2.2.2.   Window Backup   When windows overlap, we must decide what to do with the memory contents allocated to an obscured window. One possibility that helps hide window interactions from the client is to have the server copy the contents into another part of the (nonrefresh) memory, then restore it later. Unfortunately this simple solution is not supported by the X Window System. The decision was made not to place responsibility for backing up obscured windows on the display device (server) because it exceeds the primary task of interpreting network messages and mapping them into refresh memory.

In X when a window is obscured, nothing happens. When a window becomes visible, the display device sends a message to the applications program, informing it of the need to redraw exposed parts of the display. Such messages are placed in the queue as expose events, and applicants programs must provide a *redrawing* function for the event handler to call. An expose event is also used to draw a window for the first time, not only when it has to be restored after having been obscured.

Although not required by X Window System specification, many servers offer a backup facility. To use this facility the application must determine if such a facility exists and also request that it be used. The application must also specify a *gravity*, which is a parameter that determines to which part of the window the drawing is attached if the window increases in size. This task is achieved with the following code that relies on window attributes:

```
if ( DoesBackingStore( DefaultScreenOfDisplay( Dpy) )==
Always) {
    XSetWindowAttributes attr;
    unsigned long valuemask = CWBackingStore;
    attr.backing_store = Always;
    XChangeWindowAttributes(Dpy, w, valuemask, &attr);
```

Note the use of a mask to select values, as discussed in Sec. 1.4.2.

The macro `DefaultScreenOfDisplay()` returns a pointer to the screen (refresh memory) of the server, and the macro `DoesBackingStore()` returns an integer with information about the availability of memory backup in the server. Both `Always` and `CWBackingStore` are predefined constants (1L<<6 for the latter). Because of this setting, the `XChangeWindowAttributes()` call tells the server to ignore all other members of the `attr` structure and update only the one determining the backup of window contents. In this example that attribute is set to the predefined constant `Always`, thereby asking the server always to make a copy of the window contents.

If a window is using backup store, we can instruct the server on recreating window contents after resizing by using a window attribute called *bit_gravity*. This attribute determines the side and corner toward to which the contents gravitate when the window size changes. The preceding code is then modified as follows:

```
if ( DoesBackingStore ( DefaultScreenOfDisplay ( Dpy) )==
Always) {
    XSetWindowAttributes attr;
    unsigned long valuemask = CWBackingStore|CWBitGravity;
    attr.backing_store = Always;
```

```
        attr.bit_gravity = NorthWestGravity;
        XChangeWindowAttributes(Dpy, w, valuemask, &attr);
}
```

The attribute `NorthWestGravity` specifies that the contents gravitate toward the top left corner of the window. A second gravity attribute `win_gravity` determines the position of subwindows when a window is resized.

If backup is used, then the server does not generate expose events. We may assume that in this case, we do not need a redrawing function, but this is not true.

Caution

When using Xt (and toolkits built on top of it such as Motif), we must always provide a redrawing function because a window may be redrawn by the toolkit in response to events other than expose. For example under Motif, when a window is resized to a larger area, it is always redrawn even if no parts were obscured and the current display conforms with the specified gravity.

Recommendation

Always provide a redrawing function and do not rely on the server backup. Even if your program is going to run only on servers with backup, the behavior may not be what you expect.

Regardless of the limitations of X, automatic backup is not always desirable. Suppose we have an application that scales a drawing to fill a window. If the user reduces the window size, then automatic backup leaves some of the drawing invisible because it does not fit in the new window. The correct solution is to redo the drawing using a smaller scale. If the user increases the window size, automatic backup leaves empty areas. The correct solution is to redraw the drawing using a larger scale.

2.2.3. Properties and Atoms—Text Type Properties have names that are character strings; For example "WM_NAME" refers to the label in the window frame created by the window manager to enclose the top window of the application (see Sec. 2.4.2). While creating that window, the window manager checks to see if the original window has such a property associated with it; if so, it uses the associated data for the label. The structure associated with the property is called the *type* of the property, and it sometimes has the same name. The type of "WM_NAME" is "TEXT" which means that data are stored in the following structure:

```
typedef struct {
    unsigned char *value;
    Atom encoding;
    int format;
    unsigned long nitems;
} XTextProperty;
```

The member `value` points to the string of characters that form the label; `format` in this case contains 8, which means that data are stored in a byte, and `nitems` is the number of characters in the label. The `Atom` type requires a bit of discussion. While properties are defined as strings, strings are not convenient for many operations, such as comparisons. Therefore X has a mechanism to map strings into integers in a unique way. The function that does this is `XInternAtom()`, it has the following prototype:

```
Atom XInternAtom(Display *Dpy, char * name, Boolean
only_if_exists)
```

If the last argument is set to `True`, the function returns an atom only if the name were already mapped into an atom. Otherwise it returns the symbolic constant `None`. If the last argument is set to `False`, a new atom is created if none exists for that name. In the latter case an atom is returned for any string whether it is useful or not. The string mapping into an atom remains for the life of the server program. Some predefined atoms in the server always have the same values and these are represented by symbolic names in the file `X11/Xatom.h`. For example the atom for "WM_NAME" has the symbolic name XA_WM_NAME, and the value for text has the symbolic name XA_STRING (in the server we use, these are numerical values 36 and 31, respectively.) Values of atoms that are not predefined depend on history.

Given an atom we obtain the string by the function:

```
char *XGetAtomName (Display *Dpy, Atom atom)
```

Atoms are used not only for property names, but also for property types, and this is the meaning of the second element of the XTextProperty structure.

There is a pair of general functions for setting and retrieving properties and many *convenience* functions. For "WM_NAME" there are two convenience functions: One to set the label (after it copied into the `value` member of the `TextProperty` structure):

```
XSetWMName(Display *Dpy, Window win, TextProperty *tp)
```

and one to read back the data:

```
XGetWMName(Display *Dpy, Window win, TextProperty *tp)
```

The function `XSetWMName()` is normally called by the application for its top window and the function `XGetWMName()` is normally called by the window manager.

This property is automatically set by Xt for the top window of an application, but other properties are not handled in this way, as we see in Sec. 2.4.2.

"WM_CLIENT_MACHINE" is another property of TEXT type; it refers to the name (as viewed from the server) of the machine on which the client is running. The symbolic value for the atom is XA_WM_CLIENT_MACHINE, and the pair of convenience functions are `XSetWMClientMachine()` and `XGetWMClientMachine()` with the same arguments as the functions for the window name. For example to set the name of the machine, we can use the following code (which assumes that that the machine name is no longer than 31 characters):

```
TextProperty tp;
tp.value =(char *)malloc(32*sizeof(char));
/* call a system function to retrieve the name  */
gethostname(tp.value, sizeof(tp.value));
/* ... */
XSetWMClientMachine(Dpy, win, &tp);
```

Now the window structure of `win` has a structure attached to it with the machine name. We can read back the information with the function call:

```
XGetWMClientMachine(Dpy, win, &tp);
```

We can determine the properties attached to a window by calling the function `XListProperties()`; see Sec. 2.5 for examples. In general properties are assigned to the top window in the application because that is where the window manager looks. The preceding code fragment may reside in the code of a window manager program that assigns values to window properties and attributes.

2.2.4. Properties and Atoms—Hints TEXT properties are relatively simple; other properties contain a variety of data. Two of these contain hints which are data that the window manager sees as suggestions.

The "WM_NORMAL_HINTS" property contains the suggested size of the window in a structure of type XSizeHints. Its type is "WM_SIZE_HINTS", and the structure contains the window location (coordinates of top left corner) and dimension (width and height). Convenience functions for setting and reading these hints are XSetWMNormalHints() and XGetNormalHints(). The predefined atom for "WM_NORMAL_HINTS" is XA_NORMAL_HINTS (actually the integer 40).

Because there are many members in a property structure, a mechanism similar to the value mask used for attributes is used. The property structure contains a member, flag, declared as long, that is used as a mask. The main difference with earlier uses of masks is that the mask is part of the data structure rather than a separate item.

The "WM_HINTS" property corresponds to a structure of type XWMHints; its type is also "WM_HINTS". It contains a rather odd assortment of data, mainly about the icon used to represent the window when it is iconified and about how to direct keyboard input to a window. The "WM_HINTS" has the predefined atom XA_WM_HINTS (actually the interger 35).

The following code fragment tells the window manager how to direct keyboard input to window win when the mouse-controlled cursor is located in that window:

```
XWMHints wmhints;
/* ... */
wmhints.flags = InputHint;
wmhints.input = True;
XSetWMHints(Dpy, win, &wmhints);
```

Here InputHint is a predefined constant, and XSetWMHints() is the convenience function. This particular code asks the window manager to direct keyboard input to window win whenever the pointer is in that window. Keep in mind that usually *the window manager has its own policy* for such matters, so hint specifications are just suggestions. They need not be followed by the window manager. The reading convenance function is XGetWMHints(); it has a different argument organization. Its prototype is

```
char * XGetWMHints(Display *Dpy, Window win)
```

2.2.5.   Examples of Properties   Table 2.1 lists some properties and how the
various toolkits handled them. The *Xt* includes Athena widgets; *St* stands for the
Starter toolkit when built with Athena widgets only. Table 2.1 is based on
information gathered while running the expanded spy program (see Sec. 2.5) on a
machine with windows created in different ways.

The Xt automatically sets up eight properties, but not the WM_PROTOCOLS.
(We return to this point in Sec. 2.4.2.) The Starter toolkit also sets up the
WM_COLORMAP_WINDOWS property, but it does so indirectly using an Xt call.
Programs created by using only Xlib (such as the one in Listing 2.1) have only the
WM_STATE property automatically attached to them; other properties must be
given explicitly.

Note: Information contained in some properties *need not be true*. The window
manager supposedly knows about the arguments with which an application was
invoked, but it does not obtain them from the Unix shell. The application must set
the appropriate property, but it may choose not to do so! For example the Starter
toolkit does not require the applications programmer to pass command line

Table 2.1.   Properties of Various Toolkits

Property		Toolkit				
Atom	Name	Xt	St	OLIT	Motif	Tk
34	WM_COMMAND[a]	Yes	Yes[a]	Yes	Yes	No
35	WM_HINTS[b]	Yes	Yes	Yes	Yes	Yes
36	WM_CLIENT_MACHINE[c]	Yes	Yes	Yes	Yes	No
37	WM_ICON_NAME[d]	Yes	Yes	Yes	Yes	No
39	WM_NAME[c]	Yes	Yes	Yes	Yes	Yes
40	WM_NORMAL_HINTS[b]	Yes	Yes	Yes	Yes	Yes
67	WM_CLASS[e]	Yes	Yes[e]	Yes	Yes	Yes
105	_SUN_DRAGDROP_INTER[f,k]	No	No	Yes	No	No
127	WM_STATE[g,k]	Yes	Yes	Yes	Yes	Yes
137	WM_COLORMAP_WINDOWS[h,k]	No	Yes	No	No	No
139	WM_PROTOCOLS[i,k]	No	Yes	Yes	Yes	Yes
294	_MOTIF_WM_MESSAGES[j,k]	No	No	No	Yes	No

Notes:
[a]Copy of the command line that invoked the application. This need not be the true line, so the Starter toolkit provides only a
guess.
[b]See Sec. 2.2.4.
[c]See Sec. 2.2.3.
[d]Label on icon window.
[e]Program name and name of program class; the Starter toolkit provides only a generic name.
[f]Example of a property special to OLIT. Note: Names special to a particular set start with an underscore.
[g]State of the application; a discussion is beyond our scope.
[h]Windows associated with a particular colormap.
[i]See Sec. 2.4.2.
[j]Example of property special to Motif.
[k]Not a predefined atom.

argument to X functions. The toolkit itself passes a string to the window manager with generic information. Programmers using the Starter toolkit who care about this issue should call the function `arguments()` before any other Starter toolkit functions. The use of this function is illustrated later in Listing 2.4 (Part 1).

2.3.   EVENTS

2.3.1.   Types of Events   We systematically categorize events here by how they are generated and selected. It is beyond the scope of this book to discuss all event types. (There are about 40.) Instead we focus on events that are most likely to concern applications.

Most events initiated by the user are selected by the `XSelectInput()` function with appropriate masks. Besides `ButtonPress`, shown in Listing 2.1, symbolic names for events generated by the user include `MotionNotify` (the mouse moved), `KeyPress` (a keyboard key was pressed), `ButtonRelease`, and `KeyRelease`. Thus the following call tells the server that when a mouse button is pressed, the mouse moves, or a key is struck while the window w has control of these devices, an appropriate event should be inserted in the queue for the application that owns window w:

```
XSelectInput ( Dp, w, ButtonPressMask | PointerMotionMask
| KeyPressMask );
```

A key issue is the conditions under which a window is considered to control the keyboard and the mouse. Normally a window receives mouse events if the cursor is inside the window, although there are exceptions to that rule, which we discuss in Sec 2.5. We say that a window *grabs* the pointer if it receives mouse events when the pointer is outside its boundaries. Such a grab can be explicit (as in the program of Sec. 2.5) or implicit. In particular whenever the cursor moves outside a window with a button pressed, the cursor is automatically grabbed by that window until the button is released. In this way the button press and subsequent button release events always go to the same window.

Things are a bit more complex for the keyboard. We say that a window has *input focus* if it receives keyboard events. Focus is assigned by the window manager under one of two policies: Focus follows the cursor (as in the case of mouse events), or it results from clicking on the window (often the default policy). We return to this topic in Sec. 4.4.1.

The function `XSelectInput()` is used to select some event types generated *indirectly* by the user. The following are of particular interest. The event `Expose` is generated when a window becomes visible and must be redrawn.

If we have opted for server backup, such events are not generated (with one exception that we explain shortly). The event type is selected with the `ExposureMask`.

The event `ConfigureNotify` is generated when the window moves or it is resized. It is selected with the `StructureNotifyMask`, and information about it is stored in the structure `xconfigure`. When the window is resized, it also generates an `Expose` event *unless* we provide a hint about how to copy the old window area into the new one. This process was discussed in Sec. 2.2.2.

Two events cannot be selected by `XSelectInput()`; these must be selected through the graphics context (see Sec. 1.2). These events are `GraphicExpose` and `NoExpose`. The first is generated when part of the refresh memory cannot be copied into another; the second is generated when copying is successful. Some programs, such as video games, perform the copying operation many times, which can flood the event queue with `NoExpose` events. Unfortunately, it is not possible to select `GraphicExpose` but not `NoExpose`. Hence we recommend including the following call right after the graphics context is created:

```
XSetGraphicsExposures (Dp, gc, False);
```

Copying may fail because the source is an invisible window. If we copy only from pixmaps (as in the case of video game animation) to a visible window, then such a failure is not possible. Since copying from one part of a window to another is useful for scrolling, we should select these events in such applications.

Some events are always selected. Of interest to us is `ClientMessage`, which is generated when one program sends a message to another.

2.3.2. Modal Windows   In Listing 2.1 a single event loop is expected to handle any kind of input. This is the rule in most window programs, not only in X. However it is possible to have many event loops (see Listing 2.2). Such programs are called *modal* or said to accept *modal input*. The most common use of modal input is for temporary windows (popups) that usually contain a message describing the next user action. Such windows are often called *dialog boxes*.

The program in Listing 2.2 goes into a waiting loop only when it expects a particular event; it exits the loop when the event occurs. This approach is convenient for programs that do significant computation but only occasionally look for user input. Because the flow of execution is controlled by the structure of the program, we do not need static storage between events. However this methodology is discouraged by various toolkits because the application user may become frustrated with a program that does not respond to any action unless it is the one the program expects.

Listing 2.2. Program with Modal Input — File modal.c

```
# include <X11/Xlib.h>
static Display *Dpy;
static Window w;
void wait_for_mouse (), wait_for_key ();
int main(void)
{
    int x, y, key;
    Dpy=XOpenDisplay ("");
    w=XCreateSimpleWindow( Dpy, DefaultRootWindow(Dpy),
        0, 0, 200, 100, 2,
        BlackPixel (Dpy, Default Screen(Dpy),
        WhitePixel (Dpy, Default Screen(DPy));
    XMapWindow (Dpy, w);
    /*  read mouse position when button 1 is pressed  */
    wait_for_mouse (1, &x, &y);
    printf("x=%d y=%d for button 1\n", x, y);
    /*  read mouse position when button 2 is pressed  */
    wait_for_mouse (2, &x, &y);
    printf("x=%d y=%d for button 2\n", x, y);
    /*  read mouse position when a key is pressed  */
    wait_for_key(&key, &x, &y);
    printf("key %o (%c) at x=%d y=%d\n", key, key, x, y);
    XCloseDisplay (Dpy);
    return (0);
}
void wait_for_mouse(int button_id, int *xp, int *yp)
{
    XEvent activity;
    XSelectInput (Dpy, w, ButtonPressMask); /*  select
    button press events  */
    while(1) {
        XNextEvent (Dpy, &activity);
        if(activity.type != ButtonPress) continue;
        if(activity.xbutton.button==button_id) break;
    }
    *cp=activity.xbutton.x;
    *yp=activity.xbutton.y;
    XSelectInput (Dpy, w, NoEventMask); /*  do not place
    events in the queue  */
}
void wait_for_key(int *cp, int *xp, int *yp)
{
```

```
    XSelectInput (Dpy, w, KeyPressMask); /* select key
    press events */
    while(1) {
        XNextEvent (Dpy, &activity);
        if(activity.type = KeyPress) break;
    }
    *xp = activity.xkey.x;
    *yp = activity.xkey.y;
    XSelectInput (Dpy, w, NoEventMask); /* do not place
    events in the queue */
}
```

2.4. WINDOW MANAGER

2.4.1. Basic Role   Typing the name of a program in a shell window starts
an application (or client). If this program requires its own window, it then asks the
server for the following sequence of operations: (1) Creation of the appropriate
window data structure, which is added to the list of windows the server maintains;
(2) allocation of a rectangle in refresh memory. The window list not only contains
information about the window position and dimensions but also the *stacking order*;
that is, the relative order with respect to the display screen. Note: A window may
obscure another window behind it in the stacking order.

When the application asks for a window to be mapped (i.e., take actual control
of the allocated piece of refresh memory), the server does not immediately perform
the operation, but instead passes the request to the window manager. The window
manager can thus control the position and size of each window.

Definition

A *window manager* is an application (client) program that mediates resource
allocation and deals with user interaction. Resources include *refresh memory*
(window display), *keyboard* (determining which window receives the input),
and *video lookup table* (deciding which colormap to load). A window
manager displays the windows of other applications (usually with additional
decorations) and modifies the size, position, and relative placement of a
window on the basis of user actions.

The window manager usually tracks the position of the mouse-controlled cursor. When the cursor is inside a window, the process associated with that window takes control of the keyboard and the video lookup table. Keyboard control by a process means that all typed input is sent to the standard input of that process. That window is usually called the *active window*.

Like other applications, the window manager sends messages to the server to implement any of those operations. Consider a program that displays the names of a set of files that each contains a picture. When the user selects a name, the program displays the respective picture in a new window. Figure 2.2 illustrates the program response to the user request. The program reads the picture file, computes window dimensions, then asks the server to create the window data structure (Message 1). Then it asks the server to map (display) the window (Message 2). The server passes the request to the window manager (Message 3), which must decide where and how to position the window relative to other windows on the screen. After doing so the program asks the server to execute the appropriate graphics primitives (Message 4).

Having the window manager as a program distinct from the server is a characteristic of the X Window System. (Actually we can run programs, albeit awkwardly, without a window manager.) Such a separation is not a requirement for window systems. It is possible to write a server program that also manages the windows. Having the functions in two separate programs has two advantages:

1. It allows users to vary the look and feel of the window system by choosing a different window manager. Thus the same server (display) can support different interface standards at different times.
2. It makes the server a simpler program. Since servers must translate protocol messages into machine instructions, they are hardware-

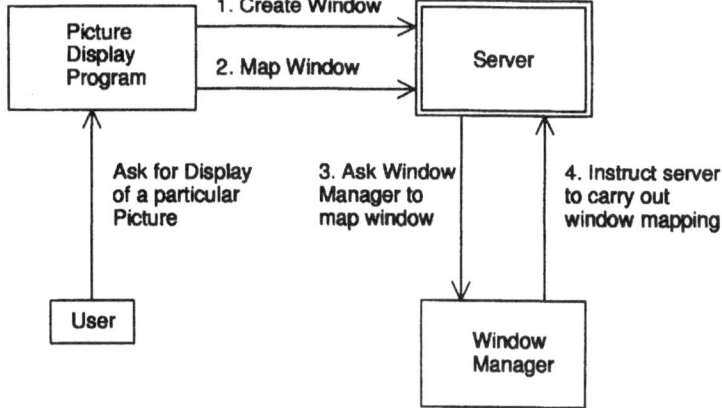

Figure 2.2. Interaction among an application program, the server, and the window manager. For clarify only major messages are shown. Confirmation messages are omitted.

dependent. To make a new device conform to the X standard, the manufacturer must provide a server. Making that task easier helps establish the standard.

This separation also has a disadvantage: A large part of the X protocol (and as a consequence of Xlib) pertains to communication between the server and window manager. Some Xlib functions are reserved for window managers only (although there is no automatic way of enforcing that). The window manager is indeed a very important client!

Because the two programs are distinct, we must invoke both to work on a machine with the X Window System. The typical sequence is to invoke the program xinit, which starts a server (given as an argument) and a single client. For example SUN workstations use the xnews server, and the first client is the *Open Look* window manager, olwm. Rather lengthy shell scripts are necessary, but in a well-maintained system, the average user has to invoke only one script to start the whole process.

One other common configuration is to have X handle the login process so that the server and window manager are started only once and users find themselves immediately in an X environment after login.

2.4.2.   Interaction among Window Manager and Application Programs
If we compile and run the program in Listing 2.1, we find that the displayed window has a fancy frame similar to other windows on the screen. Who inserted all these decorations? Actually no one did anything to the window our program created. However the window manager inserted a new window (with decorations) between the root window and the one just created. This process is called *reparenting*.

Reparenting occurs because the window manager must allow the user to move and resize windows, so offering the same facilities to any window created by an application is a good practice. Because it is impossible to force all applications programmers to do that, the window manager solves the problem by inserting a window of its own (with all the desired facilities) between the root and the top application window. (Strictly speaking the window manager can allow manipulation without reparenting and without special demands on the applications. It is simply less user friendly to do so without the facilities offered by reparenting.)

Reparenting imposes various obligations on the applications programmer. The program must respond gracefully when the user operates on the (new) top window. How does the program know that the new parent has been manipulated? The server generates events when the window is moved or resized, and the program must make provisions to look for them in the event queue and act accordingly. Because the program in Listing 2.1 does not do anything useful, it may ignore most of these events. However one event cannot be ignored even by the current trivial program: If the user terminates the top window, everything disappears from the screen. Nevertheless the program in Listing 2.1 continues running! Since the connection to the server has closed, the call to XNextEvent() causes an error with a diagnostic statement similar to:

```
XIO: fatal IO error 32 (Broken pipe) on X server "0.0"
after 5 requests (2 known processed) with 0 events
remaining.
the connection was probably broken by a server shutdown or
KillClient.
```

If we write programs using Motif, OLIT, or the Starter toolkit, interaction with the window manager is handled by the toolkit, so that problem is taken care of automatically. If we write programs using the Athena toolkit (or no toolkit at all), then we must deal with the actions of the window manager directly; in particular we must provide code to deal with events of type ClientMessage. Such events are placed in the event queue by another program, often the window manager. The generating program does so with the Xlib function XSend-Event(). To provide a response to such an event, we must use the window properties, specifically the WM_PROTOCOLS property, which is a list of atoms set with the XSetWMProtocols() function. This function takes as an argument a list of protocols. The list includes WM_DELETE_WINDOW, which causes the window manager to send a ClientMessage when the parent window is destroyed. Not all properties have predefined atoms, and WM_DELETE_WIN-DOW happens to be one that does not. The following code fragment shows how to define an atom, then set the protocol:

```
static Atom wm_quit;
...
wm_quit=XCInterAtom (Dpy, "WM_DELETE_WINDOW", False);
XSetWMProtocols( Dpy, win, &wm_quit, 1);
```

Because the WM_DELETE_WINDOW is not predefined, instead of just calling the XSetW... functions as we did with predefined atoms, we must also call the XInterAtom() function to map the property string into an atom.

The call to the function XInterAtom() converts the string WM_DELETE _WINDOW to an atom, as described in Sec. 2.2.3. The argument win in the call to

XSetWMProtocols() is the XID of the window that is going to receive the message. Number 1 is simply the number of atoms in the list.

We are now ready to remedy the problem in Listing 2.1. The solution is to give the simple program window the property WM_DELETE_WINDOW, then provide a response for an event of ClientMessage type. The code is given in Listing 2.3. The member of the XEvent union in this case is xclient, which in addition to the members of type and xany (see Fig. 2.2), contains an atom message_type, an integer for the format of the message and a union, data, 20 bytes long

Listing 2.3. An *Xlib* Program that Listens to the Window Manager

```
#include <X11/Xlib>
int main (void)
{
    Display *Dpy;
    Window w;
    XEvent activity;
    Atom wm_quit;
    Dpy = XOpenDisplay ("");
    w = XCreateSimpleWindow (Dpy, DefaultRootWindow(Dpy),
        0, 0, 256, 256, 4, 1, 0);
    XSelectInput( Dpy, w, ButtonPressMask);
    wm_quit = Xinternatom(Dpy, "WM_DELETE_WINDOW", False);
    XSetWMProtocols (Dpy, w, &wm_quit, 1);
    XMapWindow(Dpy, w);
    while(1) {
        XNextEvent (Dp, &activity);
        switch(activity.type) {
        case ClientMessage:
            if(activity.xclient.data.1[0] != w, _quit)
                continue;
            printf("Exit because of window manager action\n");
            break;
        case ButtonPress:
            printf("Exit because of user action\n");
            break:
        default: continue;
        }
        break;
    }
    XCloseDisplay(Dpy);
    return(0);
}
```

that can be interpreted as an array of 20 characters, 10 short integers, or 5 long integers. In this listing we select the long integer interpretation.

We made one minor and two major changes in Listing 2.1. We replaced the "if equal" statement with a switch that contains `printf` statements to describe the action. Major changes—setting the window manager protocol property and handling the `ClientMessage`—are highlighted.

Once we intercept the `ClientMessage` event, we may choose not to exit immediately or even *not exit at all*. For example:

```
if (activity.xclient.data.1[0]!= wm_quit) continue;
printf("You cannot quit that way\n");
continue;
```

The most common response is to ask the user for confirmation. In an editor we may save modified files or perform various clean-up tasks.

2.5. GRABBING AND SPYING

We devote this section to a spying program where the user points to a window, and the program provides information about characteristics of that window. The program is a complete application that illustrates many of the fundamental features of X. Because this section deals only with an example program, it may be skipped without affecting the user's understanding of the rest of the book.

2.5.1. Basics of a Window-Spying Program A nontrivial application requires much more code than the examples of X programs we have seen so far. Because we have not yet covered the material needed to set up such an application, we use the Starter toolkit (see Sec. 1.3) to obtain basic program functionality. Starter toolkit functions and data types carry the prefix `St`. For some parts we must use the Xt (see Sec. 1.2, it is covered in detail in Chap. 4). Functions of the Xt carry the prefix `Xt`. We are going to pass quickly over that code to focus on Xlib functions that do the real work. The program is given in Listing 2.4.

Creation of the application is shown in Listing 2.4 (Part 1). The program creates a single window and assigns to it a redrawing function (`paint`) and a function to handle user-generated events (`act`). Functions without prefixes `St`, `Xt`, or `X` are local.

Listing 2.4 (Part 2) contains the drawing code. The function `paint()` is called only once; it is used to initialize certain static variables. Subsequent redrawing (if needed) is done by the function `repaint()`. The array `buf[][]` is used to store messages displayed on the screen. The array is read and messages displayed through the `display_info()` function, which is called by the

Listing 2.4. Window Spying-File spy.c (Part 1)

```
/*  Interrogate Window Properties - The main function  */
/*  Create an application with a drawing window  */
/*  of dimensions WIDTH by HEIGHT and label "Spy"  */
/*  paint() does the window drawing in response to  */
/*  expose events and act() handles user generated  */
/*  events (mouse events)  */
#include <Stdef.h>
#define WIDTH   300
#define HEIGHT 100
void paint(), act();
main (int arc, char **arv)
{
    St_arguments(arc, arv);
    St_draw_window(paint, act, WIDTH, HEIGHT, "Spy");
}
```

Listing 2.4. Window Spying-File spy.c (Part 2)

```
/*  Interrogate Window Properties - The redrawing functions  */
#include <X11.StringDefs.h>
#include <X11/Intrinsic.h>
#include <Starter.h>
#include <cat.icon>    /*  icon for cursor in grab state  */
static Display *Dpy;
static Cursor grab_cursor;
static Window spy_window;
static int grab = 0;
#define MAX_LINES 64
static char buf[MAX_LINES][256];
static int nmsg = 0;
/*  Redraw Function (except for the first time)  */
void repaint (void)/*  see Figure 2.3  */
{
    /*  Create a black rectangle at the bottom of the
    window  */
    St_use_replace_mode();
    St_fill_rectangle(2, HEIGHT-22, 140, 20);
    /*  Display a label in reverse video  */
    St_use_xor_mode();
    if(grab) St_put_text("Click here to Ungrab", 8,
    HEIGHT-8);
```

```
    else St_put_text("Click here to Grab", 8, HEIGHT-8);
    /*  Show list of properties */
    display_info();
}
/*  Initial Redraw Function  */
void paint(Widget w)
{
    Dpy = XtDisplay(w);
    spy_window = XtWindow(XtParent(w));
    /*  Create a cursor icon to be used when the pointer is
    grabbed  */
    grab_cursor = St_true_cursor(
        St_make_color_cursor(cat_bits, 8, 8, "red",
        "white") );
    repaint ();
    St_set_redraw(repaint);
}
/*  Auxiliary Function called also from other parts of the
program  */
void display_info(void)
{
    register i;
    St_clear_screen(0, 0, WIDTH, HEIGHT-23);
    for(i=0; i<nmsg; i++) St_put_text(buf[i], 20, 20+20*i);
}
```

repaint() function, as well as from other parts of the program. Storing the characters of messages rather than the display bitmap offers an economical backup.

The function repaint() outlines a control area to which the user must point to start spying. It also calls the function display_into(), which displays information about the last window spied on. The pointer to the Display structure and the program window XID are obtained by using Xt macros. Because the Starter toolkit normally uses a different handle type than Xlib to identify cursors, the Starter toolkit function St_true_cursor() returns the type needed by Xlib functions. The function display_info() displays the contents of two text buffers containing information describing a window. Figure 2.3 shows the window, which contains information about the window where this text was being edited.

2.5.2. Connecting Cursor Location to a Window   The central part of the program is the response to mouse events (see Listing 2.4, Part 3). The key function is XQueryPointer(), which in its fourth argument returns the XID of the window were the pointer is located. It is possible for the display to contain several nested windows; thus the pointer may be in more than one window. To determine

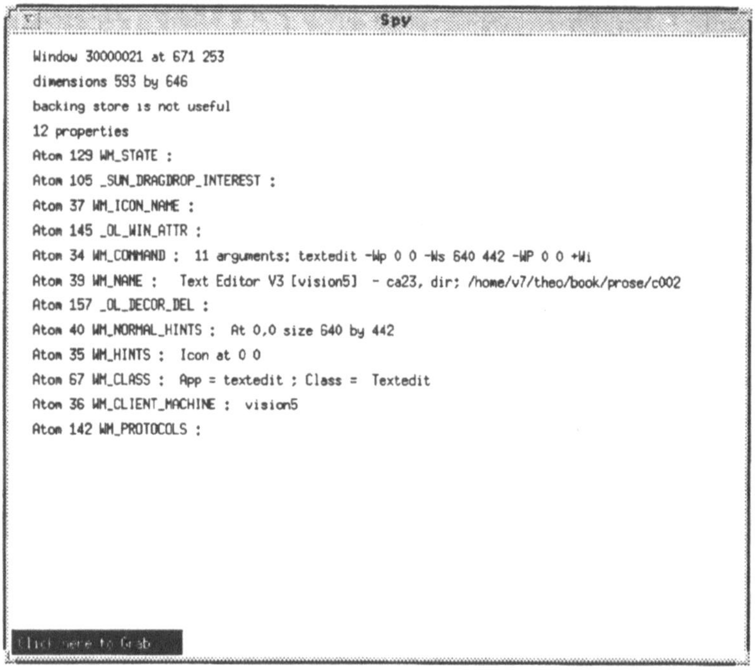

Figure 2.3.   The appearance of the spy window program.

Listing 2.4.   Window Spying-File spy.c (Part 3)

```
/*  Interrogate Window Properties - Locating the
pointer  */
#define inside_control(X, Y) ( (X) < 140 && (Y) <20 )
/*  act() is called by the Starter Toolkit with argument a
pointer to a simplified event structure. The widget pointer
is contained in the origin member of that structure.  */
void act(St_event *p)
{
    Widget w = (Widget)p->origin;
    Window basis, root, child, grandchild;
    int r_x, r_y, c_x, c_y, t_x, t_y;
    unsigned int kb;
    /*  Handle only mouse button press events  */
    if(p->kind != BTN_PRESS) return;
    /*  Exit when the right button is pressed when the  */
    /*  the pointer is not grabbed *
    if(P->key==RIGHT && &!grab) exit(0);
```

```
/*  **** Do the real spying ****  */
/*  Find the coordinates of the pointer with respect  */
/*  the root window  */
basis = DefaultRootWindow(Dpy);
XQueryPointer(Dpy, basis,
    &root, &child, &r_x, &r_y, &c_x, &c_y, &kb);
if(!child) {
    sprintf(buf[0], "No window at %d %d - Root statistics",
    c_x, c_y);
    window_stats (basis);
}
else {
    XQueryPointer (Dpy, child,
        &root, &grandchild, &r_x, &r_y, &t_x, &t_y, &kb);
    if (grandchild) {
        /*  Check if event occurred in control area  */
        if (grandchild==spy_window &&
                inside_control(p->x, HEIGHT-p->y) ) {
            if(!grab) grab_pointer(XtWindow(w));
            else release_pointer();
            return;
        }
        sprintf(buf[0], "Window %o at %d %d",
          grandchild, c_x, c_y);
        window_stats(grandchild);
    }
    else { /*  Event occurred outside shell window,
    probably in another child of the WM inserted
    parent  */
            sprintf(buf[0], "WM Decor Window %o at %d %d",
            child, c_x, c_y);
            window_stats (child);
    }
}
display_info();
return;
}
```

the window returned by XQueryPointer(), a parent window identifier is passed as the second argument. The window returned is an immediate child of this parent window. When the bottom of the nesting hierarchy is reached, zero is returned instead of a window XID. Thus to find the smallest window containing the pointer, we execute the following code:

```
child = DefaultRootWindow (Dpy);
do {
    basis = child;
    XQueryPointer (Dpy, basis,
        &root, &child, &r_x, &r_y, &c_x, &c_y, &kb);
} while (child);
```

In the code in Listing 2.4 (Part 3), we start with the root window, so the first call to XQueryPointer() returns the XID of the window inserted by the window manager between the root window and the top application (shell) window. To find the top window of the application, we must call XQueryPointer() once more. The shell window XID is in grandchild. When the window manager reparents the top window of an application, it also creates siblings for it (where the various labels and buttons reside). If the pointer is in one of these, there is no other child, so the value of grandchild is zero. If the grandchild is the same as the spy window and the pointer is inside the control area, then we change the state of the program by calling either of the functions given in Listing 2.4 (Part 4). The function grab_pointer() grabs the pointer, i.e., pointer events are sent to the grabbing application even if these occur outside its windows. The application lets the user know about the change by replacing the cursor icon. When the pointer is released, we return to the normal condition where pointer events are sent to the application that owns the window where the event occurred. In both cases the window is repainted to change the control area label.

2.5.3.   Finding Out about the Window   We are finally ready to interrogate the window. Functions window_stats_attr() and window_stats_prop() provide what we are looking for.

We can add more statements to list additional properties, foe example:

```
sprintf(buf[nmsg++], "upper left corner is at %d, %d",
        window_info.x, window_info.y);
sprintf(buf[nmsg++], "backing store: %d",
        window_into.backing_store);
```

Unfortunately the message generated by the last statement is not very informative because it has an integer value of significance only to Xlib. A better solution is to use a switch depending on the symbolic names for backing store values:

Listing 2.4.   Window Spying-File `spy.c` (Part 4)

```c
/* Interrogate Window Properties - Grabbing the pointer */
#include <stdio.h>
void grab_pointer (Window w)
{
    int gstat = XGrabPointer (Dpy, w,
        False, /* events to window */
        ButtonPressMask | ButtonReleaseMask,
        GrabModeAsync, /* for pointer */
        GrabModeAsync, /*  for keyboard */
        None, /*  no confinement */
        grab_cursor,
        CurrentTime);
    if (gstat==GrabSuccess) {
        grab = 1;
        repaint();
    }
    else fprintf (stderr, "Failed to Grab Pointer!\n");
}
void release_pointer (void)
{
    if (grab) XUngrabPointer (Dpy, CurrentTime);
    grab = 0;
    repaint();
}
```

```c
switch(window_info.backing_store) {
case Always:
    sprintf(buf[nmsg++],
    "backing store is always available");
    break;
case WhenMapped:
    sprintf(buf[nmsg++],
        "backing store is available when window is mapped");
    break;
case NotUseful:
    sprintf(buf[nmsg++], "backing store is not useful");
    break;
default:
}
```

Listing 2.4.   Window Spying-File `spy.c` (Part 5)

```
/* Ask for all information */
void window_stats(Window w)
{
    window_stats_attr(w);
    window_stats_prop(w);
}
/* Interrogate Window Attributes -
Finding out about the Window */
void window_stats_attr (Window w)
{
    XWindowAttributes window_info;
    nmsg = 1;
    XGetWindowAttributes(Dpy, w, &window_info);
    sprint (buf[nmsg++], "dimensions %d by %d"),
        window_info.width, window_info.height); /* ... */
}
```

Listing 2.4 (Part 6) shows a similar program for investigating window properties.

Note: The program in Listing 2.4 (Part 6) is not complete, see Project 4.

Listing 2.4.   Window Spying-File `spy.c` (Part 6)

```
/* Interrogate Window Properties -
Finding about the Window */
void window_stats_prop(Window w)
{
    Atom *atom_prop;
    int num_prop = 0;
    char property_name[32];
    register i;
    atom_prop = XListProperties (Dpy, w, &num_prop);
    if (num_prop < 1) return;
    sprintf(buf[nmsg++], "%d properties", num_prop);
    for (i=0; i<num_prop; i++) {
        /* Display the atom names instead of the numerical
        values */
        sprintf (property_name, "%s",
            XGetAtomName(Dpy,  atom_prop[i]));
        switch (atom_prop[i]) {
```

```
    case XA_WM_NAME:
    {
        XTextProperty data;
        XGetWMName(Dpy, w, &data);
        sprintf(buf[nmsg++], "%s: %s"", property_name,
        data.value);
    }
    break;
    case XA_WM_CLIENT_MACHINE:
    /* ... */
    default: sprintf(buf[nmsg++], "%s", property_name);
    }
}
}
```

2.6. CONCLUSIONS

Chapter 2 examines the mechanism of window creation by Xlib and briefly discusses the X protocol and interaction between window managers and other applications. For most if not all applications, the programmer need not be concerned with those issues because these are handled by various toolkits. However they are important issues because they are the basis of the X Window System,

Creating applications with Xlib alone can be a formidable process. The program in Listing 2.1 is misleadingly simple. Not only does the window lack functionality, it also lacks significant features needed to conform to the *ICCCM* (see Section 1.1.3). The Xt takes care of the latter, and it also provides mechanisms for adding functionality, so in most applications the programmer does not have to worry about conforming to *ICCCM* or attaching properties to a window.

While window creation is always hidden from the application by the toolkits, user-generated events may not be. For such events the user must deal directly with the XEvent (union of) structure(s). Depending on the toolkit being used it may even be necessary to deal with some window properties (Section 4.2.6 shows how to handle the WM_DELETE_WINDOW message from Xt).

Note: The programming style often associated with X reflects the constraints of Xt rather than Xlib. This is certainly the case with modal input.

2.7. PROJECTS

1. Locate the shell script that starts X in your system and try to identify statements that refer to the server and the window manager.

2. Investigate how to run your programs on a different machine from the one controlling the display. Normally the Unix shell variable DISPLAY contains the necessary information. (Type echo $DISPLAY to see the current destination. Most likely the answer will be : 0 . 0, which stands for local display.) If you are sitting in front of a display controlled by a machine named saturn and you want to run your program on a machine named jupiter, the following sequence may work. (Bold characters denote the machine prompt.)

```
saturn 12 % xhost +jupiter
saturn 13 % rlogin jupiter
jupiter 1 % setenv DISPLAY saturn:0
jupiter 2 % a.out
```

Details of this operation depend on the particular installation, so you should ask your instructor or system administrator for help if the preceding sequence does not work. (The third statement assumes a C shell command interpreter. Although it is the most commonly used shell in educational environments, it is not universal.)

3. Write a program to create a window in each of several displays. You must modify Listing 2.1 by enclosing all statements referring to Dpy in a loop, then replacing the empty string in Statement 1 by the appropriate machine name. To execute your program, secure appropriate permission for each machine. You can make that program useful by displaying a message in each window. (To do so requires you need material in Chap. 8, which can be read any time, since it depends only on Chap. 1.)

4. Implement the program in Listing 2.4 and complete it so that it displays information about all attributes and properties.

3

Introduction to the X
Toolkit

3.1. WIDGETS

3.1.1. Basic Definitions   Creating a window can be a complex affair because we must deal with interclient communications and other requirements not yet discussed. On the other hand creating a window is a very common operation that any X program does. These two conditions, commonality and difficulty, led to the development of Xt, which we previewed in Sec. 1.2.2.

The Xt includes some basic widgets, which are much larger and more complex window objects than the example in Listing 1.4. We later examine the internals of the widgets, but here we point out that these widgets form a hierarchy, the *widget class hierarchy*. A widget class is a type of window object. The Xt provides a *Core* widget class containing necessary information for any widget. Other widget classes are built by adding members to the core widget structure.

Definition

Widget class B is derived from widget class A, or B is a subclass of A, if the structure of B contains all members of A in addition to the other members of its own class.

Thus Xt has a *Composite* widget class derived from the Core class by adding members that deal with children. (In that sense the window object in Listing 1.4 is a composite window object.) According to the preceding definition, the Composite class is a *subclass* of the Core class. Subclass seems counterintuitive because the Composite class has more members than the Core class, but it makes sense in terms of class hierarchy.

Two classes are derived from the Composite class: *Constraint* and *Shell*. Constraint widgets can have many children, and they can control their layouts. Shell widgets can have only one child, but they can interact with the window manager. These four classes are the major *base classes* of Xt. Figure 3.1. shows the relationship between their structures, and Figure 3.2 shows the hierarchy.

Since the base classes are incomplete, additional work is needed to construct widget classes that can be used by application programs. This is where such toolkits as *Athena*, *OLIT*, and *Motif* come into play: They provide many widget classes that can be used by application programs. Each widget class has a name used by application programs, for example `commandWidgetClass` in Listing 1.2. The names are actually pointers to structures; somewhere in the system code there is a definition:

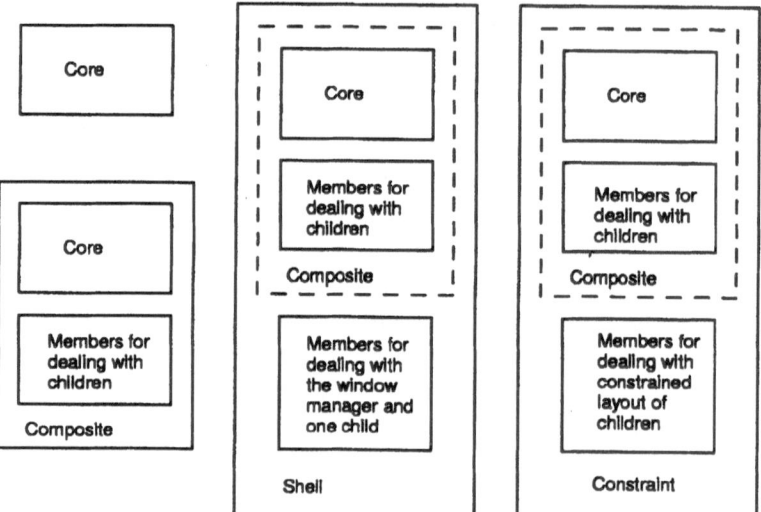

Figure 3.1. Relationship among the Core, Composite, Constrained, and Shell class structures.

```
typedef struct ...     *commandWidgetClass;
```

However application programs are not supposed to access the members of the structures directly.

3.1.2. Widget Class Hierarchy, Widget Tree, and Instances Do not confuse class hierarchy with the application widget tree (see Sec. 1.2.1). The former describes how classes are derived from one another; the latter describes which window includes another, and it is also used as a data structure for storing the widgets. The distinction becomes clearer if we distinguish between a widget class and an *instance* of a widget.

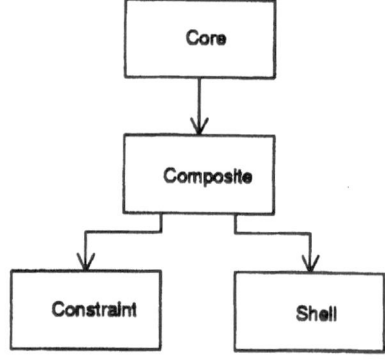

Figure 3.2.   Widget class hierarchy for the base classes.

A widget class is a structure definition, such as shown in Listing 1.4. An instance of a widget is a particular object whose type belongs to the class. Thus in Listing 1.1 variables `toplevel` and `button` each point to an instance of the window object. In the following a statement, `int` is a type of variable, while n and m are instances of that type:

```
int n, m;
```

Important Point

Class hierarchy deals with classes themselves, whereas the widget tree consists of instances of widgets.

Figure 3.3 shows the window layout and the widget tree for an application with a selection panel with buttons and a drawing window. The top widget of the widget tree is always a shell widget because it must deal with the window manager. A shell widget can have only one child, so that child must be a composite widget or even better a constraint widget. A constraint class widget is preferable because it can dynamically manage the layout of its children. In this case it has two children: A panel widget (a subclass of Composite) and a drawing widget (which may be a subclass of Core). The panel widget has as many children as buttons.

In general class hierarchy is primarily of interest to widget writers, so most application programs do not have to deal with it. However the widget tree is of

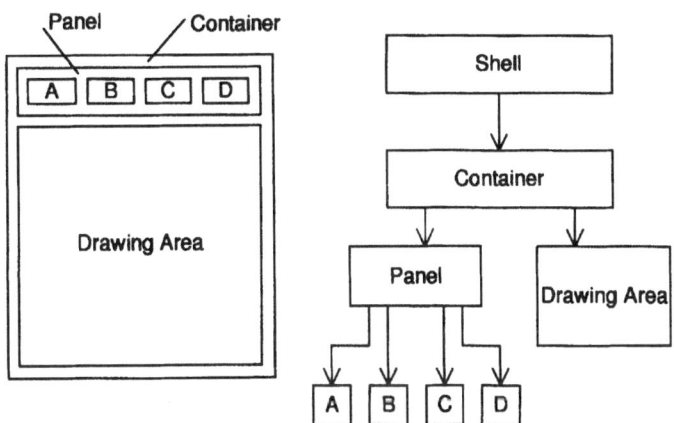

Figure 3.3. A window layout and the respective widget tree.

obvious interest: with one exception it determines the containment relationship of
an application windows.

Pop-up widgets are the exception to the containment rule. The window of a
pop-up widget is always a child of the root window, but the widget itself can be the
child of any widget in the tree, including the top shell widgets. (The rule that shell
widgets must have only one child does not apply to pop-up widgets. Shell widgets
can have only one *managed* child.) We discuss pop-up widgets in more detail in
Sec. 4.5.

3.1.3. Widget Creation and Parameter Specification Widgets are
created with the function XtVaCreateManagedWidget(), which we first
saw in Sec. 1.2.1. (Listing 1.1) with the call:

```
button = XtVaCreateManagedWidget ("button",
    commandWidgetClass, toplevel, XtNlabel, "Hello World"
    XtNwidth, 256, XtNheight, 256, NULL);
```

The first argument of the function is the name of the widget instant, the second the
widget class, the third the parent widget, and the rest refer to *resource* values. In this
case parameters are passed as pairs of names and values. There is another function
for creating that accepts resource values in a different format. The corresponding
example to the preceding call is.

```
Arg Parameters[]={
     { XtNlabel, "Hello World" },
     { XtNwidth, 256, },
     { XtNheight, 256 } };
/* ... */
    button = XtCreateManagedWidget("button",
        commandWidgetClass, toplevel, Parameters, 3);
```

The type Arg is defined as a structure with two members: A pointer to a
character string and a long integer that holds either values (as in the case of
XtNwidth and XtNheight) or pointers (as in the case of XtNlabel). The type
ArgList is a pointer to Arg.

All widget functions that accept resource values as arguments come in two
forms; in general:

```
XtSomething( /* ... */, Array_of_Arg_Structures,
    Number_of_Elements);
XtVaSomething ( /* ... */, Resource_Name, Value,
    Resource_Name, Value, NULL);...
```

The NULL value (for a resource name) tells the function that the list is finished. For example in Listing 1.1 we used

```
toplevel = XtVaAppInitialize( &app, "Trivial",
    NULL, 0, &arc, arv, NULL, NULL);
```

We could instead used

```
top = XtAppInitialize( &app, "Trivial",
    NULL, 0. &arc, arv, NULL,
    (Arg)NULL, 0);
```

Functions that accept a variable number of arguments are called *varargs* routines; these were not part of early Xt releases. While indirectly passing the XtSomething() form usually results in more economical code, explicitly passing pairs in XtVaSomething() results in more informative code; given the educational goals of this book, we prefer the latter.

Widget parameters can be set or read by a pair of functions that have the following prototypes:

```
XtVaSetValues (Widget, name and value pairs,...,NULL)
XtVaGetValues (Widget, name and value address pairs,...,
NULL)
```

There are certain restrictions on how values are specified that apply to both varargs and the original routines.

Caution

In set value functions (either XtVaSetValues() or XtSetValues()), values should be in the type expected by the program or one automatically converted into the type expected by C. (For example int will do if short is expected.) Values cannot be given as strings.

For example it is wrong to call

```
/* wrong code */
XtVaSetValue(w, XtNbackground, "blue", NULL);
```

Instead we must compute a pixel value that corresponds to blue, then call

```
Pixel blue;
/*  ...  */
XtVaSetValue(w, XtNbackground, blue, NULL);
```

Section 3.3.5 discusses how to do such a conversion. Restrictions on type are much stricter for get value functions.

Caution

When calling a get value function (either `XtGetValue()` or `XtGetValues()`), special care must be taken to provide the *exact* type for value arguments that Xt expects.

For example:

```
Dimension width, height;
XtVaGetValues(w, XtNwidth, &width, XtNheight, &height,
NULL);
```

The type `dimension` is declared by the Intrinsics to be `unsigned short`. The following code results in an error in systems where `int` is not the same size as `short`:

```
/* wrong code */
int width, height;
XtVaGetValues(w, XtNwidth, &width, XtNheight, &height,
NULL);
```

There is a way of getting around specifying values in their true type that is offered only by varargs routines. If we provide the argument `XtVaTypedArg` as the resource name, then the Intrinsics use the subsequent four arguments to compute the resource value from a string representation. For example we can set the background color to blue by using the following code:

```
XtVaSetValue(w, XtVaTypedArg,
    XtNbackground, XtRString, "blue", strlen("blue")+1,
    NULL);
```

The first of the four arguments is the resource name; the second is the type of the value. Since we plan to use this feature with value names, the second argument must always be XtRString. The third argument is the string with the name of the value, and the fourth is the length of the string. (The mechanism of XtVaTypedArg is more general than we just described, but the form we gave is enough for the scope of this book.)

We return to using set value functions in Sec. 3.4, where we give some reasons for restricting their use.

3.1.4. Some Specific Classes and Some of Their Resources   Resources are the common mechanism used to specify widget parameters because they allow parameter specification at either compilation or execution time.

The most basic class is Core, which has 18 resources; these are also resources of every other widget class. Here we discuss those most relevant to simple programs. Five of these are used to determine the window position and dimensions; these are called the *geometry* resources: XtNx, XtNy (coordinates of top left corner with default value 0), XtNwidth, XtNheight (dimensions with default value 0), and XtNborderWidth (default value 1). The type of the first two is Position (actually int), and the other three are Dimension (actually unsigned short).

The color of the window is specified by XtNbackground, whose type is Pixel (actually unsigned long). There is also XtNborderColor, with the obvious meaning. Default values for the background color is usually white and for the border color, black. Core does *not* have a XtNforeground resource (color with which to draw on). That resource exists only in some derived classes.

A few other resources describe display device properties, and these are normally used mainly for information by application programs; for example XtNdepth is the number of bits per pixel. The resource XtNcolormap refers to the colormap, the table that establishes conversion between bit patterns stored in refresh memory and actual colors (see Sec. 1.4.1). This resource may be modified by application programs (see Chap. 9).

The resource XtNmappedWhenManaged (of type Boolean and default value TRUE) is a flag whose use is explained in Sec. 3.1.5.

The Shell class is important because it is the class of the top widget of each application as well as of any pop-ups. There are actually four shell classes; the one of interest at the moment is ApplicationShell. The following are some of its most commonly used resources: XtNtitle (the string that goes on the window frame created by the window manager), XtNiconPixmap (the icon that appears when the window is iconified), XtNiconX and XtNiconY (the position of the icon), etc. We discuss shell widgets in more detail in Sec. 5.5.

3.1.5. Widget Realization, Management, and Mapping   Widgets are client structures; when they are created, their windows are not. There is a good reason for that: Container widget dimensions are not usually known until its children are created. For example menu panel dimensions depend on its button dimensions, and the dimensions of the latter are determined by their label size. Thus we normally wait until all widgets are created before creating their windows. The following function not only creates the window of w but also those of all *managed* widgets in the tree whose root is w:

```
void XtRealizeWidget(Widget w)
```

By definition a managed widget is one that is taken into account when the window dimensions of its parents are computed (see Sec. 5.1.2 for more on this topic). For now we deal only with managed widgets.

The function XtRealizeWidget() is normally called with the argument of the topmost application widget. If the resource XtNmappedWhenManaged is true, then the widget window is also mapped; i.e. it appears on the screen (see Sec. 5.1.2 for explicitly mapping and unmapping widgets). This is the most common case, but there are times when we do not want to display a widget, for example a button that can be used only after the program has reached a certain state.

The difference between a managed unmapped widget and an unmanaged widget is that the space occupied by the widget appears vacant in the former case, while no such space is shown when the widget is unmanaged. If the button in the example is initially unmanaged, then later managed, it causes a rearrangement of its parent's entire layout, which may disturb the application user. If the button is managed and initially unmapped, when mapped it simply fills a vacant space in its parent's layout.

3.2. USING RESOURCES

3.2.1. Overview Resources are a mechanism used by X (and other window systems) to facilitate customizing programs. X not only allows parameters to be specified through the command line but also through files read at execution time. We already considered this subject in Sec. 1.2.2; here we discuss it in more depth.

Resources can refer to a widget or an application. X lets you specify resources in six ways:

1. As part of a property (RESOURCE_MANAGER) of the root window of the display; this ensures that such resources are used by all applications running on that machine.
2. Within a set of files that each program searches according to certain rules (we provided an example in Sec. 1.2.2).

3. As part of the command line argument list (see Sec. 3.2.3).
4. Through a fallback mechanism (discussed in Sec. 3.2.4).
5. As part of the arguments of the widget creation function [for example `XtVaCreateManagedWidget()` in Listing 1.1] or through the `XtVaSetValues()` function.
6. As default values of the widget.

The application user has access only to the first three mechanisms; mechanisms 4–5 are used by application programmers. While a different parameter specification method may be possible during program writing, the use of resources ensures uniformity in the parameter specification mechanism.

Resources are a mixed blessing: While a degree of customization is desirable, it can also be carried too far. A common example is language customization. All text labels can reside within an application as resources, and we can place all actual text in a resource file. Then to run the program using a different language, we need change only the resource file. We believe this is too drastic a change to be left to the users: There is not much harm to a program if a user displays text labels in lime green on a peach color background (instead of black on white), but displaying the wrong text can be disastrous. X does not provide different security levels for resources, so language customization must be done through an include file that requires program compilation (but no editing of the source).

The resource mechanism assumes that the user (or the user's administrator) will do things right. This is a rather optimistic assumption, so *resource files* or *resource command line arguments* should never be used for essential program parameters. As we explain in Sec. 3.2.6, resource specification by function arguments (Mechanism 5) always overrides other specifications, and it should be used only for critical parameters. By the same token such specification should be avoided for resources where we want to allow user customization.

X has a resource database utility `xrdb`, which changes resource values in files without having to edit such files explicitly. The program operates by setting the RESOURCE_MANAGER property in the root window. Running the following piece of code displays the resource database for the root window which is used by all programs running on the server:

```
xrdb -query
```

Running the following piece of code adds the resources in the file `new_stuff` to the RESOURCE_MANAGER property:

```
xrdb -merge new_stuff
```

If the file name is missing, the following piece of code reads the standard input:

```
xrdb -merge
```

The following command copies the RESOURCE_MANAGER property into a file named junk: xrdb -file junk. The following command places the contents of the file into the RESOURCE_MANAGER property: xrdb -load junk.

Since resources specified in this way apply to all programs, we should not use it carelessly (see Sec. 3.2.6).

3.2.2.   A Minimal Program   In this section we create a minimal application consisting of an application shell and a core widget to explain how the Xt deals with resources and (see Sec. 4.2) events. The core widget can be used as a drawing widget, as we explain in Sec. 5.6, but here we are concerned only with resource specification, so, we do not provide the application with functionality. Listing 3.1 shows such a minimal program.

The call XtAppInitialize() hides many operations, including initializing Xt, establishing a connection to the server (by calling XOpenDisplay (" ")), dealing with resources, and creating an application shell widget. (Actually this is a convenience function that calls five others that do the work.) The app (of type XtAppContext) is a useful structure for programs that open connections to many servers. (It contains an array of Display pointers.) It is of no use in programs that use only one server, but we must carry it along as a price for generality. The string "Min" specifies an *applications class*—a name for related programs that may have similar resources. We ignore arguments set to NULL or 0 for the time being and point out that we pass arguments from main() to XtAppInitialize(). Since these are parsed for values recognized by Xt they offer a way to provide resource values. In particular the first argument (arv[0]), which is the name of the program, is used to label the top widget in the widget tree.

The function XtVaCreateManagedWidget() creates the drawing widget, and XtRealizeWidget() creates and maps the windows. The function XtAppMainLoop() executes an infinite loop that checks for events (see Sec. 4.1). The program can be compiled and linked with the following Make-file:

```
INCLUDE = -I/usr/local/X11R6/include
LIB     = -L/usr/local/X11R6/lib
CFLAGS  = ${INCLUDE} -I. -g
$(PGM): $(PGM).o
   $(CC)    $(PGM).o $(LIB)  -lXt -lX11 -lm -o $(PGM)
```

If we run the program, a window appears, but when we exit from the surrounding window, we notice the error message in Sec. 2.4.2. This will not

Listing 3.1. Minimal X Toolkit Program

```
/*  Minimal Xt Program  */
#include <X11/StringDefs.h>
#include <X11/Intrinsic.h>
#include <X11/Shell.h>
#include <X11/Core.h>
int main (int arc, char **arv)
{
    Widget top, canvas;
    XtAppContext app;
    /*  Initialize the X Toolkit, read the resource files,
        open a connection to the server, and create a shell
        widget
    */
    top = XtVaAppInitialize( &app, "Min", NULL, 0,
        &arc, arv, 0,
        NULL);
    /*  Create a canvas widget using the core class  */
    canvas = XtVaCreateManagedWidget ("canvas",
        coreWidgetClass, top
        XtNWidth, 200, XtNheight, 200,
        NULL);
    XtRealizeWidget(top);
    XtAppMainLoop(app);
}
```

happen if we link the program to the Motif or OLIT libraries, but it will persist if we link it to the Athena libraries. In the latter case we need the remedy in Sec. 4.2.6.

3.2.3. Passing Resource Values through the Command Line   The Xt allows us to use the resource mechanism in command line arguments. To use resources to set the application window size we must remove the dimension arguments during creation of the canvas widget, so that the call is

```
canvas = XtVaCreateManagedWidget ("canvas",
    coreWidgetClass, top,
    NULL);
```

If we compile the program and run it without arguments, it will fail because the default dimensions of core are 0 and X will not create a window with either of these equal to 0. To give different dimensions, we can execute

```
min -xrm "*width : 200" -xrm "*height : 50"
```

The command line arguments were passed to XtVaAppInitialize(), where
they were parsed to extract resources. When the argument -xrm is seen, the next
argument is parsed as a line from a resource file.

This form seems cumbersome; it is simpler to write

```
min -w 200 -h 50
```

It is possible to do that by using the third and fourth arguments of
XtVaAppInitialize() as described in Listing 3.2.

If we compile this code, then we can run it as:

```
min1 -w 400 -h 500
```

Listing 3.2. Specifying the Form of the Command Line

```
/*  Command Line Argument Specification  */
/*  Same include files as in Listing 3.1  */
/*  Instructions on parsing the command line for
    resources  */
XrmOptionDescRec command_line_syntax[] = {
        {"-w", "*width", XrmoptionSepArg, NULL},
        { "-h", "*height", XrmoptionSepArg, NULL },
        };
main (int arc, char **arv)
{
    Widget top, canvas;
    XtAppContext app;
    /*  Initialize the X Toolkit, open a connection to the
    server, look at resources, and create a shell widget */
    top = XtVaAppInitialize( &app, "Min1",
      command_line_syntax, 2,
        &arc, arv, 0, NULL);
    /*  The rest is the same as in Listing 3.1  */
}
```

to obtain a window 400 by 500 pixels in size. The entry `XrmoptionSepArg` is a symbolic constant specifying that the resource value should be taken from the next argument in the command line.

The `XrmOptionDescRec` contains four members: Two character strings— `option` (the command line argument defined) and `specifier` (the resource name); an enumerator (in effect an integer) `argKind` (for storing a symbolic name, such as the preceding `XrmoptionSepArg`); and a `caddr_t` (pointer), called `value`, where we store a value to be used if the third argument is `XrmoptionNoArg`. The type `XrmOptionDescList` is defined as a pointer to a `XrmOptionDescRec` structure.

There are a few other abbreviations known to Xt including the following:

`-bg`	Next argument is the name of the window (background) color
`-fg`	Next argument is the name of the drawing (foreground) color
`-font`	Next argument is the font name
`-title`	Next argument is the title on the window frame
`-rv`	Windows appear in reverse video (no extra argument)
`-iconic`	Applications starts in iconic form (minimized, no extra argument)
`-geometry`	Specify geometry (see discussion below)
`-sync`	Run in synchrony between client server (good for debugging)

For example the following piece of code displays a green window with the title "Green Acres" (the first two flags are specified in the code of `min1.c` in Listing 3.2):

```
min1 -w 400 -h 500 -bg green -title "Green Acres"
```

The first three flags (`-bg`, `-fg`, and `-font`) are applicable to any widget; the rest applies only to the top shell. Unique abbreviations are also acceptable, for example `-g` for `-geometry`. See Sec. 3.6 [AS90] for a complete list of command line abbreviations known to Xt.

The geometry resource has a specific syntax:

width×height+x+y

where the names in italics must be replaced by integers; $+$ may be replaced by $-$. Not all arguments must be present. The following examples are all legal:

```
... -g 500x300            # Main window to be 500 pixels wide
                          # and 300 pixels tall
```

```
... -g +400              # Main window to be 400 pixels to
                         # the right of the top left corner
... -g 500×300+400       # All of the above
... -g ×100              # Main window to be 100 pixels tall
```

Using command line arguments for resources is easy for simple programs, but it presents potential conflicts in complex programs that expect many arguments of their own. Some flags, such as -g and -t, are common letters that may have a more natural use in certain applications. On the other hand the -xrm flag is rather unique, so it should pose no problems. An even better solution is to use a common prefix, for example X, for X resources to avoid conflicts. If we modify the code in Listing 3.2 as:

```
{ "-Xw", "*width", XrmoptionSepArg, NULL },
{ "-Xh", "*height", XrmoptionSepArg, NULL },
```

then we use the following command line to define window dimensions:

```
min1 -Xw 400 -Xh 500
```

Listing 3.3. Fallback Resources

```
/*  Fallback Resources  */
/*  Same include files in Listing 3.1  */
/*  Resource values if found nowhere else (last resort)  */
String fallbacks []={
    "*width: 100", "*height: 300",
    NULL);
main (int arc, char **arv)
{
    Widget top canvas;
    XtAppContext app;
    /*  Initialize the X Toolkit, open a connection to the
    server, look at resources, and create a shell
    widget  */
    top = XtVaAppInitialize( &app, "Min",
        (XrmOptionDescList) NULL, 0,
        &arc, arv, fallbacks, NULL);
    /*  the rest is the same as Listing 3.1  */
}
```

Unfortunately, there is no way of preventing the Intrinsics from interpreting arguments as they do except by removing such arguments before passing them to `XtVaAppInitialize()`. The convention of using a special prefix for all arguments interpreted by X was not adopted, even though similar conventions were used in earlier window systems, such as SUNVIEW.

3.2.4. Fallback Resources   The seventh argument of `XtVaAppInitialize()` can be used to pass a pointer to an array of *fallback* resources. Its use is shown in Listing 3.3. `String` is defined as `char *`, and the array `fallbacks` is an array of pointers to strings treated as lines of a resource file.

If the program `min2` is run without arguments it produces a window 100 by 300 pixels in size (rather than fail as does the program in Listing 3.2). These default values can be overridden by passing arguments, for example:

```
min2 -xrm "*width: 500"
```

Fallback resources are useful if an application allows the user to specify a resource but does not use the widget default value, if the user fails to do so.

Recommended

Fallback resources should always be used to specify *noncritical* parameters instead of passing the values as arguments at widget creation time or through the set value functions.

Using the fallback mechanism allows later customization by the application user. With assignments through fallbacks, we do not have to worry about value conversion. Thus for a widget with name `pad` to have a blue background, we need the fallback entry:

```
"*pad.background: blue"
```

The order of items in the fallback array is not important. Unfortunately fallbacks make the program code more difficult to read, a major concern for beginners.

Finally we can combine all resource specification methods at application initialization to create the program in Listing 3.4.

3.2.5.   Resource Line Syntax   The following basic rules are used to specify resource lines whether in a file, command line, or fallback array.

Listing 3.4.   Using all Arguments of XtAppinitialize-File min.c

```
/* Illustration of the arguments of XtVaAppInitialize () */
#include <X11/StringDefs.h>
#include <X11/Intrinsic.h>
#include <X11/Core.h>


/*  Instructions on parsing the command line for
resources  */
XrmOptionDescRec command_line_syntax[] = {
        { "-w", "*width", XrmoptionSepArg, NULL),
        { "-h", "*height", XrmoptionSepArg, NULL),
        };
/*  Resource values if found nowhere else (last resort)  */
String fallbacks[] = {
    "*width: 100", "*height: 300",
    NULL);
int main (int arc, char **arv)
{
    Widget top, canvas;
    XtAppContext app;
    /*  Initialize the X Toolkit, open a connection to the
    server, look at resources, and create a shell widget
    */
    top = XtVaInitialize( &app, "Min",
        command_line_syntax, 2,
        &arc, arv, fallbacks, NULL);
    /*  Create a canvas widget  */
    canvas = XtVaCreateManagedWidget("canvas",
        coreWidgetClass, top,
        NULL);
    XtRealizeWidget(top);
    XtAppMainLoop(app);
}
```

Each resource line has two parts separated by a colon, the specification of the resource and its value.

Resource specification can be given in terms of instances (lower case letters) or classes (initial capital letters). A *complete* specification starts with the application name followed by names of widgets of the tree path that leads to the widget that has the resource, followed by the resource name. Each entry is separated by a period, for example for the program in Listing 3.2:

```
min1.canvas.width: 400
```

Instead of the program name, we may also use the application class (second argument of XtVaAppInitialize()) mentioned in Sec. 3.2.2, for example:

```
Min.canvas.width: 400
```

We may also replace the widget name by the class name, for example:

```
min1.Core.width: 400
```

or

```
Min.Core.width: 400
```

If there is more than one specification, the more specific one takes precedence (widget name over class name, application name over application class). In this example the order from most specific to least specific is

```
min1.canvas.width: 1000
min1.Core.width: 500
Min.canvas.width: 250
Min.core.width: 125
```

In this case all Core class widgets in application min1 have width 500, except those named canvas; those will have width 1000. (Note: A widget name need not be unique within an application if all widgets with the same name can have the same resources.) In applications other than min1 but of class Min, the width of Core class widgets will be 125 except those named canvas; those will have width 250.

It is possible to omit and replace some names by an asterisk, '*', a process called *wildcarding*. This makes sense in our example, where we have only one canvas widget, for example:

```
min1*width: 500
```

We have already used this notation in the examples of the previous section where we used *complete wildcarding* such as:

```
*width: 200
```

While starting a resource with an asterisk is perfectly safe in a command line or fallback specification, it should be used with care in file specifications because it applies to *all* programs.

Caution

The asterisk symbol (*) does *not* have the same meaning as in Unix shell commands and regular expressions. It stands for complete widget names (or classes) or a sequence of the same.

For example, the following piece of code does *not* apply to all programs whose name starts with a *z* but only to the program named *z*. z*width: 200 The correct way of specifying program classes is through the second argument of XtVaAppInitialize().

3.2.6.   Priorities   What happens if a resource is specified in more than one place? To understand the process, we must look at the places where resources are specified. The application initialization function (XtVaAppInitialize()) reads the files, parses command line arguments, and looks at fallbacks. Resource specification through function arguments (Mechanism 5 in Sec. 3.2.1) comes later in the program; therefore *resources as function arguments override all others*.

Other things being equals, command line arguments have priority over values read from files or from the RESOURCE_MANAGER property. Fallbacks come into play only if a resource is not already specified. Thus *fallbacks have the lowest priority except for widget default values*.

The situation is more complex for files, but here is a general principle: *The tighter the specification, the higher the priority.* Thus specifications tied to an application take priority over general widget specifications.

We do not discuss priorities between *different* files where a resource can be specified. When the XENVIRONMENT variable specifies a file (the mechanism discussed in Sec. 1.2.2), that file takes priority over all others. Rules for other files are rather complex; we do not need to know them until we write a program that will be made public. Many resources are kept in the file named .Xdefaults in the user's home directory; the contents of that file are normally loaded into the RESOURCE_MANAGER property at start-up time.

Priorities are clearly established by the time something is specified. Since widgets are created after the call to XtVaAppInitialize(), values specified at creation time override any values specified during that call. Since `XtVaSetVa-lues()` is called after widget creation, it has the highest priority of all.

Caution

Never specify a resource value through `XtVaSetValues()` [or `XtSet-Values()`] unless you really mean that this is the only value allowed. The same warning applies to specifications at widget creation time.

3.3. RESOURCE DEFINITION

3.3.1. Concept   So far we have discussed the resource mechanism in application programs. By associating a character string and a value, we can specify parameters for widgets through function arguments, command line arguments, and files. Here we describe how such resources are defined. All examples in this chapter apply to application resources, but the mechanism is identical for widget resources as well.

The simplest way of defining a resource is to associate a character string (resource name) with the memory location where the value is stored, for example:

```
typedef struct {
    const char *name;
    int value;
} mini_resource
```

(We use the `const` qualifier to make sure the name does not change.) Then we can use this type in a program to specify two integer parameters as follows:

```
mini_resource v[2] = {
    {"start",1 },
    {"stop", 100 }
};
```

Inside the program we use the values `v[0].value` or `v[1].value`, etc. This definition provides default values that can be changed in various ways. For example we can pass them through the command line as follows:

```
a.out -start 20
```

For this scheme to work, inside the program we need a loop with such code as:

```
for(i=1; i<arc; i++) (  /* examine all arguments  */
    if (arv [i][0]=='-') {
        for (j=0; j<2; j++) {
            if (strcmp(v[j].name, arv[i]+1)==0) {
                if (i+1 < arc) {
                    int n = atoi(arv[i+1]);
                    if (n > 0) v[j].value = n;
                }
                break;
            }
        }
    }
}
```

The function strcmp() returns 0 when the two strings match. In this case the match occurs for i equal to 1 and j equal to 0, so that:

```
v[0].value = atoi (arv[2]);
```

In this example we accept all positive values; other permissible ranges can be treated the same way.

While this simple mechanism works, it has many disadvantages. First it allows only integer parameters. Obviously we need a wider range, and we also need additional *conversion* routines besides atoi(). Second we need to separate the name definition from the value definition, since having these in the same structure makes awkward programs if there is another more natural parameter grouping. It would be better to have an address next to the name instead of a value, for example:

```
typedef struct {
    char *name;
    int *place;
} mini_resource;
```

X goes farther by including in the resource structure information about the type and default values, a class name (so that values can be specified for a group of resources), etc.

3.3.2.   Resources in X   We continue with the example in Sec. 3.3.1, but now we create a new structure to store values of the two parameters:

```
typedef struct {
    int kstart;
    int kstop;
} Parameters;
```

Then we use X facilities to create a *resource* array with elements of type XtResource, which in this case has the form:

```
static XtResource my_resources[] = {
    {"start", "Start", XtRInt, sizeof(int),
    XtOffSetOf(Parameters, kstart),
    XtRImmediate, (XtPointer)1},
    {"stop", "Stop", XtRInt, sizeof(int),
    XtOffsetOf(Parameters, kstop),
    XtRImmediate, (XtPointer)100 },
};
```

While the initialization statement of my_resources[] is more complex than the initialization of the array v[] in Sec. 3.3.1, it is also more general. The resource structure not only connects parameters with strings, it also provides instructions to a parsing function. The first two elements of each item are the resource name and the resource class name. The third item is a symbolic string specifying its type from a set supported by the Intrinsics; in this case XtRInt defined as "Int". We use a string rather than the C type int to adhere to the type definitions of the Intrinsics that need not always be equivalent to C types. The fourth item is the size of the parameter. The fifth member precomputes the offset of the resource variable from the start of the structure using the macro XtOffsetOf(). This associates the resource named "start" with the variable parameter kstart.

The last two members refer to the default value of the resource: The sixth is the default type (XtRImmediate in this case) and the seventh the address where the default value may be stored. In general the default type should be the same as the resource type (the third member). However there are two major exceptions to this policy. The type XtRImmediate (used in the preceding example) specifies that the seventh member is the default value rather than the address of the default. In our example default values of kstart and kstop are 1 and 100, respectively, cast to XtPointer to match the structure element type. The type XtRCallProc (demonstrated later) specifies that the value in the address field is a procedure pointer.

One of the tasks of the XtVaAppInitialize() [more specifically of one of the functions it calls: XtOpenDisplay()] is to find resource values. It collects them from files, command arguments, fallbacks, etc. To make them accessible to the rest of the application we must call the function

```
XtVaGetApplicationResources(),
```

which has the following prototype:

```
XtVaGetApplicationResources(Widget w,
XtPointer where_to_store,
XtResource *resource_specs,
int number_of_resource_specs, NULL);
```

This function looks at the resource data base for names matching those present in the array of resource structures `resource_specs` (first or second members), then stores the corresponding values in the location by the fifth member of the resource structure. In our example we must first create the database, then call this function:

```
static Parameters v;
/* ... */
   toplevel=XtVaAppInitialize( /* ... */);
   /* ... */
   XtVaGetApplicationResources(toplevel, (XtPointer) &v,
       my_resources, 2, NULL);
```

After this call we can use values `v.kstart` and `v.kstop` any place in the program. The reason for computing the offset in the resource specification is to convey in effect the structure of `v` to the `XtVaGetApplication-Resources()` function.

Listing 3.5 shows a trivial program that prints the values, then exits.

If we compile this program into `a.out` and execute (using the notation in Sec. 3.2.3):

```
a.out -xrm "*start: 40"
```

we obtain the following:

```
start=40 stop=100
```

Note: We let Xt do all the command line parsing and error checking. Clearly these values can also be stored in a resource file like any other resource.

There is no limitations in specifying a parameter as a resource as long as we can describe it through the mechanism of the `XtResource` structure.

Listing 3.5.   Minimal Application Resources — File apres.c

```
#include <X11/StringDefs/h>
#include <X11/Intrinsic.h>
typedef struct {
    int kstart;
    int kstop;
} Parameters;
static XtResource my_resources[] = {
    {"start", "Start", XtRInt, sizeof(int),
    XtOffsetOf(Parameters, kstart),
    XtRImmediate, (XtPointer)1 },
    {"stop", "Stop", XtRInt, sizeof(int),
    XtOffsetOf (Parameters, kstop),
    XtRImmediate, (XtPointer)100 },
};
main (arc, arv)
    char **arv;
{
    XtAppContext app;
    Widget toplevel;
    static Parameters v;
    toplevel=XtVaAppInitialize (&app, "Test",
        NULL, 0, &arc, arv, NULL, NULL);
    XtVaGetApplicationResources (toplevel, (XtPointer) &v,
        my_resources, 2, NULL);
    printf ("start=%d stop=%d\n", v.kstart, v.kstop);
}
```

3.3.3.   Quarks   Because resources are expressed through character strings, functions dealing with resources must perform many string comparisons (as in the example in Sec. 3.3.1). It is desirable to map strings to an integer to replace string comparisons with integer comparisons. We already saw one such mapping in Sec. 2.4.2: Atoms were introduced as string mappings used for window properties.

The X Window System provides another set of unique mappings for strings: *Quarks*. While atoms are used to represent strings uniquely within the server, quarks are used to represent strings uniquely *within an application*. The type of these numbers is XrmQuark (actually an integer). The following two Xlib functions perform conversions between strings and quarks:

```
XrmQuark XrmStringToQuark (char * string)
char * XrmQuarkToString (XrmQuark quark)
```

While quarks are used mainly for resource management, they can be used for any string conversion in the application.

3.3.4. XtResource Structure   The type XtResource is defined formally as:

```
typedef struct {
    String resource_name;           /* name for the particular
                                       resource */
    String resource_class;          /* name for a class of
                                       resources */
    String resource_type;           /* describes what type
                                       of variable is the
                                       resource value */
    Cardinal resource_size;         /* how many bytes */
    Cardinal resource_offset;       /* bytes from start of
                                       structure in program
                                       using the resource */
    String default_type;            /* maybe the same as
                                       resource_type */
    XtPointerdefault_addr;          /* address of default
                                       value */
} XtResource, *XtResourceList;
```

We used resource names extensively in Secs. 1.2 and 3.2, often given in symbolic form, for example XtNwidth, defined as "width" in a definition file. Class names are supposed to cover related resources; for example in a program we may have resource for text color ("textcolor"), line color ("lineColor"), and the color of filled areas ("fillColor"). Having a resource class "Color" allows us to assign a common color to text, lines, and filled areas.

The member resource_type is a string describing either a basic C type or a defined C type. We already saw the XtRInt type and its use in the previous section. We discuss additional types in the following examples. (See [AS90], pp. 777–778, for a complete list of resource types.) Members resource_size and resource_offset are used by XtVaGetApplicationResources() to store resource values in as structure provided by the program. (The structure is v in Listing 3.1.) Default type and address were discussed in the previous section.

We devote the rest of this section to examples of different resource types, starting with strings. We assume that our program has the following structure for the parameters it uses.

```
typedef struct {
    Pixel text_color;
    Pixel line_color;
    Bollean fixedwindow;
    int (*work)();
    String work_type;
} OptionsRec;
```

It also contains a declaration, such as:

```
static OptionsRec options;
```

In the current discussion we do not need a detailed explanation of how X handles color (covered in Chap. 9). Here we need know only that a type, `Pixel` (in reality a long integer), stores the value that Xlib functions use to produce a particular color.

Resource specification entries for color parameters may be

```
static XtResource my_resources [] = {
    /* ... */
    {"textColor", "Color", XtRPixel, sizeof(Pixel),
    XtOffsetOf(OptionsRec, text_color),
    XtRString, "red" },
    {"lineColor", "Color", XtRPixel, sizeof(Pixel),
    XtOffsetof(OptionsRec, line_color),
    XtRString, "orange" },
    /* ... */
};
```

The following string in a resource file or in a command line (following a –xrm flag) assigns the color blue to all text labels in the program, but it leaves lines drawn in orange:

```
*textColor: blue
```

The following string assigns the color blue to both text labels and lines:

```
*Color: blue
```

Of course nothing happens until we call

```
XtVaGetApplicationResources( /* top widget name */,
    (XtPointer) &options,
    my_resources, XtNumber(my_resources), NULL);
```

and then use a function to set foreground color, for example (if we use the Starter toolkit to draw):

```
St_set_foregr (options.text_color);
St_put_text (/* ... */);
St_set_foregr (options.line_color);
St_put_line (/* ... */);
```

The Boolean variable fixedwindow can be used to control window resizing (see Sec. 5.5.2); the entry for it in the resource structure may be as follows:

```
{"fixedwindow", "Fixedwindow", XtRBoolean, sizeof(Boolean),
XtOffsetOf(OptionsRec, fixedwindow),
XtRImmediate, (XtPointer) TRUE },
```

It is initialized as true.

The structure OptionsRec includes a function pointer (work) that can be made a background procedure by the call:

```
XtAppAddWorkProc(/*application*/, options.work, /* ... */);
```

We may consider using the resource mechanism to specify different background procedures at execution time; however this does not work because functions *cannot be specified outside the program*. As we saw in Chap. 3, such specifications can be made only through a translation table. This is overkill in our case (the function is not going to be tied to events), so it is best to use a string resource, work_type, then create our own private translation mechanism. The resource specification can be

```
{"work", "Work", XtRString, sizeof(String),
XtOffsetOf(OptionsRec, work_type),
XtRString, "play()" },
```

To remind the application user that this resource leads to selecting functions, we provide resource string values that look like function calls: "play()", "travel()", etc. This is the same notational convention used in translation tables. Listing 3.6 shows a relevant code fragment that translates resource values into function pointers. Using quarks allows us to avoid string comparisons.

Other externally specified resources include (listed with the corresponding C or Intrinsic type)

Listing 3.6. Simple Translation Table

```c
/*  Simple Translation Table  */
static struct {
    XrmQuark q;
    int (*f)();
} F[4];
/* ... */
int travel_f(), play_f(), /* ... */
/* ... */
    F[0].q = XrmStringToQuark ("travel()");
    f[0].f = travel_f;
    F[1].q=XrmStringToQuark ("play()");
    F[1].f=play_f;
/* ... */
    XrmQuark q=XrmStringToQuark(options.work_type);
    for (i=0; i<4; i++) {
        if (q==F[i].q) {
            XtAppAddWorkProc(app, F[i].f, /* ... */);
            break;
        }
    }
```

```
XtRFloat             float
XtRLongBollean       long
XtRPixel             Pixel
XtRShort             short
XtRString            String (char *)
StRStringArray       String* (char **)
```

3.3.5. Resource Conversion One reason for using the Xt resource mechanism is that it provides type conversion facilities. For example we can specify a color by name, then rely on the resource conversion to provide the appropriate bit pattern for its display. (Recall Sec. 1.4.1 on generating color displays). Conversion functions use the following type:

```c
typedef struct {
    unsigned int size;
    caddr_t addr;
} XrmValue, *XrmValuePtr;
```

The basic function for conversions is XtConvertAndStore(), which takes five arguments: A widget, a source type, a source pointer, a destination type, and a destination pointer. Types are (symbolic) strings; the source and destination have type XrmValue. The function returns TRUE when successful, FALSE otherwise. The only reason for including a widget among arguments is to extract information about server resources from its resources, such as the color map (the table linking bit patterns and colors discussed in Sec. 1.4.1). Therefore it is not important which particular widget we pass. We illustrate the use of this function with two examples: One for converting color names into bit patterns and the other for converting character font names into the structure pointers needed by Xlib.

Listing 3.7 shows how resource conversion is used for color. We created a function color_convert() with a simple argument structure that creates arguments needed by XtConvertAndStore(), then calls the latter. The returned Pixel value can be used in the appropriate Xlib structures and functions (discussed in Chap. 8 and 9).

Listing 3.8 shows how to use XtConvertAndStore() to find a pointer to a font structure from a font name. The details of how X handles fonts are discussed in Secs. 8.3.4–8.3.4.6, but we do not have to worry about these now—the resource conversion mechanism does all the work for us. The returned structure pointer can be used in Xlib functions requiring font information.

Besides hiding conversion details from us, the function XtConvertAnd-Store() has a caching mechanism that can avoid unnecessary trips to the server. A discussion of memory management for the cache is beyond our scope (see [AS90], pp. 166–168). The preceding examples also show that the conversion mechanism can be used outside the resource framework. The conversion mechanism is also invoked when we pass an XtVaTypedArg argument to an XtVaSetValues() call (see Sec. 3.1.3). The four arguments that follow

Listing 3.7. Color Name to Pixel Conversion

```
Boolean color_convert(Widget w, String color_name, Pixel
*color_value)
{
    XrmValue source, dest;
    source.size = strlen(color_name)+1;
    source.addr = color_name;
    dest.size   = sizeof(Pixel);
    dest.addr   = (caddr_t)color_value;
    return XtConvertAndStore (w, XtRString, &source,
      XtRPixel, &dest);
}
```

Listing 3.8.   Font Name to Font Structure Conversion

```
Boolean font_convert(Widget, w, String font_name,
 XFontStruct **value)
{
    XrmValue source, dest;
    source.size = strlen(font_name)+1;
    source.addr = font_name;
    dest.size   = sizeof(XFontStruct *);
    dest.addr   = (cadd_r)value;
    return XtConvertAndStore(w, XrRString, &source,
      XtRFontStruct, &dest);
}
```

XtVaTypedArg provide arguments for XtConvertAndStore. The first is the resource name that provides information about the destination. The second argument is used as the second argument of the conversion function, while the third and fourth arguments are used to construct the source argument.

3.3.6.   Finding out about Class Resources   It is possible to find widget class resources by calling the function XtGetResourceList(), which has the following prototype:

```
XtGetResourceList(WidgetClass wc, XtResourceList *rp,
Cardinal *n)
```

The class of a widget w is obtained by the convenience function XtClass(w). The type XtResourceList is simply a pointer to an XtResource array; n points to the number of resources. After calling this function, we can print resource names and types by using the following code fragment:

```
XtResourceList r;
Cardinal n;
XtGetResourceList (XtClass(w), &r, &n);
for (i=0; i<n; i++)
    printf("%s %s\n", r[i].resource_name,
    r[i].resource_type);
```

If the widget is not realized, this function returns only its own resources—if it is realized it returns all inherited resources as well. We must be careful to check type before printing the remaining values of the resources.

There is a similar function for obtaining constraint resources (see Sec. 6.1.1), `XtGetConstraintResourceList()`. These functions are useful for debugging programs or analyzing the structure of compound widgets.

There is no simple way of printing the class name. The Intrinsics have a function that checks whether a guess is correct. The function prototype is

```
Boolean XtIsSubclass(Widget w, WidgetClass w_class)
```

It returns TRUE if w is of class `w_class` or one of it subclasses, for example:

```
if( XtIsSubclass (w, paperWidgetClass) )
    printf ("paper widget\n");
```

Having a sequence of such statements and *assuming* that we know all class names used in the program, we can print class information other than the widget name. The difficulty is that class names, such as `paperWidgetClass`, are pointers to structures, not strings.

A more direct way requires looking at the private structure of the widget and the Intrinsics. The following code does that:

```
#include <X11/IntrinsicP.h>
#include <X11/CoreP.h>
char *class_name(Widget w)
{
    return XtClass(w)→core_class.class_name;
}
```

We explain this code in Chap. 11.

3.3.7.   A Warning on the Use of Resources   While specifying parameters through resources offers many advantages, there are cases where this is not recommended.

Advice

Parameters that must be frequently changed during the execution of a program should not be defined through the resource mechanism.

The main reason is that when a widget resource changes value (through an `XtSetValues()` call for example), the intrinsics redraw the widget, and redrawing a widget with complex appearance not only wastes computation cycles, it also interferes with the operation of the application. The following two examples illustrate such a situation.

Example 1: Assume the user selects a different color from the palette in a drawing program. If the drawing color is specified as resource (possibly the foreground color of the widget) the whole display will be redrawn, even though nothing has changed but the palette selection.

Example 2: Assume we want to change the color of the icon depicting a character to indicate a changed state in a video game. The most economical way of doing this is to erase and redraw that particular icon rather than the whole display.

Furthermore the main advantage of the resource mechanism (customization by the application user) does not apply to parameters that change during program execution. If we want to allow customization of the *initial* value of a parameter, then we must use different parameters for that purpose. In Example 2 we may have resources `CoolColor` and `Hotcolor` and a *nonresource parameter* that holds the current color of he character. During the game that parameter is given values from either of the two resources.

3.4. CONCLUSIONS

Chapter 3 discusses general methods for creating widgets and specifying their parameters through resources. We also discuss resource specification. The resource mechanism may be used directly in applications without associating it to a widget. Chapter 3 shows also how to define resources for applications as well as widgets and how to use the resource conversion mechanism for variables that are not resources.

Widget parameter specification is a rather complex topic in X because of the multiple ways that such specifications can be made. Consider for the moment specifying window dimensions. Listing 3.1 sets values, so we do not expect to have them changed through command line resource specification. Indeed if we compile the program and name the executable `min`, then running the following piece of code does not affect the dimension:

```
min -xrm "*canvas.width: 50"
```

However running the following piece of code (or min -g 50) does:

```
min -xrm "*width: 50"
```

What is happening? When we omit the widget name, the parameter is applied to all widgets in the application, including the top shell widget. If shell widget dimensions are not specified, the shell widget wraps itself around its child widget. However if they are explicitly specified, they take precedence, so the child is adjusted to fit exactly inside the parent!

Suppose now that we specify dimensions of the shell widget in Listing 3.1. If we compile the program, then the following piece of code no longer has effect on the dimensions, as we would expect:

```
min -xrm "*width: 50"
```

But the following piece of code does:

```
min -g 50
```

The flag -g refers to a shell resource XtNgeometry, and geometry specification overrides specific parameter specification. (Of course the application user can change the dimensions of a shell window by resizing the window through interaction with the window manager. The effect of such resizing on the interior windows is discussed in Chap. 6.)

We can explore the RESOURCE_MANAGER property by using the Xlib function XGetWindowProperty(), as shown in Listing 3.9. This function is also used to read and modify properties, so it has many arguments that are of no particular interest here.

The items in the return string are separated by new lines, so we need not worry about formatting the output. The output of this program usually shows resource settings of the desktop environment.

3.5. PROJECTS

1. Implement the program in Listing 3.4, then experiment with various ways of specifying parameters.
2. Modify the program in Listing 3.4, by including other resources, such as color, border width, icon position, etc. Then experiment with different specification forms.
3. Use the resource mechanism to write a program that displays four colored squares in a 2 by 2 matrix, with color and square size specified at execution time. (The challenge is to create four widgets that are identical in all respects except one. Therefore the widget resource mechanism is not sufficient.) Compare the complexity of this program with one that creates the same display without using the resources mechanism. (Do not forget the * prefix in resource names when you run this program.)

Listing 3.9. Resource Manager Property — File rprop.c

```
/*  Find Resource Manager Property  */
/*  Equivalent to xrbd -query  */
#include <X11/Xlib.h>
#include <X11/Xatom.h>
int main (void)
{
    Display *Dpy = XOpenDisplay ("");
    Atom type_ret;
    long offset=0, length = 512;
    int form_ret;
    unsigned long nitems;
    unsigned long left_over;
    char *prop
    XGetWindowProperty (Dpy, DefaultRootWindow(Dpy),
        XA_RESOURCE_MANAGER,   /*  property atom  */
        offset, length,        /*  the values used for all
                                   the data  */
        False                  /*  do not modify the prop-
                                   erty  */
        AnyPropertyType,       /*  We do not specify the
                                   type  */
        &type_ret,             /*  in this case it returns
                                   STRING  */
        &form_ret,             /*  In this case returns 8
                                   (i.e. byte)  */
        &nitems,               /*  in this case returns
                                   1  */
        &left_over,            /*  in this case it should
                                   return 0  */
        &prop_return);         /*  where the property con-
                                   tents are stored  */
    printf(
    "%d items of type %s read, each of %d bits \
    (%d leftover)\n",
            nitems, XGetAtomName(Dpy, type_ret), form_ret,
            left_over );
    printf ("%s\n", prop_return);
    return (0);
}
```

4

Event Handling in
the X Toolkit

4.1. OVERVIEW

In the Xt environment applications do not deal directly with events. Events are taken from the queue by an Intrinsics function that then processes them according to certain policies set up by the application. The basic function is `XtAppMain-Loop()`, which is a convenience function with code similar to the following:

```
XtAppMainLoop(XtAppContext app)
{
    XEvent activity;
    while (1) {
        XtAppNextEvent(app, &activity);
        XtDispatchEvent (&activity);
    }
}
```

The function `XtAppNextEvent()` examines the event queue as well as alternative sources of input (see Sec. 4.2). When the function finds an event, it returns. The event is then passed to the dispatch routine that does all the work. Among other things, the dispatch routine finds the widget in whose window the event occurred by using the method in Sec. 2.1.4. We say that the "event is delivered to the widget." Associated with each widget are arrays of function pointers; depending on prespecified policy, one of these is called with the event as an argument. Applications specify the policy and assign values to these function pointers. There are three types of such functions: *Event Handlers*, *Callbacks*, and *Action Procedures*.

We say that an event handler function (or other type) is *registered with the Intrinsics* if the function is given as a value to any of the function pointers accessed by `XtDispatchEvent()`. Details of the assignment are hidden from the applications programmer—the function to be used is simply passed as an argument to a messenger function.

Event handlers are invoked immediately once an event is delivered to the widget. Action procedures rely on translation tables (see Sec. 1.2.2). If such tables exist, `XtDispatchEvent()` calls an internal function, `_XtTranslate-Event()`, which identifies the function to be called from the table. Callbacks are handled by widget methods. Depending on the event an internal widget function is called that looks at function pointer arrays associated with it.

This rough description of what happens mainly indicates the degree to which the application controls event processing. Event handlers provide the most general way, since the handler is invoked with a pointer to the event as an argument without other preprocessing. Action procedures are a little more restrictive: Conditions for calling an action procedure must be specified in conformation with translation table rules. Callbacks are the most restrictive because all event analysis is done by the Intrinsics and widget methods. In essence for callbacks and action procedures, an event is first processed by the Intrinsics or widget event handlers before application-defined functions are invoked. The common usage of the term event handler refers to an event handler that the application programmer is aware of.

It is possible for an application or a widget to use all three methods, each for different types of events. For example a program may use an event handler to deal with mouse events, a callback to deal with exposure events, and an action procedure to deal with keyboard events. It is also possible to have multiple event handlers, callbacks, or action procedures, for even the same event. It is not uncommon to call a sequence of event handlers for the same event.

We discuss each of the three ways of dealing with events in Sec. 4.2, and we also compare these methods by implementing an application in two different ways.

In addition to dealing with events, we discuss other means of interaction between a program and its environment. There are three things that a program can do while waiting for events: Run a process, accept input from or place output to a file, or respond to a timeout. When there are no events in the queue, the function XtAppNextEvent() looks at alternative input sources and timeouts; if nothing is happening there, it may execute what is called a work (rather than background) procedure. We examine each of these action sources in Sec. 4.3.

In Sec. 4.4 we discuss entering text.

Note

To present complete examples that contain drawing commands and at the same time avoid using elaborate Xlib functions in some examples, we use drawing functions from the Starter toolkit (see Sec. 1.3.2 and the Appendix). Such functions can be used to draw only on a paperClass widget that is part of the Starter toolkit.

4.2.   EVENT PROCESSING

4.2.1.   Event Handlers   An *event handler* is a function that takes as one of its arguments a pointer to an XEvent, say, ep and normally includes a switch statement examining the value of ep -> type. It then executes the appropriate code. Each widget maintains an array of pointers to event handlers (the *Event Handler list*). The function prototype is

```
void g(Widget w, XtPointer client_data,
    XEvent *ep, Boolean *pass_the_event)
```

It is added to the event handler list of a widget by the function:

```
void XtAddEventHandler(Widget w, EventMask em,
    Boolean nonmaskable, void (*g)(),
    XtPointer client_data)
```

Highlighted items indicate correspondence between the two functions. The mask em specifies events for which the handler is called, for example:

```
ButtonReleaseMask | ButtonPressMask | PointerMotionMask
```

(See Sec. 1.4.2 for a discussion of masks.) The nonmaskable argument is TRUE if the event handler receives events that cannot be selected with masks (such as those described in Sec. 2.3.1). Finally client_data is a pointer to a structure or a function that will be part of the arguments of the event handler when it is called. The pass_the_event argument is TRUE if the rest of the event handler list is called for that event.

The event handler is the most general and flexible way of dealing with events, and it is the preferred solution when the interpretation of events depends on preceding events, as in a rubber band drawing program. The event handler also involves less work when the widget class is created because the event handlers are called directly by the Intrinsics, so there is no need to provide a widget method for that purpose. Listing 4.1 shows a simple handler that deals with mouse clicks—a quick succession of button press and button release events.

Event handlers can be modified or removed by the function:

```
void XtRemoveEventHandler(Widget w, EventMask em,
    Boolean nonmaskable, void (*g)(),
    XtPointer client_data)
```

In spite of its name, the function does not immediately remove an event handler. Three of the arguments, the widget, the procedure g(), and the client_data data must match those of a previously added event handler otherwise the function has no effect. If a match is found, the function acts on its second and third arguments in the opposite way that XtAddEventHandler() does. For example the handler stops mouse-tracking button events if the mask is:

```
ButtonReleaseMask | ButtonPressMask
```

Listing 4.1. Simple Event Handler

```
void click_response(Widget w, XtPointer client_data)
{
    /* ... code to run in response to a click ... */
}
/*  Event Handler  */
void click (Widget w, XtPointer client_data, XEvent *ep,
    Boolean *disp)
{
    static Time time = 0; /*  when button was pressed  */
    if(ep->type==ButtonPress) time=(ep->button).time;
    else if (ep->type==ButtonRelease) {
        Time dt = (ep->xbutton).time - time; /* in msecs */
        if (dt<500) click_response(w, client_data);
    }
}
```

The event handler is removed only when there are no events left to track. To make sure that the handler is removed, pass the mask XtAllEvents for the second argument and TRUE for the third.

Changing event handlers is useful for changing the state of complex programs. For example in a drawing program, one event handler may let the user draw new shapes, and another event handler may let the user edit shapes. Appropriate visual feedback is important—for example a pencil icon for the cursor when drawing and an icon with a pencil and an eraser for editing.

4.2.2. *Callbacks*   A *Callback* is a function called by a widget (rather than the Intrinsics) in response to a particular condition. The condition may be an event or a sequence of events, but it can also be unrelated to any event. Therefore a callback function does not include in its arguments a pointer to an event, but it includes two pointers to data, one specified by the application and the other by the widget. The prototype of a callback is

```
void f (Widget w, XtPointer client_data,
    XtPointer call_data)
```

where client_data has the same significance as for the event handler and call_data is a value generated by the widget, as we explain later. A callback list is an array of pairs, each consisting of a function pointer to an X pointer. The formal definitions of a callback function and a callback list are

```
typedef void (*XtCallbackProc) (Widget, XtPointer,
    XtPointer);
```

```
typedef struct_XtCallbackRec {
    XtCallbackProc callback;
    XtPointer closure; /* really client data */
} XtCallbackRec, *XtCallbackList;
```

There are two ways of specifying callbacks for a widget. The most common is to add a function to the callback list of a widget by the call:

```
XtAddCallback(Widget w, String name, void (*f)(),
    XtPointer client_data)
```

where name is the resource name of the callback list.

The second way assigns the whole list at creation time, for example:

```
static XtCallbackRec helpcallbacks[] = {
    {generic_help, NULL}, {local_help, NULL}, {NULL, NULL}
    };
w = XtVaCreateManagedWidget ("button", ...,
    XtNhelpCallback, helpcallbacks, NULL);
```

The example assumes that we have a widget class with a callback list resource whose name is XtNhelpCallback. We assign two functions to the list: generic_help() and local_help(). Neither uses client data, hence the NULL pointers. Setting the callback through the explicit use of the callback list seems to be more cumbersome than the first, but we use only one call rather than many XtAddCallback() calls.

Callback lists are specified for each widget class, and these must be looked up in the widget documentation. For example the Core class has only one callback list for functions to be called when the widget is destroyed. The Shell class has two more lists, one for popups and one for popdowns. The Athena Command class has one list for button clicking. The Starter toolkit Paper class has two lists one for redrawing and the other for user-generated events. (Of course all widgets inherit the callback list of the Core class.)

The particular callback list names tend to be rather arbitrary. Consider a push button widget where we want to specify a function called when a user clicks a mouse button while the pointer is on the button window. Symbolic names for that event combination (pressing and releasing a button in quick succession) are XmNameCallback for Motif, XtNcallback for Athena, and XtNselect for OLIT. If we use such a widget, then we do not need the event handler in Listing 4.1; instead we can register the function click_response() as a callback using the code of Listing 4.2 (assuming OLIT widgets). In this example we do not register

Listing 4.2. Simple Callback

```
void click_response(Widget w, XtPointer client_data)
{
    /* ... code to run in response to a click ... */
}
main()
{
    /* ... */
    XtAddCallback(w, XtNselect, click_response, NULL);
    /* ... */
}
```

client data. In contrast to the event handler, we have no direct control over the time between button press and release. That interval may be set only through widget resources.

　　We illustrate the client_data argument with an example of a set of canvas widgets that each displays a different raster image. The Starter toolkit paper widget has a callback list with resource name XtNredrawCallback that is called after an Expose event. Let: (1) show_image be a function that takes as an argument a pointer to an image and displays the image; (2) Im[] be an array of images (of St_Image type in the Starter toolkit for example); and (3) W[] be an array of widgets used to display the images. The following code assigns the proper exposure callbacks:

```
for (i=0; i<Nimages; i++)
   XtAddCallback( W [i], XtNredrawCallback, show_image,
       &(Im[i]) );
```

When there is a need to redraw the widget, the function show_image() is called with a pointer to the widget where the event occurred and a pointer to the image that corresponds to that widget.

　　Quite often the callback needs information about the widget before performing its operations. For example, if we resizes a window, we wish to scale an image accordingly. Some times such information can be obtained from the widget itself. For example we can find the window dimensions width and height by calling the function:

```
XtVaGetValues(w, XtNwidth, &width, XtNheight, &height,
NULL);
```

However there are situations when the information does not exist in the widget structure. Suppose we do not attempt to scale an image to fit in a window, but we use a set of scrollbars to control placement. The display widget must now store the scrollbar positions, which should be passed to the display functions through the call_back argument. Because we can pass only one argument, but we have two numbers, we must use a pointer to a structure with two members, the x and y offsets.

Caution

The call_data argument must be provided by the widget writer. The applications programmer may use it or ignore it.

For example the person who writes the image display widget must create the code that passes the scrollbar positions to the display callbacks.

Widgets also have predefined methods for dealing with particular events. For example all Xt widgets contain a method of type XtExposeProc that redraws the widget window in response to Exposure events. For widgets with predefined form (push buttons for example) the function is implemented by the widget writer. For a canvas widget that function should do some basic tasks only, then invoke a callback list, passing the necessary client and call data. (In the case of the Paper class, it is the redrawCallback list.)

An applications programmer must remember that there need not be a one-to-one correspondence between XEvent types and callbacks. It may take more than one event to cause a widget to invoke a callback, and there may be additional operations besides the callback in response to a particular event.

Callbacks can be removed by the function:

```
XtRemoveCallback(Widget w, String name, void (*f)(),
    XtPointer client_data)
```

Both the function and client data arguments must be matched to remove a callback. The following function removes all callbacks of the named list:

```
XtRemoveAllCallbacks (Widget w, String name)
```

Changing a callback is a way of changing the state of a program; it is similar to changing event handlers as described in Sec. 4.2.1.

4.2.3. Action Procedures   An *Action procedure* is similar to a callback, but it allows customization through the resource database.

Caution

The *condition* that triggers an action procedure and the *arguments* passed to it can be customized. The procedure itself cannot be changed.

The prototype or an action procedure is

```
void h( Widget w, XEvent *ep, String *params, int *n)
```

where w is the widget where the event occurred. While an action procedure is written for a particular event (or combination thereof), it still takes a pointer to an XEVent as an argument both to obtain parameters from the structure and to check errors. (Nothing prevents an application user from incorrectly assigning an action procedure written for keyboard events to a mouse button event.)

The third argument is a pointer to an array of strings, and the last argument points to a number specifying how many strings in that array are to be used. It is necessary to limit the type of arguments to character strings to be able to specify these through the resource database.

To use action procedures the program must contain an *actions table* consisting of pairs of strings and function pointers of the form:

```
"Name_of_h", h, ...  .
```

and the program must have access to a translation table that links strings to events with entries of the form:

```
<Event_name> : Name_of_h()
```

Note the somewhat misleading syntax. Parentheses following Name_of_h are purely decorative. Name_of_h is a character string linked to an actual function name through the action table. Action procedures associate functions to events in two steps by using an intermediary string. For example to use an action procedure to specify the response to a button click (Listings 4.1 and 4.2) we need Listing 4.3. The function XtAppAddActions() passes the correspondence between strings and functions to the Intrinsics. The macro XtNumber() returns the number of elements in an array. The translation table can be either in an internal array (as in Listing 4.3) or in a resource file. (We discuss its format in detail in Sec. 4.2.4.) When the translation table is internal, it must be passed to the widget through resource arguments.

Listing 4.3. Simple Action Procedure

```
void click_response(Widget x, XEvent *ep, char **params,
int *n)
{
    /* ... code to be run in response to a click ... */
}
static XtActionRec my_actions [] = {
    { "click", click_response}
};
static char translations[] = "<BtnDown><BtnUp> : click()";
main()
{
    /* ... */
    XtAppAddActions(app, my_actions, XtNumber(my_actions));
    /* ... */
    XtVaCreateManagedWidget( ...,
        XtNtranslations,
        XtParseTranslationTable(translations), ...
        NULL);
    /* ... */
}
```

A slightly more complex example is given by the following pair of action and translation tables:

```
static XtActionRec acts [] = {
    ( "refresh", Scribble}, {"focus", Get_focus },
    {"bye", Quit}
};
static char translations[] =
"<Expose> : refresh() \n <Enter> : focus() \n <Key>q : bye()";
```

Note: The translation table is a *single* string, not an array of strings. If the table is in the resource file, it takes the form:

```
z*translations: <Expose> : refresh() \n\
    <Enter> : focus() \n <Key>q : bye()
```

(We assume that the name of the application is z.) We dropped quotation marks and used a backslash to fit the string in two lines. In this case we do not need to pass the

XtNtranslations argument to the widget creation function, although the call
to XtAppAddActions() is still needed.

The preceding examples show that a translation table is a resource item.

Listing 4.4 contains a complete program using action procedures. It starts an
application, then creates a canvas widget using the paper class and drawing
functions from the Starter toolkit. The user controls the size of the window through
ordinary resources and the color of the window and how to exit the program
through a translations table.

Listing 4.4.   Use of Action Procedures—File ap.c

```
/*  Demonstration of Action Procedures  */
/*  Program draws a filled rectangle with color */
/*  and margins determined by arguments of the   */
/*  action procedure  */

#include <X11/StringDefs.h>
#include <X11/Intrinsic.h>
#include <Paper.h>        /*  Starter Toolkit widget  */
#include <Stdef.h>

/*  Associate strings with functions  */
void good_bye(), draw();
static XtActionsRec actionsTable [] = {
        { "quit", good_bye }.
        { "paint", draw },
    };

int main (int arc, char **arv)
{
    Widget      toplevel, canvas;
    XtAppContext app;
    /*  Initialize the application  */
    toplevel = XtVaAppInitialize(&app, "Toy",
        (XrmOptionDescList)NULL, 0,
        &arc, arv, (String *)NULL, NULL);

/*  Pass the action table to the Intrinsics  */
    XtAppAddActions( app, actionsTable,
        XtNumber (actionsTable) );
    /*  Create a canvas widget  */
    canvas = XtVaCreateManagedWidget( "canvas",
```

```
        paperWidgetClass, toplevel, NULL);
    XtRealizeWidget (toplevel);
    XtAppMainLoop (app;
}
/*  Exit function  */
void good_bye (Widget w)
{
    exit (0);
}
/*  Redraw function: specified as action procedure  */
void draw(Widget w, XEvent, *ep, String *param, int *np)
{
    Dimension width, height;
    int margin = 10;

    if(ep -> type != Expose) return;

    /*  Find dimensions of the widget  */
    XtVaGetValues(w, XtNwidth, &width, XtNheight, &height,
    NULL);

    St_draw_area(w); /*  Direct all graphics output to w  */
    if(*np > 0) St_fore_color(param[0]);
    else St_fore_color("gray70");

    /*  Compute margin and make sure it has a reasonable
    value  */
    if(*np > 1) {
        margin = atoi(param[1]);
        if(margin < 0 || margin > width/2 || margin > height/2)
            margin = 10;
    }
    /*  Draw a filled rectangle with a margin  */
    St_fill_rectangle(margin, margin, width-2*margin,
        height-2*margin);
}
```

The resource file may contain the following lines:

```
y*canvas.width:   400
y*canvas.height: 200
y*canvas.translations: <Key>Escape: quit() \n\
    <Expose>: paint( green 40 )
```

The program illustrates the use of parameters in the translation table. The user can specify the drawing color and margins.

Placing a redrawing function in a translation table, as in Listing 4.4, is somewhat contrived. In this case it may have been simpler to specify color and margin parameters as resources. On the other hand a program can have more than one function used to redraw the window, and a translation table is the only way of selecting one of them. In general action procedures tend to be better suited for changing the user action for causing something to happen, for example exiting a program.

4.2.4.   Translation Table Syntax   Translations are resources, but they have a more complex specification than those described in Sec. 3.2.5. The first part of the specification is the same as for all other resources, for example: the following stand, respectively, for translations of events in all widgets of program z and in widget canvas of program y:

```
z*translations:
```

and

```
y*canvas.translations:
```

The table consists of items separated by new line characters (\n), and each item contains two entries separated by a colon. The first entry is an event (or combination thereof) and the second a reference to a function.

The function is specified by a name that must appear in the action table of the polygram, while arguments are strings that are actually passed as arguments to the function when it is called. Thus in the example from the previous section, the entry in the translation table means that when an Expose event occurs, a code fragment similar to the one below is executed:

```
Widget w;
XEvent e;
String param[] = { "green", "40" };
int n = 2;
draw(w, *e, param, &n);
```

The correspondence between draw() and paint was made in the action-sTable[] array. It is possible to have more than one function, for example:

```
<Key>q: ring_bell() quit()
```

The first entry of translation table items is the one most under user control. It is formed by the following rules:

1. It can be an event name (or an abbreviation) enclosed in angular brackets ('<', '>'), for example `<KeyPress>` (abbreviated to <Key>), `<ButtonPress>` (abbreviated to <BtnDown>), `<MotionNotify>` (abbreviated to <Motion>), etc.

2. It can be an event name followed by a *detail*, for example `<Key>q` (the 'q' key was pressed), `<BtnDown>1` (the left mouse button was pressed), etc. Abbreviations exist for events with details, in particular `<Btn1Up>`, `<Btn1Down>`, etc., have the obvious meanings.

3. It can be a *modified* event, such as `Ctrl <key>d`, other modifiers being `Shift`, `Lock`, `Alt`, `Button1`, etc. Modified events can have details.

4. It can be a sequence of entries of the first three types, separated by commas, for example:

   `<Key>q, <Key>u, <Key>i, <Key>t : quit()`

   Note: Be aware that the preceding notation means to type all four characters in the right sequence (i.e., the word quit) rather than just one of them. To be able to quit by pressing *any* of a certain number of keys, we must create a translation table entry for each key.

5. It can be an entry of the first three types followed by a number in parentheses, for example:

   `<Key>q(2) : quit()`

   This means that the program exits if the key q is pressed twice in *quick* succession. The actual time allowed to elapse between repetitions is an installation parameter. If we do not want to be confined by that constraint, we use the following:

   `<Key>q, <Key>q : quit()`

   In this case there is no time limit between occurrences of the event.

Finally a few words about the apparently bizarre notation of adding a new line character, then escaping it, as in:

```
<Key>q: quit() \n\
<Expose>: paint()
```

A translation table is expected to be a single string. The last escape character ('\') is needed to continue the string across new lines. Explicit new line characters ('\n') are needed inside the string so that the translations manager can separate items! If there is a gap between the new line character and the escape, \n\ will not parse correctly.

4.2.5. Comparisons It is possible to write an application with either an event handler or a translation table. (Callbacks are usually not an alternative because they are limited to the widget's predefined conditions for invoking callbacks.) We use a rubber band drawing program to illustrate the two alternatives. Listing 4.5 shows the part of the main program common in both versions; numbered comments mark places where code must be added according to the chosen solution.

Listing 4.5. Main Program for the Rubber Band Program—File rb.c

```
/*  Rubber Band Drawing Program  */

#include <X11/StringDefs.h>
#include <X11/Intrinsic.h>
#include <Paper.h> /*  St widget class  */
#include <Sdef.h>

/*  1 - Declarations  */

int main(int arc, char **arv)
{
    Widget         toplevel, canvas;
    XtAppContext app;
    /*  Initialize the application  */
    toplevel = XtVaAppInitialize( &app, "Toy",
        (XrmOptionDescList)NULL, 0,
        &arc, arv, (String *)NULL, NULL);
    /*  Create a canvas widget  */
    canvas = XtVaCreateManagedWidget( "canvas",
        paperWidgetClass, toplevel, NULL); /*  St widget
        class  */

    /*  2 - Activation of Event Handling Mechanism  */

    XtRealizeWidget (toplevel);

    /*  Initialize the drawing functions of the Starter
    Toolkit  */
    St_draw_area (canvas);
    St_use_xor_mode();
    XtAppMainLoop(app);
}

/*  3 - Event handling functions  */
```

The program starts an application, then creates a canvas widget from the Starter toolkit. As it stands, the program does nothing. In either version we need a set of functions to perform the basic application operations. These, shown in Listing 4.6, use the Starter toolkit line-drawing function.

The function anchor() fixes a point on the screen that can be used as an anchor for the rubber band. The function erase_and_draw() erases the previously drawn line, then draws a new one from the anchor point to the mouse position; it does nothing

Listing 4.6. Rubber Band Functions—File rb.c

```
/* Common Functions to both versions */

static int initialized=0;
static int x0, y0, x1, y1;

void anchor(Widget w, XEvent *ep)
{
    x0 = x1 = (ep->xbutton).x; y0 = y1 = (ep->xbutton).y;
    initialized = 1;
}

void erase_and_draw(Widget w, XEvent *ep)
{
    if(initialized) {
        St_draw_area(w);
        St_put_line(x0, y0, x1, y1); /* erase */
        x1 = (ep->xbutton).x;
        y1 = (ep->xbutton).y;
        St_put_line(x0, y0, x1, y1); /* draw */
    }
}

void terminate(Widget w, XEvent *ep /* not used */)
{
    if(initialized) {
        St_draw_area (w);
        St_put_line(x0, y0, x1, y1);
        initialized = 0;
    }
    else exit(0);
}
```

if an anchor point is not defined. If the function terminate() is called when a rubber band is being drawn, it erases the last line drawn and stops further drawing; if nothing is being drawn, it causes the program to exit.

Listing 4.7 shows the code that must be added to Listing 4.5 for the event handler solution. The event handler rubber_band() is registered with the Intrinsics (Position 2); it is called whenever a button is pressed or the mouse moves. A more efficient version replaces the code of the three functions inside the event handler, thereby avoiding the overhead of function calls. External static variables can also reside within the event handler.

Listing 4.8 shows the code to add for translation table implementation. A table of pairs of strings and functions is defined, then passed to the intrinsics (Position 2). The overall code is simpler, but we also need something else, an entry in the resource data base, for example:

Listing 4.7.   Rubber Band Using an Event Handler—File rb1.c

```
/*  In Position 1  */
void rubber_band(), anchor(),. terminate(),
    erase_and_draw();
/*  In Position 2  */
XtAddEventHandler(canvas,
      ButtonPressMask | PointerMotionMask,
      False, rubber_band, NULL);
/*  In Position 3  */
/*  Rubber band event handler  */
void rubber_band(Widget w,
    XtPointer client_data/ *  not used  */,
    XEvent *ep, Boolean *pass_the_event /*  not used  */)
{
    switch (ep->type) {
    case MotionNotify:
        erase_and_draw(w, ep);
        return;
    case ButtonPress:
        if((ep->xbutton).button == 1) anchor(w, ep);
        else terminate(w, ep);
        return;
    }
}
```

Listing 4.8.   Rubber Band Using a Translation Table—File `rb2.c`

```
/*  In Position 1  */
void anchor(), terminate(), erase_and_draw();
static XtActionsRec actionsTable [] = {
        { "pick", anchor },
        { "quit", terminate },
        { "paint", erase_and_draw },
    };
/*  In Position 2  */
    /*  Pass the action table to the Intrinsics  */
    XtAppAddActions( app, actionsTable,
        XtNumber(actions Table) );
/*  In Position 3 - NOTHING  */
```

```
rb*canvas.translations: <Btn1Down>: pick() \n\
    <Motion>: paint() \n\
    <Btn2Down>: quit() \n <Btn3Down>: quit()
```

(We assume that the name of the program is `rb`.) We must make sure that the resource file exists before we can run the program. We must also add an error-checking statement in two of the functions in Listing 4.6 to confirm that the structure of `ep -> type` contains information about the pointer coordinates. (These are `KeyPress`, `KeyRelease`, `ButtonPress`, `ButtonRelease`, and `MotionNotify`.)

On the other hand it is very easy for a user to change the behavior of the program by using a different translation table, such as:

```
rb*canvas.translations:<Btn1Up>: pick() \n\
    <Motion>: paint() \n\
    <Btn2Up>: quit() \n <Btn3Up>: quit()
```

or

```
rb*canvas.translations:<Key>a: pick() \n\
    <Motion>: paint() \n\
    <Key>Escape: quit()
```

The second version is acceptable because keyboard events contain mouse coordinates when a key is struck. We can even replace `<Motion>` by, say, `<Key>z` and still have a working program (though not a good one).

The code for the event handler version is much tighter (and easier to maintain), but the program's behavior is far more rigid than that of the translation table version. Because the three functions are closely linked, translation table entries must be coordinated, for example the following code is a particularly bad choice:

```
rb*canvas.translations:<Key>a: pick() \n\
    <Key>p: paint() \n\
    <Key>Escape: quit()
```

The mouse must be moved to select the new point location, and after each move, the application user must press a key to see the effects of the move.

The event handler seems to be a better solution for the rubber band program. On the other hand in programs where the different functions are independent, the translation table seems preferable.

Note

Section 4.2.6 covers material beyond the needs of most simple programs, especially those relying on a toolkit; it may be skipped at first reading.

4.2.6. **Dealing with Window Manager Messages** We conclude the section on events with a discussion of window manager messages of the type described in Secs. 2.3.5 and 3.3. If we use the Motif or OLIT toolkit, we need not worry about these, but we must provide code to handle these if we use the Athena toolkit or Xt with the paper widget alone (as in this chapter's examples). We present two solutions: First with an action procedure then with an event handler. Listing 4.9 repeats code in Listing 4.4, which we modify by adding code from Sec. 2.4.2 in the context of Xt.

The following remarks are pertinent.

The atom wm_quit is global because it is used by two functions: The action procedure shutdown() and the initialization procedure create_protocol(). The former contains code in the switch statement (case ClientMessage) in Listing 2.2; the latter contains the initialization code with a few modifications. In particular it uses three macros to examine the structure of the widget. XtIsShell() returns to zero if the widget is not in Shell class (in which case it is meaningless to establish a protocol); XtDisplay() and XtWindow() return the display structure pointer and window XID needed for the Xlib functions used.

Listing 4.9.   Window Manager Protocol (Action Procedure)—File
wmap.c

```
/*  Demonstration of Action Procedures, including dealing
    with Window Manager Events
*/
#include <X11/StringDefs.h>
#include <X11/Intrinsic.h>
#include <Paper.h>

static Atom wm_quit;

/*  Action procedure for communication with WM  */
void shut_down(Widget w, XEvent *ep,
    String *param, int *n)
{
    if(ep->type != ClientMessage) return;
    if( ep->xclient.data.l[0] == wm_quit) exit(0);
}
void create_protocol(Widget w)
{
    Display *dpy = XtDisplay (w);

    if (!XtIsShell(w)) {/*  issue warning and return  */}
    wm_quit = XInternAtom (dpy, "WM_DELETE_WINDOW", False);
    XSetWMProtocols( dpy, XtWindow(w), &wm_quit, 1);
}
/*  Associate strings with functions  */
void good_bye(), draw();
static XtActionsRec actionsTable [] = {
      { "quit", good_bye },
      { "out", shutdown },
      { "paint", draw ),
    },
static char internal_transl[]="<ClientMessage>: out()";

int main(int arc, char **arv)

    /*  Code from Listing 4.4  */
    XtVaSetValues (toplevel,
        XtNtranslations,
        XtParseTranslationTable(internal_transl), NULL);
    XtRealizeWidget (toplevel);
    create_protocol (toplevel);
    XtAppMainLoop (app);
}
    /*  Rest of the Code from Listing 4.4  */
```

Listing 4.10.   Window Manager Protocol (Event Handler)—File wmeh.c

```c
/* Demonstration of Event Handler for WM messages */
#include <X11/StringDefs.h>
#include <X11/Intrinsic.h>
#include <Paper.h>

static Atom wm_quit;

/* Event handler for communication with WM */
void shut_down(Widget w, XtrPointer client_data,
    XEvent ep, Boolean *continue_dispatch)
{
    if(ep->type != ClientMessage) return;
    if(ep->xclient.data.1[0] == wm_quit) exit(0);
}
void create_protocol (Widget w)
{
    Display *dpy = XtDisplay(w);
    If(!XtIsShell(w) )
    own_error(1, "Tried WM protocol for non shell widget");
    wm_quit = XInternAtom(dpy, "WM_DELETE_WINDOW", False);
    XSetWMProtocols( dpy, XtWindow(w), &wm_quit, 1);
    XtAddEventHandler(w, 0, True, shut_down, NULL);
}
/* Associate strings with functions */
void good_bye(), draw();
static XtActionsRec actionsTable [] = {
        { "quit", good_bye },
        { "paint", draw },
    };
int main (int arc, char **arv)
    /* Code from Listing 4.4, NOT 4.9 */
    XtRealizeWidget (toplevel);
    Create_protocol(toplevel);
    XtAppMainLoop (app);
}
    /* Rest of the Code from Listing 4.4 */
```

Since there is no point in customizing this event, the translation table is internal and attached to the widget with the call XtVaSetValues(). The protocol function *must* be called after the XtRealizeWidget() function call because this function creates as well as maps windows.

It is possible to use an event handler instead of an action procedure; this is shown in Listing 4.10, again, using, the program in Listing 4.4 as a basis.

The code with the event handler is somewhat clearer than the code with the action procedure. The function shut_down() need not be known to other parts of the program than the function that sets the protocol, and there is no need to worry about translation tables.

4.3. DEALING WITH NONEVENT INPUT

4.3.1. Work Procedures and Animation

The Xt function XtAddWork-Proc() registers a function with the *Intrinsics*, which is called when there are no events in the queue. Its prototype is

```
XtAppAddWorkProc(XtAppContext app,
    int (*f)(XtPointer), XtPointer client_data)
```

The function f() is invoked within XtAppNextEvent() with client_data as its argument. Its return value is important: If nonzero, then the function is removed from the system. More than one such function may be added by calling XtAppAddWorkProc() more than once. These are invoked in the reverse order in which they were added.

Caution

While there may be many work procedures registered, only one of these is called between events. If there are no events for awhile, the same function is called repeatedly.

When the highest priority work function is removed, the next one is executed between events. This is one reason for not using the term background process. Normally operating systems invoke all background processes periodically.

We must make sure that a work function returns quickly so that events do not pile up in the queue. For example the following function packs too much computation into one call:

```
int f()
{
    /* ... A ... */
    for (i=0; i<N; i++) { /* ... B ... */ }
```

```
    /*  ...  C  ...  */
    return (0);
}
```

Its code must be distributed into three functions, as shown in the following example. Static variable can be used to pass information from one to the other, or information can be kept in a structure associated with the **client_data** pointer.

```
int f1()
{
    /*  ...  A  ...  */
    return(1);
}
int f2()
}
    static i=0;
    /*  ...  B  ...  */
    i++;
    if (i<N) return (0);
    else return(1);
}
int f3()
{
    /*  ...  C  ...  */
    /*   register again f3, f2, and f1  */
    return(1);
}
```

Because work procedures are called in the reverse order of registration, f3 () must be registered first, followed by f2 () and f1 (). With this arrangement the loop is executed only once between checking for events.

Work procedures can be used for animation in the following manner. Let frame [] be an array of N_FRAMES images, each containing an animation frame. Then the following work procedure performs animation:

```
#define IDLE_TIME 50000 /*  time in microseconds  */
int show_frame (void)
{
    static i=0;
    if(i>= N_FRAMES) return 1;
    /*  Display Frame+i (see Section 9.5.2 for an
    example)  */
    i++;
```

```
    /* flush the buffer to the server using XFlush()  */
    usleep (IDLE_TIME);
    return 0;
}
```

The function usleep() suspends execution for as many microseconds as its argument, so that frames stay visible for a while. (In our example for one-twentieth of a second.) It is important to flush the client–server buffer before idling so the user can see the new display. Animation stops after all frames are shown. We could have made a continuous animation by resetting i to zero.

Besides showing precomputed frames, we can modify a given image by moving and redrawing objects. In this way we can create video games. We may still need a delay so that objects do not move too fast. For a game the looping function f2() takes the form:

```
#define IDLE_TIME 5000
int f2()
{
    static i=0;
    /* ... redraw one object ... */
    i++;
    /*  Flush the buffer to the server using XFlush()  */
    usleep(IDLE_TIME);
    if(i<N) return (0);
    else return (1);
}
```

Listing 4.11 shows a simple work procedure that produces a display of blinking text.

The program registers the work procedure blink() with the intrinsics and asks the canvas widget to be passed as argument. While widgets are passed automatically as arguments to callbacks and event handlers, this is not the case with work procedures. The work procedure calls the redraw procedure, which, because of the exclusive OR mode erases, then displays the text every other call, thereby creating the blinking effect.

To turn the blinking on and off, the static variable stop_work is complemented when button 1 or 2 is pressed. If it is 1, the work procedure is removed after the next call; if it is 0, we must register blink() with the *Intrinsics*. Because XtAppAddWorkProc() requires the application context as its first argument, we use the convenience function XtWidgetToApplicationContext() to find the application context.

Caution

The long sleep interval used in the code in Listing 4.11 is not a good idea because the event queue is left unexamined for all that time. A better way of creating animation that requires long idle periods is through timeouts, described in Sec. 4.3.2. The code there is given in terms of specific modifications to the code in Listing 4.11.

Listing 4.11. Blinking Display—File blink.c

```
/*  Blinking display using Starter Toolkit (St) functions
for drawing  */
#include <X11/StringDefs.h>
#include <X11/Intrinsic.h>
#include <Paper.h>
#include <Starter.h>
#define VERTICAL_SPACE   20
#define MARGINS   10
#define CHAR_WIDTH   8
void paint(Widget),
act(Widget, XtPointer, XEvent *, Boolean *);

int blink(XtPointer);

static char msg[] = "BLINKING MESSAGE";
int main(int arc, char **arv)
{
    XtAppContext app;
    Widget top, canvas;

    top = XtAppInitialize( &app, "Blink",
        NULL, 0, &arc, arv, NULL, NULL, 0);

        /*  Create a canvas widget big enough to contain the
        message  */
    canvas = XtVaCreateManagedWidget("canvas",
        paperWidgetClass, top,
        XtNwidth, strlen (msg)*CHAR_WIDTH+MARGINS,
        XtNheigth, VERTICAL_SPACE,
        NULL);
```

```
    /*  Specify the function that draws the window  */
    XtAddCallback(canvas, XtNredrawCallback, paint,
        NULL);

    /*  Add an event handler, not essential for this
    example  */
    XtrAddEventHandler (canvas, ButtonPressMask, False,
        act, NULL);

    /*  Register the work procedure to be called with canvas
    as argument  */
    XtAppAddWorkProc(app, blink, (XtPointer) canvas);

    XtRealizeWidget(top);

    XtAppMainLoop(app);
}
static int stop_work = 0; /*  Let us turn blinking on and
                             off  */

/*  Work Procedure  */
blink(XtPointer w)
{
    paint((Widget)w); /*  Re-paint window  */
    St_xflush();
    usleep (500000); /*  sleep for half a second - bad
                       implementation  */
    return (stop_work);
}
void paint (Widget w)
{
    St_draw_area(w);
    St_use_xor_mode();
    St_put_text(msg, 5, 15);
}
void act(Widget w, XtPointer client_data,
    XEvent *ep, Boolean *pass_the_event)
{
    if(ep -> type! = Button Press)return;
    switch((ep -> xbutton).button) {
    case 1:
    case 2:
        stop_work = 1 - stop_work;
```

```
    if (!stop_work) XtAppAddWorkProc(
        XtWidgetToApplicationContext(w),
        blink, (XtPointer)w);
    return;
  case 3:
      exit(0);
  }
}
```

4.3.2. Timeouts and Animation   The Intrinsics provide a function for registering timeouts. Its prototype is

```
unsigned long XtAppAddTimeOut( XtAppContext app,
    unsigned long time_interval,
    void (*f)(), XtPointer client_data)
```

The meaning of the first and fourth arguments is self-explanatory. The time_-interval is the time in *milliseconds* before f(), given as the third argument, is called. This function is called with the following arguments:

```
void f( XtPointer client_data, unsigned long *timer_id)
```

The argument timer_id points to the value returned by XtAppAddTime-Out() when it registers the time out. The argument is a pointer rather than a value for reasons pertaining to the use of Xt by languages other than C. It is not something that the function is supposed to modify.

Since the *Intrinsics* look at timers only when there are no pending events, the time is not particularly accurate. If we really care about the correct time, we must call one of the system clock functions shown later in this section. It is possible to create a blinking message using timeouts rather than work procedures by modifying the code in Listing 4.11 as follows:

1. Replace the declaration:

   ```
   int blink();
   ```
   by
   ```
   void time_blink();
   ```

2. Replace the call to XtAppAddWorkProc(app, ...) in the main procedure by:

   ```
   XtAppAddTimeOut(app, 500, time_blink,
       (XtPointer)canvas);
   ```

3.   Change the function definition blink (w) to:

```
void time_blink (w)
```

4.   Inside this function, replace statements:

```
usleep (500000);
return (stop_work);
```

with the following:

```
if(!stop_work)XtAppAddTimeOut(
    XtWidgetToApplicationContext((Widget)w),
    500, time_blink, w);
```

5.   Inside the event handler act (), replace the call:

```
If(!stop_work) XtAppAddWorkProc(
    XtWidgetToApplicationContext(w),
    blink, (XtPointer)w);
```

with the following:

```
if(!stop_work) XtAppAddTimeOut(
    XtWidgetToApplicationContext(w),
    500, time_blink, w);
```

Once a timeout occurs, it is unregistered; to keep it occurring at regular intervals, we must register it again. This is best done from the function called in response to it. Note the different unit of time measurement in usleep() (microseconds) and XtAppAddTimeOut () (milliseconds).

The similarity of the code implementing animation by using work procedures with that using timeouts should not be surprising. Both work procedures and timeouts are called by XtNextEvent () when there are no pending events. The only difference is that a work procedure is always called, while a timeout is called only after a certain amount of time (since registration) has elapsed. The mechanism of work procedures is a little simpler (see item No. 4 in the preceding list), especially when we divide a function into many work procedures. Timeouts have the following advantages:

- The event queue is being checked while waiting for the timeout, but it is not checked when the work procedure goes to sleep. (Note: This does not apply in cases of large computation where we divide a function into many work procedures.)

- We may have more than one active timer but only one work procedure. This is useful for animating asynchronously different windows in an application.

If the exact value of the time is pertinent, use code similar to the following:

```
#include <time.h> /*  may be omitted if Intrinsic.h is
                   included  */
void get_time(char *bfr)
{
    struct tm tm;
    time_t seconds;

    time(&seconds);
    tm=*localtime(&seconds);
    sprintf(bfr, "%02d", tm.tm_sec);
}
```

The function time() obtains the time in seconds since January 1, 1970. (The type time_t is normally just long.) The function localtime() converts that value into a more usable form, including hours (in tm_hour), minutes (in tm_min), etc. In the preceding example, the function get_time returns a string that can be used to update a *digital clock*. The following code fragment contains the timeout function:

```
/*  update every second  */
#include <Stdef.h>
#define T_SPAN    1000
static char buffer[] = " ";    /*  two blanks and a null  */
static int x, y;

void time_out(Widget w)
{
    St_draw_area(w);
    St_use_xor_mode();
    St_put_text(buffer, x, y); /*  erase old display  */
    get_time(buffer); /*  get new value  */
    St_put_text(buffer, x, y); /*display new line value*/
    /*  restart timer  */
    XtAppAddTimeOut(XtWidgetToApplicationContext(w),
        T_SPAN, time_out, w);
}
```

By calling system time functions, we avoid falling behind if time_out() is called after an interval longer than one second.

True animation can be achieved if we have successive frames from a motion picture. Suppose we store frames in an array of image structures Frame[] and that there are N_FRAMES of them. In the following code we assume that we defined an appropriate image structure and we also have a display function available for such image structures. In this case the timeout function follows (we assume copy mode in drawing):

```
/*  update 30 times a second  */
#define T_SPAN    33
#define N_FRAMES 100
static /*  Image structure  */ Frame [N_FRAMES];
void time_out(Widget w)
{
    static i=0;

    /*  display Frame+i on window of widget w  */
    i++;
    if(i<N_FRAMES)/*    restart timer  */
       XtAppAddTimeOut(XtWidgetToApplicationContext(w),
          T_SPAN, time_out, w);
}
```

4.3.3. File and Pipe Input—Graphical Front Ends

The function XtAppAddInput() registers a file descriptor and a function with the *Intrinsics*; when there is input in the file descriptor, the function is called. The prototype for the function that registers such input is

```
XtAppAddInput (XtAppContext app, int fid, int mask,
      int (*fun) (XtPointer, int *), XtPointer client_data)
```

Its second argument fid, is a file descriptor returned from an open() call. The fourth argument, fun(), is the function that reads data corresponding to the file descriptor. The third argument is a symbolic constant that specifies interaction with the file. The value XtInputReadMask states that the file descriptor is used for reading. The last argument is a pointer to structure that is used as the first argument of fun() when the latter is invoked by the *Intrinsics*.

This function is useful when we create a graphical front end for an existing program that expects keyboard input and prints out characters.

We now outline how to create the basic communication mechanism for such a graphical front end. Let old_program be the name of the existing program (in /usr/local/bin) for which we want to create the front end. The code in the main procedure follows:

```
/*  inclusions, declarations, etc  */
static int to_child, from_child;
extern read_from_child(XtPointer, int *); /*  Function to
                                            read the pipe */

int main (int arc, char **arv)
{
    XtAppContext app;
    Widget canvas;
    /*  XtVaAppInitialize(), creation of a canvas  */
    /*  widget, etc. to XtRealizeWidget();  */

    /*  Open two-way pipe between programs  */
    two_way_pipe ("/usr/local/bin/old_program", &to_child,
        &from_child);
    /*  ask the Intrinsics to co-operate  */
    XtAppAddInput(app, from_child, XtInputReadMask,
        read_from_child, (XtPointer)canvas);

    XtAppMainLoop(app);
}
```

We pass the canvas widget to the function that will read the input as client data, so that what is read can be displayed on that widget. The function two_way_pipe() uses Unix system functions to create a two-way pipe between processes; it is given in Listing 4.12. The variables from_child_p and to_child_p are pointers to Unix file descriptors, and cmd is the program path to be invoked. The function relies on Unix system functions fork(), execl(), and dup(). The function fork() creates a copy of the current process, then returns 0 for the copy (the child process) and 1 for the original (the parent process). The function dup() returns the lowest unused file descriptor. Thus calling dup() right after closing 0 returns 0. The function execl() replaces the copy of the original with the cmd process.

From now on a statement read(from_child, ...) will read the output of old_program [or whatever command was the first argument of two_way_pipe()]. An example of implementation that simply displays the input read follows:

Listing 4.12.   Two-Way Unix Pipe

```
/*  Code written by Bill Sakoda, October, 1994  */
int two_way_pipe(char *cmd, int *to_child_p,
    int *from_child_p)
{
    static int popen_pid;
    int p[2];
    int q[2];
    /*  create two pipes - return on failure  */
    if(pipe(p) <0) return(0);
    if(pipe(q) <0) return(0);
    /*  Unix fork returns 0 for child, 1 for parent  */
    if ((popen_pid = fork ()) == 0) {   /*  child code  */
        close (p[1]); close(q[0]);       /*  close what is
                                             not  needed  */
        close (0); dup(p[0]);            /*  this copies
                                             p[0] to child
                                             stdin  */
        close (p[0]);                    /*  no longer
                                             needed  */
        close(1); dup(q[1]);             /*  this copies
                                             q[1] to child
                                             stout  */
        close (q[1]);                    /*  no longer
                                             needed  */
        /*  execute cmd command  */
        execl ("/bin/sh", "sh", "-c", cmd, 0);
        /*  if call succeeds we should never reach here  */
        exit(1);
    }
    else { /*  parent code  */
        if(popen_pid == -1) return (0); /*  failure  */
        close (p[0]); close (q[1]);      /*  close what is
                                             not needed  */
        *to_child_p = p[1];              /*  p[1] is parent
                                             stdout  */
        *from _child_p = q[0];           /*  q[0] is parent
                                             stdin  */
        return (1);
    }
}
```

```
#include <Stdef.h>
#define BFSIZE 256
static int x, y;

void read_from_child (XtPointer w, int *source)
{
    int n;
    static char read_bf[BFSIZWE+1];
    St_draw_area( (Widget)w );
    n = read(*source, read_bf, BfSIZE);
    if(n > 0) {
        read_bf[n] = 0;  /* Make string null terminated */
        St_put_text (read_bf, x, y);
        y += 20;       /* for placing the next message */
    }
}
```

Notice that as in the two previous sections, we explicitly request that the widget be used as an argument when the input function is called. We also pass a pointer to the file descriptor rather than its value, even though havoc results if read_from_child() changed its value. The Intrinsics insist on that for the sake of portability to languages other than C.

In most cases we expect the user to initiate input to the program on the other side of the pipe. Therefore a statement write(to_child, ...) is typically located inside callbacks or event handlers. The file descriptor can be passed as client data to such procedures, but it can also be made an external variable, as in the example of p. 126.

4.4.   ENTERING TEXT

4.4.1.   Tools for Entering Text   So far we discussed mouse input (Sec. 4.2) as well as file input (Sec. 4.3), but we only briefly mentioned keyboard input (in connection with action procedures in Sec. 4.2.3). Entering text through the keyboard is a complex process in X (or for that matter in most window systems) for two reasons: (1) The keyboard is a shared resource among different windows, so we must decide how to allocate it to a particular application; (2) each key stroke generates an event, so we must do all the work to assemble lines of text.

Keyboard allocation is discussed in Sec. 4.4.2. The collection of typed text itself can be dealt with by using a text-entry widget. All toolkits have at least one such widget; the topic is covered in Sec. 7.1. These widgets provide a resource that corresponds to the buffer of collected text and a callback in response to pressing a particular key or key combination. For example Motif uses the RETURN key for one-line text entry and the CONTROL–RETURN key combination for multiline text entry. Application writers can write a simple callback around a XtVaGet-Values() call that extracts collected text from the resource.

If we want to mix text and graphics entries (for example to label a drawn figure), then a text widget is not appropriate. The Starter toolkit provides a set of functions for entering text in a paper class widget, so we can use those to label a drawing. The functions are as follows:

- void St_init_text(int x, int y, int stop_rule) specifies the location where the lower left corner of the first line of the typed text appears on the screen (x and y), if the third argument is nonzero, text entry terminates with a new line; otherwise it terminates when a nonprintable character (such as Escape) is entered. It also performs the necessary initializations. It must be called before calls to collect_text().
- void St_set_string_use(void (*f)(char *)) specifies the function to be called with the typed string as an argument when text entry terminates. It must be called before call to collect_text().
- void St_collect_text(Event *p) does the real work, and it must be called from inside the event handler. If it is called before init_text(), it returns immediately. If it is called before call to set_string_use(), the typed text is not used.

If we do not want to use the Starter toolkit or a text-entry widget, then we must write our own text collection facility (see Sec. 4.4.3).

4.4.2. Getting the Focus   We say that a widget (window) has the *focus* when it receives keyboard events. It is a responsibility of the window manager to direct such events to a specific widget, and there are various possible policies. The simplest policy is to have keyboard events sent to the widget whose window contains the pointer. If this is not already the default policy in the system we are using, we must explicitly specify it. When using the Athena or OLIT toolkit (or Xt by itself) the specification is made by the statement:

```
XtVaSetValues (toplevel, XtNinput, True, NULL);
```

When using Motif the specification is made by the statement:

```
XtVaSetValues(toplevel, XmNKeyboardFocusPolicy,
    XmPOINTER, NULL);
```

Note: In both cases only the widget name (toplevel) is a variable. Other values refer to symbolic names, so these are fixed. In the absence of the above, the translation `<Enter> : focus()` accomplishes the task for simple programs provided `focus` refers to a function with the following Xlib code:

```
void Get_focus (w)
    Widget w;
{
    XSetInputFocus (XtDisplay(w), XtWindow(w),
        RevertToParent, CurrentTime);
}
```

In addition to asking the window manager to direct keyboard events to widget w whenever the pointer is inside the window of w, this call also provides other instructions for the window manager. The third argument provides instructions about what to do with keyboard events when the window of w is no longer visible; the fourth argument specifies when the focus policy becomes effective.

Note:

Section 4.4.3 covers material beyond the needs of most programs. Read this section only if planning to write an application for which text-entry widgets or the Starter toolkit functions are inadequate.

4.4.3.   Low-Level Functions for Text Entry   The Xt has a function that looks at an XEvent union and extracts a code for the key that was pressed. The function has the following prototype:

```
KeySym XtGetActionKeysym(XEvent *ep, Modifiers *modp);
```

Both KeySym and Modifiers types are in effect long. The second argument indicates whether a shift key was used. (It equals 1 if not locked, 2 if locked). It does not indicate if CONTROL or ALT were pressed. The return contains a symbolic code, the keysym defined in the file X11/keysymdef.h. Only the least significant 18 bits are used. The key symbol code is designed to be the same as the ASCII code whenever feasible. Its values differ mainly when special pad keys or modifier keys are pressed, such as the SHIFT, CONTROL, and ALT keys. Table 4.1 lists the returned values of keysym when the 'A' key is pressed either alone or in combination.

Table 4.1.   Pressing the 'A' key

| Combination | Number of Returns | Return | | Modifier |
		Octal	ASCII/keysym	
Alone	1	0141	'a'	0
With the SHIFT key	2	0177741	XK_Shift_L	0
		0101	'A'	1
With the CONTROL key	2	0177743	XK_Control_L	0
		0141	'a'	0
With the ALT key	2	0177751	XK_Alt_L	0
		0141	'a'	0

Pressing any key generates an event, so it is correct to have two returns; however it is up to the application to interpret two key combinations when the modifier is not the shift key.

The keyboard can be used for two purposes: To invoke action procedures (Sec. 4.2.3) or menu accelerators (Sec. 5.2.6), where all key combinations are important, and to enter text strings. In this case we may ignore some but not all of the modifier keys. The following rules are pertinent:

- The returned value for printable keys is the 7-bit ASCII value.
- The returned value for return, backspace, tab, and escape keys is 0177400 ORed with the 7-bit ASCII value. For example the escape key's code is 0177433.
- The returned value for control keys is 0177400 ORed with an 8-bit code.

The preceding rules suggest that we can ignore a key if keysym&0200 is nonzero. However there is an exception. Many people are used to using the delete key as a character erasure key, but the code returned for it is 0177777 (sixteen 1s). These rules are sufficient for simple programs—complex programs must use symbolic names, such as XK_Control_L, etc.

Listing 4.13 contains the necessary code for collecting text lines and looking for special characters. It is given so that it can be used either from inside an event handler or as an action procedure tied to <Key>. The code assumes that characters are echoed on the screen at position _x, _y and the user is prompted with an underscore. The collected text is placed in a buffer pointed by _cp. All three are static variables, so we are not concerned here with their definitions. Typically these are initialized by the procedure that requests the user to provide text. In filling a form _x, _y is near the lower left corner of the text entry box, and _cp is initialized to point to the buffer where the typed text is placed. Listing 4.13 uses

Listing 4.13. Collecting Text—File keys.c

```
static int_x,_y;
static char *_cp;
void collect_text(Widget w, XEvent *ep)
{   KeySym keysym;
    Modifiers mods;
    static char bf[2] = " ";

    St_draw_area(w);
    St_use_xor_mode();
    keysym = XtGetActionKeySym(ep, &mods);
    if(!keysym) return;
    if(keysym &0200) {/*  control character  */
                        /*  handle special case for DEL  */
        if(keysym == 0177777) keysym &= 0177577;
        else return;
    }
    St_put_text ("_",_x,_y); /*  erase underscore  */
    if(keysym&0400) { /*  Tabs, new lines, etc  */
        switch(keysym&0177) {
        case XK_Tab:
            _x += 20; /*  for example  */
            *_cp++ = '\t ';
            break;
        /*  other cases, such as new line  */
        }
    }
    else {
            bf[0] = keysym;
            _x += St_put_text(bf, _x, _y); /*  echo character
                        and advance horizontal position  */
        *_cp++ = bf[0];
    }
    St_put_text("_",_x,_y); /*  place new underscore  */
    return;
}
#ifdef EVENT_HANDLER
void event_handler(Widget w, XtPointer client_data,
        XEvent *ep, Boolean *pass_the_event)
{
    /* ... */
    switch (ep->type) {
    case KeyPress:
```

```
        collect_text(w, ep);
        break;
   /*  other cases  */
}
#else /*  Action Procedure  */
static XtActionsRec acts [] = {
   /* ... */
   { "collect_text", collect_text},
   /* ... */
};
static char translations[] = " ... <Key> : collect_text() ... "
#endif
```

Starter toolkit functions for drawing. These can easily be replaced by Xlib functions (see Chap. 8). The code in Listing 4.13 must be completed by providing ways of dealing with new lines and erasures.

4.5. CONCLUSIONS

We discussed event handlers, callbacks, and action procedures; gave examples of their use; and made comparisons. We also discussed work procedures, timeouts, and file input and animation applications (for the first two topics) and building graphical front ends (for the third topic). Finally we discussed text entry.

Simple X programs may ignore most of these issues because events are dealt through the widget callbacks. On the other hand material in Chap. 4 is essential for programs with mixed input (both file and user) or those that do animation.

4.6. PROJECTS

1. Use the resource fallback mechanism (see Sec. 3.2.4) to modify programs in Listings 4.5–4.7 so these will work even if there is no resource file.
2. The program in Listing 4.11 stops at a random state when the user presses mouse button 1 or 2. If the display were blinking before, it may be either on or off now. Modify the program so that when steady, the display is always on.
3. Modify the program in Listing 4.11 so that it scrolls the message (instead of blinking).
4. Compare the performance of animation with work procedures and timeouts by running the program in Listing 4.11 in its original form and with the modifications suggested in Sec. 4.3.2.

5. Modify the program in Listing 4.11 by using timeouts and providing for the following application user inputs: (1) when Button 1 is pressed the rate of blinking increases; (2) when Button 2 is pressed, the rate of blinking decreases; and (3) when Button 3 is pressed, blinking pauses/restarts.

6. Create a graphics front end for an interactive Unix command, for example dc, the desk calculator, using functions described in Secs. 4.3.3 and 4.5. When the user types a line, a line returns with the result. This is not very interesting, but once we ensure that the pipe is working, we can create a true graphical front end using material from subsequent chapters.

5

Programming with Widgets

5.1. WIDGETS AS BUILDING BLOCKS

5.1.1. Introduction So far all the examples have had two widgets, one a shell widget and the other usually a paper class widget. The shell widget window is tightly wrapped around the window of its child widget, so it is not visible. In addition such programs have a window inserted by the window manager that usually has a few subwindows of its own. For practical purposes, we can think of such applications as *one-window* applications, since there is only one window that is both visible to the user and under the control of the application. (Indeed in other systems, such as Microsoft Windows, such a construct is considered a single window.) Figure 5.1 shows this arrangement on the left.

Complex X programs can be built by assembling different widgets. All programs need a shell widget that interacts with the window manager and contains all other widgets. Because shell widgets can have only one child, programs with many windows need a basic container widget that is a child of the shell and in turn contains all other widgets. Some of these widgets may be containers themselves, and so forth. Such an arrangement is shown on the right of Fig. 5.1.

The term *simple* widget refers to widgets that have no children. The word simple is misleading, since some simple widgets such as labels or buttons, are

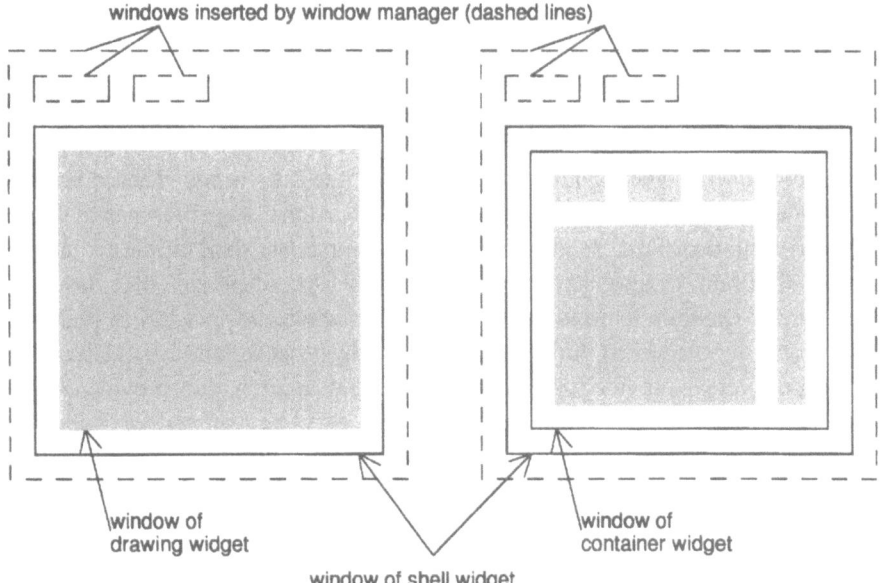

Figure 5.1. Layouts of windows in different applications. Shell and window manager windows are drawn expanded. (In reality there is no gap between them and the window they enclose.) Windows whose appearance is of special interest to the application are shown in gray.

indeed simple, but others, such as sliders, can be quite complex from both a programmer's and a user's perspective. There are also many different kinds of container widgets. These are characterized mainly by the complexity of the rules specifying the layout of their children. At one extreme are container widget classes that arrange their children according to a fixed policy (for example in a vertical column). In the other extreme are widgets where the application specifies placement directly through plane coordinates. A strict application-specified policy may seem attractive but it has one disadvantage: The policy may not provide a good arrangement if the parent widget is *resized*. Therefore it is desirable to have a set of rules by which the parent widget lays out children widgets.

In Chap. 5 we discuss widgets with relatively simple modes of interaction—simple widgets, simple container widgets, shells (including pop-ups), and drawing widgets.

The Xt provides only rudimentary widgets, so for nontrivial applications, we must use widget from another toolkit. The *Athena* toolkit is free with all distributions of X, but it is rather limited. The most advanced toolkit is *Motif*, but since it is not free, it may not exist in some installations. The OLIT, distributed with SUN systems, lacks the full functionality of Motif, but it has some widgets that provide more advanced features than the corresponding Motif widgets.

Since most X programs can be written equally well with any of these toolkits, in the rest of the text, we attempt as much as possible to provide descriptions that are independent of a particular toolkit.

5.1.2.   Relations between Children and Parents   X distinguishes between *managed* and *unmanaged* children of a container widget. A parent must provide space for each managed child by taking into account its needs. This is normally done within the function XtRealizeWidget(). At that stage most parent widgets compute their own size, so that they can accommodate their managed children. Afterward parent widgets have complete control over their children's layout (in response for example to window resizing). If an application wishes to preserve a layout form, it must do so through constraint widgets, as we discuss in Chap. 6.

While parents provide space for their managed children, they provide no space for *unmanaged* children. A managed widget may be *mapped* or *unmapped*, depending on whether its window is mapped or not. The parent of an unmapped widget leaves space for it in the display, but the widget is not visible. Widgets are managed from the start if created by XtCreateManagedWidget() (as in our examples). Widgets start unmanaged if they are created with XtCreateWidget(). That status can be changed with the following functions:

```
XtManageChild(Widget w)
XtUnmanageChild(Widget w)
```

These functions are not likely to be of use for the type of applications discussed in this book. In general it is best to change the mapping rather than the management status of a widget to make it invisible. Mapping can be changed with the functions:

```
XtMapWidget(Widget w)
XtUnmappWidget(Widget w)
```

These functions leave the position of other widgets unchanged, so these present a more consistent environment to the user.

As we mention in Sec. 3.1.4, the core class has a boolean resource XtMappedWhenManaged that ensures widgets are automatically mapped when managed if its value is TRUE.

All composite widgets have resources XtNchildren (pointer to a list of widgets), XtNnumChildren (integer), and XtNinsertPosition (pointer to procedure that determines position in the array of children). An example illustrating the use of some of these functions is given in Sec. 5.1.3.

5.1.3.   Finding the Widget Tree   Here we discuss a simple program that constructs the widget tree of an application. The program uses the resources of composite widgets and the information function, XtName(), that provide a widget's name. Listing 5.1 shows a recursive procedure that can be called with the top widget as first argument [for example tree(toplevel, 0);] just before calling XtAppMainLoop() in such programs as Listings 1.2, 5.8, etc. The essential statements are highlighted.

The function of Listing 5.1 uses tabs to denote depth. Figure 5.2 shows a simple window layout with the output of the tree() function next to it. The function is useful for extracting information from a poorly documented program provided the source is available. It is a weak relative of the spy program discussed in Chap. 2. That program extracted information from applications whose source code was not available. Because widgets are client structures and their names are known only inside an application, the "widget spy" code must be compiled with the application

The function tree() can be called from inside any callback or event handler by using the XtParent() information function in the following manner:

```
some_callback(Widget w, ... )
{
    Widget wtop = w;
    /* ... */
```

Listing 5.1. Printing the Widget Tree

```
/*  Traversing the Widget Tree  */
#include <X11/StringDefs.h>
#include <X11/Intrinsic.h>

void tree(Widget w, int depth)
{
    register i;
    Widget *kids;
    int nk=0;

    for (i=0; i<depth; i++) printf("\t");
    XtVaGetValues(w, XtNnumChildren, &nk, NULL);
    printf("%s(%d children)\n", XtName(w), nk);
    if(nk==0) return;
    XtVaGetValues(w, XtNchidlren, &kids, NULL);
    for(i==0; i<nk; i++)tree(kids [i], depth+1);
    for(i=0; i<depth; i++) printf("\t")
    printf ("- - - - - - - -\n");
}
```

```
    while(XtParent(wtop) != NULL) wtop = XtParent(wtop.);
    tree(wtop, 0);
  /* ... */
}
```

In this way we can add a menu button in an application to print the widget tree.

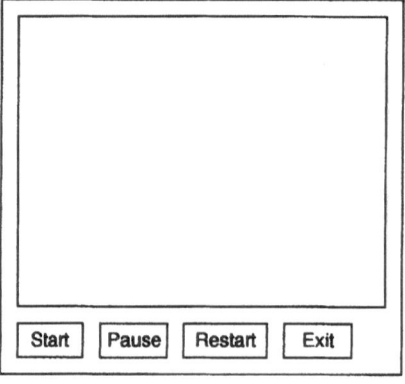

```
game (1 children)
    frame (2 children)
        canvas (0 children)
        menu (4 children)
            start (0 children)
            pause (0 children)
            restart (0 children)
            exit (0 children)
            --------

        --------

    --------
```

Figure 5.2. Window layout (*left*) and widget tree printout (*right*) in an application with a drawing area and a four-button menu. The application name is game.

Note: The widget tree computed in this fashion is correct only for applications that do not include pop-up windows. We return to this topic in Sec. 5.5.

5.2.   SIMPLE WIDGETS

5.2.1. Introduction   All widget sets have a class that is a subclass of Core and a superclass for all simple widgets. For Athena the class is `simpleWidgetClass`, for Motif `XmPrimitiveWidgetClass`, and for OLIT `primitiveWidgetClass`. These classes contain various resources that are inherited by all simple widgets. We do not consider these separately now; we refer to their resources when discussing specific simple widgets. Table 5.1 gives class relationships for some simple widgets of the three major toolkits. Each widget class is derived from the class in the row above it. The terms simple and primitive are somewhat misleading; they mean only that the widget has no children. Some simple widgets are indeed simple; for example those that serve as menu buttons. Others, such as scrollbars or text editors, may have quite complex functionality.

5.2.2. Label Widgets   One of the simplest possible widgets is a *label* widget whose window displays either (noneditable) text or a pixmap. Athena has the class `labelWidgetClass` (definitions in `Xaw/Label.h`), which is a subclass of Simple, itself a subclass of Core. This class has a large number of resources that determine its appearance; the most pertinent for simple applications are

- `XtNbitmap`: Takes as value a bit map (pixmap type) that is displayed.
- `XtNlabel`: Takes as value a string of characters; the text may include new line characters ('\n') that are interpreted correctly. If both a label and a pixmap are defined, the pixmap has priority.
- `XtNleftbitmap`: Takes as value a bit map (pixmap type); it is displayed *in addition* to the label to the left of it.

Table 5.1.   Class Relationships of Simple Widgets

Motif		OLIT		Athena
Core (Xt)		Core (Xt)		Core (Xt)
Primitive (Motif)		Primitive (Motif)		Simple
Label		Button		Label
Push Button	Toggle Button	Oblong Button	Rectangular Button	Command
				Toggle

- `XtNforeground`: The color (pixel value) used to draw the text or the bit map. Note: The widget also has a `XtNbackground` resource inherited from Core.
- `XtNFont`: Takes as value a font information structure (see Sec. 8.3.4) that specifies the font used to draw the text.

Other resources specify margins, text justification, cursor, cursor color, etc. (The last two are inherited from Simple.)

Listing 5.2 is a version of the Hello World program that uses this widget. Note: This program does not exit gracefully (see Sec. 4.2.6 on how to fix the problem).

Motif has a similar label widget class, `xmLabelWidgetClass` (definitions in `Xm/Label.h`), which is a subclass of `XmPrimitive`. Resources `XmNla-belPixmap` and `XmNlabelString` refer to the pixmap or label string. Note: The expected string is not an ordinary ASCII string but a special `XmString` that may include font specification; it allows us to use character systems other than ASCII. The simplest way of specifying a label is through the function `XmStringCreateLocalized()`, which takes as an argument an ordinary ASCII string, for example:

```
XtVaSetValues(motif_label, XmNlabelString,
   XmStringCreateLocalized("Price of generality"),
   NULL);
```

An additional resource, `XmlabelType`, has the symbolic strings `XmSTRING` and `XmPIXMAP` as possible values specifying the type of label.

The OLIT has no label widget class as such; the static text widget class, `statictextWidgetClass` (definitions in `Xol/staticText.h`), with resource `XtNstring`, has a similar functionality, but it does not provide for pixmaps (images stored on the server). Another related class is the caption widget class, but it is a composite widget whose label is used to describe a child widget.

Note

In this text we do not provide detailed documentation on widgets; we focus instead on their main features. Consult an appropriate manual for documentation of *all* features.

Listing 5.2. Hello World Program

```
/*  Hello World  */

#include <X11/StringDefs.h>
#include <X11/Intrinsic.h>

#include <X11/Xaw/Label.h>

main(int arc, char **arv)
{
    Widget toplevel, label;
    XtAppContext app;

    toplevel = XtAppInitialize( &app, "Play",
        NULL, 0, &arc, arv, NULL, NULL, 0);

    label = XtVaCreateManagedWidget("Label",
        labelWidgetClass, toplevel,
        XtNlabel, "The End of the World is Near",
        NULL);

    XtRealizeWidget(toplevel);
    XtAppMainLoop(app);
}
```

5.2.3. Command or Button Widgets   Command widgets are constructed in the Athena toolkit from Label widgets by adding a callback function, which is usually invoked when the user clicks the mouse button on the widget. Their counterpart in Motif and OLIT are button widgets, which have a three-dimensional appearance to provide the illusion of actually pushing a button. (Motif has a widget class called command, but it is used for typing commands.)

The command widget class, commandWidgetClass for the Athena set, is a subclass of Label having the additional resource, XtNcallback, which is a callback list. Listing 5.3 is an implementation of the Hello World program with a graceful exit. (However the program still cannot properly handle an exit through the window manager.)

The corresponding class in Motif is PushButton, xmPushButtonWidget-Class (definitions in Xm/PushB.h), which has three callback lists. The one corresponding to the Athena XtNcallback is XmNactivateCallback. The corresponding class in OLIT is OblongButton, oblongButtonWidgetClass (definitions in Xol/OblongButt.h), with callback resource XtNselect.

Listing 5.3.   Enhanced Hello World Program

```
/*  Hello World  */

#include <X11/StringDefs.h>
#include <X11/Intrinsic.h>

#include <X11/Xaw/Command.h>

void quit() {
    exit(0);
}
main(int arc, char **arv)
{

    Widget toplevel, button;
    XtAppContext app;

    toplevel = XtAppInitialize( &app, "Play",
        NULL, 0, &arc, arv, NULL, NULL, 0);

    button = XtVaCreateManagedWidget("Button",
        commandWidgetClass, toplevel,
        XtNlabel, "The End of the World is Near",
        NULL);
    XtAddCallback(button, XtNcallback, quit, NULL);

    XtRealizeWidget(toplevel);
    XtAppMainLoop(app);
}
```

Since button widgets are normally used in selection menus, we present examples of their use when we discuss menus.

Buttons can be labelled with icons in addition to text. Motif and Athena require the specification of a pixmap, while OLIT requires an X Image (image stored on the client).

5.2.4. Toggle Widgets   Command widgets have no memory. Once a button is pushed, it pops out immediately, and it is available for another selection by the user unless explicitly disabled by the application, as discussed in Sec. 5.2.8. Toggles are command widgets with memory—after a button is selected, it stays off.

For example in an animation program, we may have play and pause buttons. Toggles are often used in *radio boxes*. These enforce the rule that only one button can be selected at any one time. We discuss this arrangement in Sec. 5.4.4.

The toggle widget for each of the three major toolkits follow:

- Athena: `toggleWidgetClass` (definitions in `Xm/Toggle.h`)
- Motif: `xmToggleButtonWidgetClass` (definitions in `Xm/ToggleB.h`).
- OLIT: `rectButtonWidgetClass` (definitions in `Xol/RectButton.h`).

The callbacks are the same for command buttons except in Motif, where it is `XmNarmCallback`.

Toggle widgets have a *state* resource used by functions to impose radio box behaviour. The state resource is Boolean; it is called `XtNstate` in Athena, `XmNset` in Motif, and `XtNset` in OLIT. To change the state of a toggle from the application, we need a statement such as:

```
XtVaSetValues(w, XmNset, FALSE, NULL);
```

In general applications should avoid setting the state explicitly; instead these should rely on a container widget to enforce such rules as "only one choice at a time."

Toggle buttons are good for specifying parameters in a program, for example, the color used in a painting program.

5.2.5. Utility Function for Creating Buttons   Many applications need to create selection buttons without worrying too much about their particular appearance; the code in Listing 5.4 does that.

Capitalized variables are defined according to the widget set used, as shown in Listing 5.5.

The code of `make_button()` for a toggle button is identical to what is given because we use defined constants. We have to change only definitions of `BUTTON_CLASS` and in the case of Motif, of `CALLBACK`. However before trying to combine the pieces of code remember the correct procedure for changing definitions in C:

```
#define THING something
/* ... */
#undef THING
#define THING something else
```

Listing 5.4.   Button Creation Function—File button.c

```
#include <X11/StringDefs.h>
#include <X11/Intrinsic.h>
#include "button_defs.h"

Widget make_button(Widget parent, char *s, void (*f)(),
    XtPointer callback_argument)
{
    Widget w = XtVaCreateManagedWidget(s, BUTTON_CLASS,
        parent, TEXT(s), NULL);
    XtAddCallback(w, CALLBACK, f, callback_argument);
    return w;
}
```

Listing 5.5.   Widget-Set-Dependent Definitions for Buttons—
File Button_defs.h

```
#ifdef ATHENA
#include <X11/Xaw/Command.h>
#define BUTTON_CLASS commandWidgetClass
#define TEXT(A)     XtNlabel, A
#define CALLBACK    XtNcallback
#endif

ifdef MOTIF
#include <Xm/PushB.h>
#define BUTTONCLASS XmPushButtonWidgetClass
#define TEXT(A) XmNlabelString, XmStringCreateLocalized (A)
#define CALLBACK XmNactivateCallback
#endif

#ifdef OLIT
#include <Xol/OblongButt.h>
#define BUTTON_CLASS oblongButtonWidgetClass
#define TEXT(A)     XtNlabel, A
#define CALLBACK    XtNselect
#endif
```

5.2.6.   Accelerators   Buttons let us invoke actions with a mouse button
click. Some users however prefer the keyboard instead of the mouse, particularly
for such applications as text editors, which involve considerable typing anyway. It is
easy to define a second callback for a button that responds to a keyboard event.
However that requires the button to be visible and the pointer to be inside it (to have
the keyboard focus). That is almost as much work as clicking the button and it
certainly does not work with pop-up or pull-down menus, where buttons are not
visible all the time.

The Xt provides a mechanism for associating events in one widget with actions
in another. The core widget has a resource, XtNaccelerators, that points to a
translation table (see Sec. 4.2.3 and 4.2.4) whose actions can be tied to other
widgets. Suppose the accelerator table for a button contains the entry:

```
Ctrl<KeyPress>q: quit()
```

If we associate the table with all the widgets in the application, then pressing
CONTROL q causes an action procedure corresponding to quit to be called. The
name *accelerator* refers to the functionality obtained from such a mechanism. For
example in a text editor, the normal way of saving a file may require pressing a save
button. Instead of leaving the keyboard, the user could press a key combination that
would also save the file. That key combination is an accelerator for the save button.
We say that the text widget is the *destination* and the button widget is the *source* of
the accelerator. Clearly the destination widget must have the keyboard focus for
keyboard accelerators to be effective (Sec. 4.4.1).

Both Motif and OLIT provide a simpler way of specifying accelerators than
does Xt. The following code illustrates the definition of an accelerator for a Motif
pushbutton:

```
out = XtVaCreateManagedWidget("Exit",
    xmPushButtonWidgetClass, menu, XmNlabelString,
    XmStringCreateLocalized("quit"), NULL);
XtAddCallback(out, XmNactivateCallback, quit, NULL);
XtVaSetValues(out, XmNaccelerator, "Ctrl<Key>q",
    XmNacceleratorText, XmStringCreateLocalized("(^q)"),
    NULL);
```

Note: Two strings are involved: (1) a string with the syntax of the translation
table that specifies simultaneously typing CONTROL and q is the accelerator; and
(2) an XmString that specifies the text to be added to the regular label. After the
accelerator is added, the button label is quit (^q). The relevant OLIT resources
are XtNaccelerator (there is no s at the end) and XtNacceleratorText.

While accelerators in Motif and OLIT can be defined for many widget classes, they tend to be supported only under special circumstances, namely, for buttons and toggles that are normally invisible. This is the case when the parent is a pop-up or pull-down menu (see Chap. 6). No warning of any kind is issued if the parent is the wrong kind except that the accelerator text (if specified) does not appear in the label. The reason is that defining the accelerator for the source (usually a button) does only half the work. We must make sure that the destination widget knows about it. Motif and OLIT do that automatically, but they impose some policies during this process.

5.2.7. Gadgets and Objects   Creating a separate window for each menu button seems wasteful, and it often is. For this reason all toolkits provide *gadgets* as alternatives to simple *widgets*. A gadget looks and acts like a widget except that it has no X window associated with it.

To understand the implementation of gadgets, we must look at the full class hierarchy of Xt. In Chap. 3 we started with the Core class but there are actually two classes above it in the class hierarchy. The true base class is Object. It has a subclass RectObj that has dimension and position information but no window associated with it. Core is a subclass of RectObj, although the definition file of Core does not make explicit references to its superclasses; instead it repeats their definitions.

Gadgets are defined as subclasses of RectObj. Note: *There is no type Gadget*; whenever necessary we must use the Object as the type. All simple widgets described so far also have gadget counterparts. For example to create a gadget push button in Motif, we use the following code:

```
#include <Xm/PushBG.h>
#define BUTTON_CLASS xmPushButtonGadgetClass
/*  other definitions are the same as in Listing 5.5  */

Object make_button(Widget parent, char *s, void (*f)(),
    XtPointer callback_argument)
{
    Object w = XtVaCreateManagedWidget(s, BUTTON_CLASS,
        parent, TEXT(s), NULL);
    XtAddCallback(w, CALLBACK, f, callback_argument);
    return w;
}
```

The callback function should have the form

```
void f( Object w, ... )
{
/* ... */
}
```

Using gadgets reduces demands on the server but increases demands on the application. For example the server delivers events only to windows, so there is no way of directly associating events to gadgets. Thus if a widget has gadget children, it must handle events for them. In particular when the parent widget receives an event, it must perform the necessary geometric calculations to find the gadget where the pointer was when the event occurred. Then it invokes the callback associated with the gadget. Such toolkits as Motif hide these calculations from the applications programmer, so programmers sometimes forget the difference between gadgets and widgets.

Caution

Since a gadget has no window, it cannot have resources normally associated with a window, for example background pixel or pixmap. It also cannot be mapped or unmapped.

5.2.8. Widget Sensitivity   There are situations when it is inappropriate for the application user to execute a command, so we may wish to disable the widget. For example we may wish to disable a start button in an animation if the animation has already begun. There are three ways of accomplishing this: Unmanage the widget, unmap the widget, and make it insensitive. When a widget is unmanaged, it disappears from the screen, and other widgets are rearranged to assume its place. This is usually too drastic a step, and it can be confusing to the user. When a widget is unmapped, it also disappears from the screen, but its place remains empty. This is a more gentle change than when a widget is unmanaged, but it may still be deemed undesirable by application users.

The preferred way of disabling a widget is to make it insensitive using the core resource XtNsensitive. The following call makes a widget indifferent to events:

```
XtVaSetValues(w, XtNsensitive, False, NULL);
```

The following call revives it:

```
XtVaSetValues(w, XtNsensitive, True, NULL);
```

Suppose we have two button widgets, on_widget and off_widget, with respective labels "on" and "off", but we want to have only one of them sensitive. To start we call

```
XtVaSetValues(on_widget, XtNsensitive, True, NULL);
XtVaSetValues(off_widget, XtNsensitive, False, NULL);
```

Then inside the callback of the "on" button, we include statements:

```
on_callback(Widget w, ... )
{
    Widget sibling;
    /* ... */
    XtVaSetValues(w, XtNsensitive, False, NULL);
    sibling = XtNameToWidget(XtParent(w), "off");
    XtVaSetValues(sibling, XtNsensitive, True, NULL);
}
```

and a symmetric set of statements in the callback of the "off" button. Instead of using the XtNameToWidget() function, we could pass the other widget as part of the client data. However explicit use of the name makes the code easier to understand at the cost of very little computation.

While mechanisms for enabling or disabling a widget are very simple, their *use* requires special care. We must identify program states and select which command buttons are meaningful in each state. We present a less trivial example in Sec. 5.5.3.

5.2.9.   Finding Widgets by Name   When we discussed widget sensitivity, we used the information function XtNameToWidget() to find the sibling of a widget to change its sensitivity. This function has the following prototype:

```
Widget XtNameToWidget(Widget w, String names);
```

If the string names has only one name the function returns the direct child of w if any matching that name. The string may also have a list of names (separated by periods or asterisks) that specify a path in the tree. Thus to find the widget with the name "on", starting from the top of the tree, we must call

```
XtNameToWidget(toplevel, "*on");
```

The start character (*) matches any path name. If there is more than one widget named "on", the function returns the one closest to the root. Ties are broken in an unpredictable way. The following call locates a widget named "on" only if it is a direct child of toplevel. (See [AS90], pp. 415–17, for more on this topic.)

```
XtNameToWidget(toplevel, "on");
```

5.3.   WIDGET GEOMETRY

The term widget geometry refers to the size of its window (width and height), coordinates of its top left corner (with respect to the parent window), border width, and depth or stacking position. Stacking refers to which window is displayed on top of another: If windows of widgets A and B overlap and the stacking order is A, B, the window of B will be (partially) hidden by the window of A. Note: Stacking order is always defined even if windows do not overlap. (Widget geometry is information that resides on the client, while window geometry is information that resides on the server; thus the two are not the same.)

The general policy in Xt is that window dimensions and positions are calculated *bottom up* before windows are created. First each widget that has no children determines its size, then passes that information to its parent. Then each parent calculates its own size based on the size of its children, and so forth. (Parents may override some size requests, see the following discussion.) In Fig. 5.2 widgets canvas, start, pause, restart, and exit compute their size first, then menu, and then frame. After windows are created and mapped, the geometry is controlled top down. Requests by a child to change its size are restricted.

Simple widgets such as those we have seen so far have their dimensions either specified through the resources XtNwidth and XtNheight or computed based on the displayed label. Composite widgets follow different policies, so they may *ignore* some of the geometry requests from their children. Some composite widgets have a fixed *layout policy*. Their children are laid out along a particular direction (vertically or horizontally) in the order in which they were created. For example in a vertical layout, the first child is at the top. A container widget may compute the maximum width (in a vertical layout) or height (in a horizontal layout), then assign those values to all children; Fig. 5.3 shows the final appearance.

Container widgets with a specific layout policy generally ignore position requests (resources XtNx and XtNy). Other container widgets honor position requests (see Sec. 5.4.5).

The major dilemma facing an application writer is caused by conflicting requirements: On one hand we want to specify the appearance of the windows as we would like them to be; on the other hand we want to avoid burdening our code with

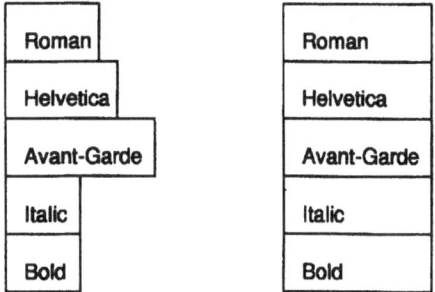

Figure 5.3. Widget layout (for a font-selection menu): *Left*—requested width; *right*—assigned widths.

detailed geometric calculations. Delegating the layout to a composite widget relieves us from the latter task, but we give up some control over window appearance. Another difficulty is the need to respond to resizing by the user.

A compromise is to specify constraints on the layout rather than the layout itself. Container widgets that accommodate such constraints are discussed in Chap. 6.

5.4.   CONTAINER WIDGETS

5.4.1.   Simple Layout Widgets   The simplest kind of container widgets are those that lay out their children in particular predefined order, *either* vertically *or* horizontally. Athena has a Box widget class `boxWidgetClass` (definitions in `Xaw/Box.h`) that is a direct subclass of composite. In addition to the resources it inherits from core and composite widgets, it has three resources of its own: `XtNorientation` can have one of two symbolic values: `XtorientVertical` or `XtorientHorizontal`. In the former case children are laid out vertically, in the latter horizontally; the default value is horizontal. However if there are no constraints on a widget dimension and all children do not fit in the requested direction, additional rows (or columns) can be created.

`XtNhSpace` and `XtNvSpace` take values in pixels that represent horizontal and vertical gaps between children and between the children and the widget frame; the default value is 4 pixels.

Similar functionality (and more) is provided by `xmRowColumnWidgetClass` of Motif and `controlAreaWidgetClass` of OLIT. The relevant resource of the former is `XmNorientation`, with values `XmVERTICAL` and `XmHORIZONTAL`. The OLIT widget has resource `XtNlayoutType`, with values `OL_FIXEDCOLS` and `OL_FIXEDROWS`. These widgets also create multiple rows or columns if all children do not fit in one.

The Motif row/column widget have a type resource, `XmNrowColumnType`, that further specifies its functionality through symbolic values; these include `XmMENU_PULLDOWN`, `XmMENU_POPUP`, and the default value `XmWORK_AREA`. If we create menus using Motif convenience functions (see Chap. 6), we need not be concerned with type specification.

5.4.2.   Application with a Visible Menu   We can combine two container widgets with a paper widget and a set of command/button widgets to construct an application with a drawing area and a visible menu with four buttons arranged horizontally beneath it. The window layout is shown in Fig. 5.2 (Sec. 5.1.3).

The program is given in Listing 5.6; widget classes definitions are given in Listing 5.7. The function `make_button()` is as in Listing 5.4 (with definitions in

Listing 5.5). Definitions of capital letter variables are straightforward, although OLIT layout specifications are rather cryptic.

It is quite easy to modify the program in Listing 5.6 to obtain different layouts. If we create the menu widget before the canvas widget, the menu appear on top. To have a vertical menu to the side of the canvas, we interchange the layout parameters of the frame and menu widgets. In this case the menu appears on the right if the canvas is created first and to the left otherwise.

The contents of the drawing window are specified by whatever the function `paint()` draws. The response to events depends on the four callbacks not been included in Listing 5.6. We added the canvas as client data to the callbacks, so when one of these functions is called, it can draw on the canvas. For example to produce an animation, we may use the following code:

```
int animate(Widget w)
{
    St_draw_area(w);
    /* ... */
}
static XtWorkProcId animation_id;
void start(Widget w, Widget sibling)
{
    draw_area(sibling);
    /* perform any initialization tasks needed */
    /* ... */
    /* pass the drawing area to the work procedure as
    well */
    animation = XtAppAddWorkProc(
        XtWidgetToApplicationContext(w),
        animate, (XtPointer)sibling);
}
```

If the application user resizes the application, all windows keep their size and positions. This is probably a desirable property for an animation or game program, but not for a drawing program where a user may want a larger canvas. For that we need a constraint widget. (The Motif Row Column widget is a constraint widget, but we used it in a naive mode in this example.) We need change only the class of the first container to a constraint widget. The menu container widget should remain in the same class because we want to keep the button layout constant, since changes are likely to confuse users. On the other hand we may wish to provide the user with the option of displaying the menu at the top rather than the bottom.

Before we deal with constraint widgets, we discuss some topics pertinent to any container widgets.

Listing 5.6.   Menu and Drawing Widget—File game.c

```c
#include <X11/StringDefs.h>
#include <X11/Intrinsic.>
#include "box_defs.h" /*  See Listing 5.6  */
#include <Paper.h>

void start(), pause(), restart(), quit();
void paint(),
Widget make_button(); /*   From Listing 5.4  */

main(int arc, char **arv)
{
    Widget toplevel, frame, menu, canvas;
    Widget start_button, pause_button, restart_button,
      exit_button;
    XtAppContext app;

    toplevel = XtVaAppInitialize( &app; "Play",
       NULL, 0, &arc, arv NULL);

    frame = XtVaCreateManagedWidget("frame",
       BOX_WIDGET_CLASS, toplevel, VERTICAL_LAYOUT,
       NULL);

    canvas = XtVaCreateManagedWidget("canvas",
       paperWidgetClass, frame,
       XtNwidth, 300, XtNheight, 200,
       NULL);
    XtAddCallback (canvas, XtNredrawCallback, paint,
      NULL);

    menu = XtVaCreateManagedWidget("menu",
       BOX_WIDGET_CLASS, frame, HORIZONTAL_LAYOUT, NULL);
    start_button = make_button(menu, "Start", start,
      (XtPointer)canvas);
    pause_button = make_button(menu, "Pause", pause,
      (XtPointer) canvas);
    restart_button = makebutton(menu, "Restart", restart,
      (XtPointer)canvas);
    exit_button = make_button(menu, "Exit", quit, NULL);

    XtRealizeWidget (toplevel);
    XtAppMainLoop (app);
}
```

Listing 5.7. Widget-Set-Dependent Definitions for Containers—File box_def.h

```
#ifdef ATHENA
#include <X11/Xaw/Box.h>
#define BOX_WIDGET_CLASS        boxWidgetClass
#define HORIZONTAL_LAYOUT XtNorientation, XtorientHorizontal
#define VERTICAL_LAYOUT XtNorientation, XtorientVertical
#endif

#ifdef MOTIF
#include (<Xm/rowColumn.h>
#define BOX_WIDGET_CLASS        xmRowColumnWidgetClass
#define HORIZONTAL_LAYOUT       XmNorientation, XmHORIZONTAL
#define VERTICAL_LAYOUT         XmNorientation, XmVERTICAL
#endif

#ifdef OLIT
#include <Xol/ControlAre.h>
#define BOX_WIDGET_CLASS        controlAreawidgetClass
#define HORIZONTAL_LAYOUT       XtNlayoutType, OL_FIXEDROWS
#define VERTICAL_LAYOUT         XtNlayoutType, OL_FIXEDCOLS
#endif
```

5.4.3. More on Widget Sensitivity   The program in Listing 5.6 is a concrete example of how to change widget sensitivity for proper functionality. For the sake of generality, we use the terms enable and disable a button, since this lets us use other means to change functionality. In particular we may define a pair of macros in one of the following ways, then experiment with the program's behavior:

```
/* Too drastic */
#define enable(A) XtManageChild(A)
#define disable(A) XtUnmanageChild(A)

/* Less drastic */
#define enable(A) XtMapWidget(A)
#define disable(A) XtUnmapWidget(A)

/* Preferred way */
#define enable(A) XtVaSetValues(A, XtNsensitive, True,\
NULL)
#define disable(A) XtVaSetValues(A, XtNsensitive, False,\
NULL)
```

We probably want to keep the exit button enabled at all times. In the beginning the start button must be enabled and the pause and restart buttons disabled. After start is pressed, it should disable itself and enable pause, etc. Therefore we modify the code in Listing 5.7 as follows (buttons are normally enabled after creation):

```
/* ... */
XtRealizeWidget(toplevel);
disable(pause_button);
disable(restart_button);
XtAppMainLoop(app);
}
```

We must also include corresponding statements to each of the callbacks just before returning. Listing 5.8 shows examples of callbacks for the game program.

5.4.4. Radio Boxes   Radio boxes are containers of toggle widgets that enforce the rule only one toggle can be set at any given time. Such behavior is achieved by different means in each toolkit. In Motif the parent is required to be a *row–column* container widget (xmRowColumnWidgetClass), with its resource XmNradioBehavior set to TRUE. In OLIT the parent is required be an *exclusive* container widget (exclusiveWidgetClass); there is no need to specify resources.

Things are more complicated in Athena. Radio box behavior is not enforced by the container widget but by establishing a *widget radio group*. Let the array button[] contain widgets of the toggle class. Then the following code puts them in one radio group:

```
for(i=0; ... ) {
    button[i] = XtVaCreateManagedWidget( ... );
    if(!i) first_button = button[i];
    else XtVaSetValues (button[i], XtNradioGroup,
        first_button, NULL);
```

This is more flexible than the behavior imposed in Motif or OLIT, but it is unclear whether such flexibility is useful enough to be worth the price of complexity.

If an application uses a radio box, it should avoid explicitly setting the toggle state, since that may interfere with widget functions that keep track of the state.

5.4.5. Application-Specified Layout   Both Motif and OLIT (but not Athena) have *Bulletin Board* classes where widgets are placed at values specified by the XtNx and XtNy resources of the child. For motif the class is xmBulletin-

Listing 5.8.   Callbacks for Listings 5.6 and 5.7

```
void start(w, sibling)
    Widget w, sibling;
{
    /* ... */
    disable (w);
    disable( XtNameToWidget(XtParent(w), "restart") );
    enable( XtNameToWidget(XtParent(w), "pause") );
}

void pause(w, sibling)
    Widget w, sibling;
{
    /* ... */
    disable(w);
    enable( XtNameToWidget(XtParent(w), "start") );
    enable( XtNameToWidget(XtParent(w), "restart") );
}

void restart(w, sibling)
    Widget w, sibling,
{
    /* ... */
    disable( w );
    disable( XtNameToWidget(XtParent(w), "start") );
    enable( XtNameToWidget(XtParent(w), "pause") );
}
```

BoardWidgetClass (definitions in Xm/BulletinB.h) and for OLIT
bulletinBoardWidgetClass (definitions in Xol/BulletinBo.h).
These do not respond well to resizing, but they are good for implementing
complex *two-dimensional* arrangements.

Suppose we display a picture, and we want to display next to it profiles of
vertical and horizontal scan lines, as shown in Fig. 5.4. When the user selects a
point (*A*) on an image, variations of image intensity along the vertical (dashed) line
through *A* are displayed in Window *V*, while those along the horizontal line are
displayed in Window *H*. It is very important that the top and bottom of Window *V*
line up with the top and bottom of the image window. Similarly the left and right
sides of Window *H* must line up with the respective sides of the image window.

A bulletin board widget is the right container for such an application. The
following code fragment creates the arrangement in Fig. 5.4 using Paper class

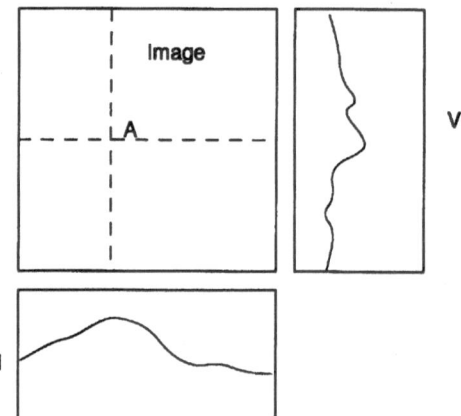

Figure 5.4.   Restricted window arrangement. Windows *V* and *H* must line up with the image window.

widgets for display windows. Variables in bold are assumed defined elsewhere in the program.


```
#ifdef MOTIF
#include <Xm/Xm.h>
#include <Xm/BulletinB.h>
#define B_BOARD_CLASS          xmBulletinBoardWidgetClass
#else    /*  assume OLIT  */
#include <Xol/OpenLook.h>
#include <Xol/BulletinBo.h>
#define B_BOARD_CLASS          bulletinBoardWidgetClass
#endif

#define MARGIN 10
    /* ... */
    Widget bb, image, vert, horiz;
    /* ... */
    bb = XtVaCreateManagedWidget ("Board",
        B_BOARD_CLASS, toplevel, NULL);
    image = XtVaCreateManagedWidget ("Image",
        paperWidgetClass, bb,
        XtNx,    MARGIN,    XtNy,    MARGIN
        XtNwidth,  img_width,
        XtNheight, img_height,
        NULL);
```

```
vert = XtVaCreateManagedWidget("Vertical",
    paperWidgetClass, bb,
    XtNx,   img_width+2*MARGIN, XtNy,     MARGIN,
    XtNwidth,   max_img_value,
    XtNheight,   img_width,
    NULL);
horiz = XtVaCreateManagedWidget("Horizontal",
    paperWidgetClass, bb,
    XtNx,     MARGIN, XtNy,     img_width+2*MARGIN,
    XtNwidth,   img_width,
    XtNheight,   max_img_value,
    NULL);
```

5.5.   SHELL WIDGETS AND POP-UPS

5.5.1.   Overview   Many times an application needs more than one window
that interacts with the window manager. The most common case is *pop-up* windows
that open outside the main application window. (This includes pop-up menus that
appear in response to user action.) Other examples are applications running in more
than one display: for example an instructor draws on his/her window, which then
appears on each student's display. One possible implementation is to have only one
application with windows on many servers.

All such windows require a *shell* widget to handle communications with the
window manager. The Xt provides different kinds of shell widgets, which are
discussed in Sec. 5.5.2; Sec. 5.5.3 discusses pop-ups.

5.5.2.   Shells   The Xt has four kind of shell widgets:

- Application shell (class `applicationShellWidgetClass`) used to
  hold the main window of an application as well as the top window in
  another display.
- Top-level shell (class `topLevelShellWidgetClass`) for pop-ups
  that may stay for the life of the application.
- Transient shell (class `transientShellWidgetClass`)
- Override shell (class `overrideShellWidgetClass`) for pop-ups of
  very short duration. As a rule window managers provide no decorations for
  override shell windows.

Typically an override shell holds a pop-up menu (it stays up only while the
user presses a button). Typical uses for top-level and transient shells include dialog
boxes and image display windows that have their own color map. Many window
managers have difficulty dealing with color maps of widgets that are not shells; if

an application requires windows with different color maps, pop-ups are the solution. The main difference between a transient and a top-level shell occurs when the main application window is iconified, transient shells are automatically unmapped, but top-level shells stay mapped. (Applications shells are discussed in Chap. 3).

All shell classes are subclasses of Composite; therefore they inherit the resources of the Core and Composite classes. Resources of special interest for simple applications include the following:

- For all shells except override shells: XtNtitle (title placed in the window frame inserted by the window manager, as described in Sec 2.4.2) and XtNinput (controlling keyboard input as described in Sec. 4.4.2).
- For all shells: XtNsaveUnder can be True or False. If True, the server saves screen contents beneath the window, so no expose events are generated when the window is dismissed. The default value is True for override and transient shells and False for the other two classes.

While shells inherit width and height resources from Core, these are not useful to them, since shells wrap themselves tightly around their only managed child. Shells can be resized by the window manager, usually in response to a user action. When the user attempts to resize a window, the window manager checks the values of the following set of dimension resources, XtNminWidth, XtNminHeight, XtNmaxWidth, and XtNmaxHeight, then refuses resizing requests outside specified limits. In particular values may prohibit resizing the top window of an application. (This could be useful in a game program for example.) The function in Listing 5.9 does this; it must be called right after XtRealizeWidget(), which (among other things) calculates the size of the top window.

By setting the minimum and maximum values of the dimensions to the current ones, we do not allow resizing. Note: We must ask for current dimensions after the shell is realized because then its dimensions are defined. We program defensively by checking whether the function is indeed called with a shell widget as argument.

Note: Do not be confused by the resource XtNallowShellResize. That resource determines whether the shell can be resized from inside, for example with such code as:

```
Dimension ww, wh;

XtVaGetValues(w, XtNwidth, &ww, XtNheight, &wh, NULL);
XtVaSetValues(w, XtNwidth, ww+20, XtNheight, wh+20, NULL);
```

Listing 5.9. Fixing the Window Size

```
Boolean fix_window_size(Widget w)
{
    Dimension current_width, current_height;

    if(!XtIsShell(w)) return FALSE;
    XtVaCreateValues(w,
        XtNwidth, &current_width,
        XtNheight, &current_height, NULL);
    XtVaSetValues(w,
        XtNminWidth, current_width,
        XtNminheight, current_height,
        XtNmaxWidth, current_width,
        XtNmaxHeight, current_height, NULL);
    return TRUE;
}
```

where w is a child of the shell. If XtNallowShellResize is set to TRUE, the preceding resizing request is granted. The resource has no bearing on resizing by the user. Thus it is possible to have a window that cannot be resized by the user but can be resized internally, a window that cannot resized either by the user or internally, etc.

5.5.3. Widget Forests   We use the term widget forest to denote a collection of widget trees, each with a separate top application shell. Such a forest is pertinent for programs that run in many displays, for example a program posting a message to a group of people. For such programs we need explicit calls to XtOpenDisplay() to establish a connection to each server and XtVaAppCreateShell() that creates each application shell. Both of these functions are called by XtVaApp Initialize(), which is all that is needed in programs with only one top window.

The function XtOpenDisplay() has the following prototype:

```
display *XtOpenDisplay( XtAppContext app,
    char * display_name,
    char * app_name, char * app_class,
    XrmOptionDescRec *resources,
    int res_length, int *arc, char **arv)
```

The first argument is the application context returned by XtVaAppInitialize
(), and the second argument is the display name, which is the sole argument of the
Xlib function XOpenDisplay() (see Sec. 2.1.1). Remaining arguments pertain
to resource handling. If app_name is specified as NULL, it is taken to be the
name of the program (arv[0]). The rest of the prototype correspond to arguments
of XtVaAppInitialize() shifted by two: the fourth (app_class) to the
second, the fifth to the third, etc.

The function XtVaAppCreateShell() has the following prototype:

```
XtVaAppCreateShell( char * app_name, char * app_class,
    WidgetClass widgetclass, Display Dpy,
    /*  resource list  */, NULL)
```

The application name (first argument) is the same as that passed to XtOpen-
Display() as third argument; the value NULL is the best choice in most
programs. The second argument is the same as that used in XtVaApp-
Initialize(), while the third is toplevelShellWidgetClass. The
fourth argument is either the return of XtOpenDisplay() or if the window will
be in the same display, XtDisplay(toplevel), where toplevel is the
return of XtAppInitialize().

When we create a new application shell, we also create a new widget tree, so
that the function XtRealizeWidget() must be called for each such shell.

Listing 5.10 shows the main procedure of a program that creates a widget
forest with trees in different displays. The program creates N-1 widget trees, each
starting with an application shell containing a set of widgets created by the function
create_tablet(). Details of this function are irrelevant for the time being. It
creates a widget that is a child of its first argument, then places that child in the ith
place in the widget array that is its third argument. We could use the following
construct except for the reason stated below:

```
tablet[i] = create_tablet(toplevel)[i]);
```

To communicate, each widget must know about the others, so the array tablet[]
must be passed as client data to callbacks and event handlers. To avoid passing N to
those functions, we set the last member of the array tablet[] to zero. The
function may create a widget tree of any complexity; the function is also supposed
to realize it before returning.

Widget forests are an example of where it is desirable *not* to have unique
widget names. Since each tree uses a different server with its own resource files,
ambiguity in resource selection is not likely to be an issue. On the other hand
common names make convenient communication between widgets by using the

Listing 5.10. Widget Forest—File rpt.c

```
/*  Classroom Repeater  */

#include <X11/StringDefs.h>
#include <X11/Intrinsic.h>
#include <X11/Shell.h>

#define N 4
static char *display_name[] = { "", "desk_1", "desk_2",
"desk_3", 0 };

main(int arc, char **arv)
{
    register i;
    XtAppContext app;
    Widget toplevel[N], tablet[N+1];
    Display *Dpy;

    toplevel[0] = XtVaAppInitialize( &app, "Repeater",
        (XrmOptionDescList)NULL, 0,
        &arc, arv, (String *)NULL, NULL);
    XtVaSetValues(toplevel[0], XtNtitle, "Leader", NULL);
    create_tablet(toplevel[0], 0, tablet);

    for(i=1; i<N; i++) {
        Dpy = XtOpenDisplay(app, display_name[i], NULL,
          "Repeater", (XrmOptionDescList)NULL, 0,
            &arc. arv, (String *)NULL, NULL);
        it(Dpy){
            toplevel[i] = XtVaAppCreateShell( (String)NULL,
              "Repeater", toplevelShellWidgetClass, Dpy
                XtNtitle, "Follower", NULL);
            create_tablet(toplevel[i], i, tablet);
        }
        else { /* message about failed connection */ }
    }
    tablet[N]=0;

    XtAppMainLoop(app);
}
```

function XtNameToWidget(), described in Sec. 5.2.9. In the case of our current example, the tree may contain, for example, an input widget and an echo widget. If the user causes a callback in an input widget, the action must produce a message on all echo widgets. If the array of all the tree tops is in client data, we may have the following callback:

```
void buzz(w, all)
   Widget w, *all;
{
   int i;
   Widget current;
   /*  here because of events in w  */
   /*  ... */
   for (i=0; all[i]; i++) {
      current = XtNameToWidget(all[i], "*Echo");
      XtVaSetValues(current, /* ... */);
   }
}
```

5.5.4. Pop-up Widgets   Pop-up widgets are useful for applications that need many top windows on the same display. Pop-ups have dual parenthood: The main pop-up window is a child of the root window of the display. The corresponding widget though can be the child of any other widget in the application. The later type of parenthood is needed to place the pop-up in the widget tree. In this way the event dispatcher can send events to the pop-up widget.

Pop-up widgets are not automatically displayed even if realized. To display these we must invoke XtPopup() and to dismiss them XtPopdown(). Both of these functions take the top widget of the pop-up as an argument; XtPopup() also takes a second argument that describes its *input modality*. If a pop-up is displayed for only a short time, we may want to direct all input to it. This is achieved by the call:

```
XtPopup(w, XtGrabExclusive);
```

where w is a shell widget. This is appropriate for dialog windows for example. If the pop-up will stay up for a long time, as in the case of image-display pop-ups mentioned earlier, the appropriate call is

```
XtPopup(w, XtGrabNone);
```

A third choice is

```
XtPopup(w, XtGrabNoneExclusive);
```

This is a bit more liberal than the first. A discussion of situations where that call is appropriate is beyond our scope.

The pop-down call is simply:

```
XtPopdown (w);
```

The following call creates a pop-up shell:

```
popup = XtVaCreatePopupShell ("popup",
    POP_SHELL, toplevel,
    XtNtitle, "Hello World", NULL);
```

where `toplevel` is another widget in the application and POP_SHELL can be defined in one of three ways: The first provides maximum flexibility when interacting with the window manager, and each pop-up window can be closed and opened separately:

```
#define POP_SHELL topLevelShellWidgetClass
```

The second has limited interaction with the window manager; in particular if one window is closed all the others are also closed

```
#define POP_SHELL transientShellWidgetClass
```

The third provides no means of interaction with the window manager—the pop-up window is not reparented:

```
#define POP_SHELL overrideShellWidgetClass
```

The Xt provides a special way of invoking pop-ups, called *spring-loaded*. These pop-ups appear when the user presses a button, and they disappear when the button is released. (In this case `overrideShellWidgetClass` is the appropriate choice.) The following code fragment illustrates their use:

```
/* Event handler with popup widget passed as client data */
void show_popup(w, client_data, ep, continue_dispatch)
    Widget w;
    XtPointer client_data;
```

```
    XEvent *ep;
    Boolean *continue_dispatch;
{
    switch(ep->type) {
    case ButtonPress:
        XtPopupSpringLoaded( (Widget) client_data);
        break;
    case ButtonRelease:
        /* not needed because of spring loading */
        break;
    }
}
```

Spring-loaded is useful for pop-up menus (their top widget should be an override shell), so we return to them in Sec. 6.3. The important point here is that spring-loaded refers to how the widget is called rather than how it is created.

5.5.5.   Image Pop-ups   Code fragments in Listing 5.11–5.13 shows pop-ups used to display a set of images whose file names are given as arguments in the command line. The program creates a set of buttons for each filename. When the user selects a button for the first time, an attempt is made to read the file as an image; if the program is successful, it creates a pop-up. Code in the main program is given in Listing 5.11.

Listing 5.12 shows the procedure that creates pop-up windows. The procedure is a callback of the button widgets, with the file name as client data. When the procedure is called, it creates a shell widget and an image display widget; it realizes and pops up the display; then it changes the button callback to a pop-down. When an image window is popped up, an expose event is automatically generated, and the show_image() function is called that creates the actual display. To allow repeated displays of images, each time a pop-up is called, it changes the callback to a pop-down, as shown in Listing 5.13.

5.6.   DRAWING WIDGETS

The appearance of all widgets discussed so far is determined by the widget program itself. Thus an application can change the text that appears on a button, but it cannot add graphics to the button. A drawing widget should allow an application to create arbitrary graphic displays. It is easy to create a basic widget that does so: All we need is an instance of Core and an action procedure for expose events. Listing 5.14 shows an example.

Listing 5.11. Using Pop-Ups for Image Display—File pop.c

```
/* ...include statement and declarations omitted... */
main(int arc, char **arv) {
    /* ... */
    /* prepare main application window */
    toplevel = XrAppInitialize( &app, "Images",
        NULL, 0, &arc, arv, NULL, NULL, 0);
    XtVaSetValues(toplevel, XtNtitle, "Image Display",
      NULL);
    /* prepare container for selection buttons */
    bb = XtVaCreateManagedWidget("frame",
        boxWidgetClass, toplevel,
        XtNorientation, XtorientHorizontal,
        XtNwidth, 400, XtNheight, 400,
        NULL);

    /* create buttons with files names */
    for(i=1, j=0, i<arc, i++, j++) {
        sprintf(bf, "button_%s", arv[i]);
        pix[j] = XtVaCreateManagedWidget(bf,
            commandWidgetClass, bb, XtNlabel, arv[i], NULL);
        XtAddCallback(pix[j], XtNcallback,
          make_image_popup, arv[i]);
    }
    /* create an exit button-see Listing 5.4 */
    out = make_button(bb, "Exit", quit, NULL);

    XtRealizeWidget(toplevel);
    create_protocoltoplevel); /* to exit with WM command */
    XtAppMainLoop(app);
}
```

The function draw() could be made much more complex by using various Xlib functions. Normally we would like a bit more support, such as callbacks for expose events and user actions (pressing a mouse button for example). Both Motif and OLIT drawing widgets are also container widgets. The Motif drawing widget is Drawing Area, xmDrawingAreaWidgetClass (definitions in Xm/Drawing A.h); it has three callbacks: XmNexposeCallback, XmNresizeCallback, and XmNinputCallback. The latter is called in response to button, mouse, and keyboard events. (A pointer to the event union is part of the call_data.) However it is not called in response to mouse motion events, so we cannot use the callback for a rubber band routine. Of course we can always add an event handler or

Listing 5.12.   Using Pop-Ups for Image Display—File pop.c

```
static Im_kount = 0;

void make_image_popup(w, name)
    Widget w;
    String name;
{
    /*  image structure  */ *imp;
    int add_on;
    static char bf[256];

    /* read an image in structure pointed by imp */

    pop[Im_kount] = XtVaCreatePopupShell("imageShell",
        toplevelShellWidgetClass, toplevel,
        XtNtitle, name,
        NULL);

    image[Im_kount] = XtVaCreateManagedWidget(name,
        paperWidgetClass, pop[Im_kount],
        XtNwidth, imp->width,
        XtNheight, imp->height,
        XtNborderWidth, MARGIN/2,
        NULL);
    XtAddCallback( image[Im_kount], XtNredrawCallback,
      show_image, imp);
    /* ... prepare colormap, XImage structure, etc. ... */
    /*  show the image  */
    XtRealizeWidget(pop[Im_kount]);
    XtPopup(pop[Im_kount], XtGrabNone);

    /*  Change the button callback  */
    XtRemoveAllCallbacks(w, XtNcallback);
    XtAddCallback(w, XtNcallback, pop_down, pop[Im_kount]);
    Im_kount++;
}
```

Listing 5.13. Using Pop-Ups for Image Display—File pop.c

```
void pop_up(w, pix_w);
    Widget w, pix_w;
{
    XtPopup(pix_w, XtGrabNone);
    XtRemoveAllCallbacks(w, XtNcallback);
    XtAddCallback(w, XtNcallback, pop_down, pix_w);
}

void pop_down(w, pix_w)
    Widget w, pix_w;
{
    XtPopdown(pix_w);
    XtRemoveAllCallbacks(w, XtNcallback);
    XtAddCallback(w, XtNcallback, pop_up, pix_w);
}
```

use the translation mechanism, but that increases the complexity of application programs. The widget also requires the creation of a graphics context and the use of low-level Xlib functions.

The corresponding OLIT widget is drawAreaWidgetClass (definitions in Xol/DrawArea.h); it has callbacks for both expose and resize events, but not for user input. It also requires the creation of a graphics context and the use of low-level Xlib functions.

It is probably accurate to describe Motif and OLIT widgets as *allowing* rather than *supporting* drawing. In contrast the Paper widget discussed in earlier sections is a drawing widget that *supports* drawing. In addition to a callback for expose events, XtNredrawCallback, it also has a user event callback, XtNuser-Callback, which is called for *all* mouse and keyboard events. Call data provide a simplified event structure, such as that described in the Appendix. A graphics context is automatically provided; a large number of convenience functions eliminates the need to deal with Xlib except on rare occasions.

5.7. CONCLUSIONS

There is a bewildering collection of widgets in the various toolkits and an even more bewildering set of parameters (resources) for them. There are widgets with over 50 resources of their own and the same number inherited from their superclasses. My advice is to select a small number of classes from the toolkit of

Listing 5.14.   Minimal Drawing Widget

```
/*  Minimal Xt Drawing Program  */

#include <X11/StringDefs.h>
#include <X11/Intrinsic.h>
#include <X11/Core.h>

void draw();

static XtActionsRec actions[] = { "draw", draw };
static char translations[] = "<Expose> :draw()";

main (int arc, char **arv)
{
    Widget top, canvas;
    XtAppContext app;

    top = XtVaAppInitialize( &app, "Min", 0, 0, &arc, arv,
        0, NULL);
    XtAppAddActions( app, actions, XtNumber(actions) );
    canvas = XtVaCreateManagedWidget("Canvas",
        coreWidgetClass, top,
        XtNwidth,        200,        XtNheight,        200,
        XtNtranslations,
        XtParseTranslationTable(translations),
        NULL);
    XtRealizeWidget(top);
    XtMainLoop(app);
}

void draw(Widget w)
{
    static GC gc = (gc)0;
    if(!gc) {
        XGCValuesvalues;
        values.foreground = 1;
        gc = XtGetGC(w, GCForeground, values);
    }
    XDrawRectangle(XtDisplay(w), XtWindow(w), gc, 25, 25,
    150, 150);
}
```

choice, then try to program using only these. A suggested essential list with the Motif names in parentheses includes: Label (xmLabel), a button with a state (XmToggle) and one without (XmPushButton), a button container for permanently displayed menus (XmRowColumn), a bulletin board container (XmBulletinBoard), and a drawing widget (XmDrawingArea or paper that can be used within Motif). Additional suggestions are given in the next chapter for more complex widgets. A good way of customizing widgets involves attaching your own data structure to them. All Motif widgets have a resource XmNuserData, and OLIT widgets have XtNuserData. The corresponding resource of the Paper widget is XtNuser-Data. Let mydata be a structure that contains information required to associate with the widget; the following piece of code attaches the data to the widget:

```
Widget fancy_button;
struct special_effects mydata;
/* ... */
XtVaSetValues(fancy_button, XtNuserData, (XtPointer)
(&mydata), NULL);
```

We access this information from within a callback by the call:

```
struct special_effects *data;
/* ... */
XtVaGetValues(w, XtNuserData, &data, NULL);
```

We could use client data to store the pointer to the structure, but we wish to leave that for other uses. User data, may be common to a family of applications, while client data differs from application to application. This feature is particularly useful when combined with a drawing widget, as we show in Sec. 11.3.5.

5.8. PROJECTS

1. Write a program that displays two rows of buttons with the same labels in each row, for example alpha, beta, gamma, and delta. When a button is selected in one row, that button is unmanaged; the button with the same name in the other rows is managed. The program should start with all buttons visible, but eventually each label should appear in only one row. [*Hint*: Use the functions XtName() and XtNameToWidget().]
2. Implement the function tree () in Listing 5.1 that prints the widget tree.
3. Instead of printing the widget tree, provide routines to display it in a specially created pop-up window. Use the Paper or another drawing

widget as the canvas. The major challenge in writing this code is the need for it to be *re-entrant*. After the new function tree() is called, it should create a static structure that is read by the expose and other callbacks of the display window. However each call must create a new structure, since tree() may be called many times from within an application.

(*Hint*: It will help if the tree() function computes the label width, say, label_width at each level by using the XTextWidth() function with XtName(w) as the text argument. If the value is returned, then the loop in Listing 5.1 could be modified to:

```
for(i=0; i<nk; i++)
    tmp_width +=tree(kids[i]; depth+1);
```

The larger of label_width or tmp_width should be returned.

6

Constraint and
Compound Widgets

6.1. CONSTRAINT WIDGETS

6.1.1. Overview   Constraint widgets include rules for relatively position-ing their children. These rules are expressed through resources that are specified for the parent, but the parameter values are kept within the children. Every widget contains a hook (a member called `constraints` of type `XtPointer`) where the parent can hang constraint information. The hook is NULL unless the widget is a child of a constraint widget; in that case it points to a structure with all the constraint information. When the parent lays out the children, it looks at this structure for each one of the children.

Suppose for example we want to arrange a set of widgets in rows of three and `XtNbelow` is the name of a resource known to the container. This is achieved by the code:

```
for (i=3;...)
XtVaSetValues (panel [i],  XtNbelow,  panel [i-3],  NULL);
```

Normally the function `XtVaSetValues()` looks for resources in the widget that is its first argument. However if the resource is not found, the Intrinsics check if the parent is a constraint widget and if it has the specified resource. That resource points (in effect) to a parameter in the `constraints` structure of the widget `panel [i]`. In this case that parameter is given the value `panel [i-3]`. The actual implementation is more complicated, but the preceding description should suffice to explain the concept. Figure 6.1 shows the arrangement of the information. A resource table (see Chap. 3) connects resource names with widget parameters.

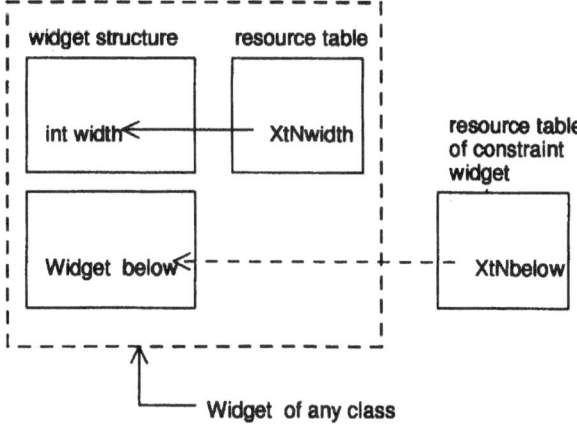

Figure 6.1.   Conceptual relationship between resources and parameters for ordinary and for constraint resources.

Normally both resource and parameter are part of the same widget, but for constraint resources, resource and parameter belong to different widgets.

During the layout process, the parent reads those records and establishes a set of relationships. It is helpful to view these in the form of a graph whose nodes are widgets and whose branches correspond to *binary* relationships, such as the preceding. Figure 6.2 shows nine widgets for this case. The graph in Fig. 6.2 is not sufficient to specify the widget layout because it does not impose any left–right relationships; however these can be added in a similar way.

Specifying the layout through a set of binary relations is particularly useful when a window is resized by the application user. Because users can normally directly resize only the top window (the one inserted by the window manager), such rules aim to translate resizing the top window into properly resizing subwindows. For example if an application contains a text-editing window and a menu window, we may want any changes in size to be taken up by only the text window. This can be achieved by assigning constraints to the sides of these windows. In addition the application does not have to be concerned with calculating dimensions, as in the case of bulletin board widgets discussed in Sec. 5.4.5 because the container widget does all calculations internally.

If we look at a Motif or OLIT manual, we encounter the resources `XtNresizable`, or `XmNresizable`, since the preceding discussion suggests a rather tortuous way of dealing with resizing. These resources refer to resizing initiated by the child widget, not to resizing induced by the application user. The situation is analogous with shell resizing described in Sec. 5.5.2.

Direct subwindow resizing is possible for certain classes of widgets, `Paned` in Athena, `XmPanedWindow` in Motif. These are container widgets that include handles with which the application user can resize subwindows. These widgets are useful for such applications as text editors, where the user may want to change the relative size of various subwindows. Such widgets may not be appropriate for simple layouts where the basic resizing mechanism is sufficient provided the right set of constraints is specified. (Remember: We want to make life easy for the application user, not the programmer.)

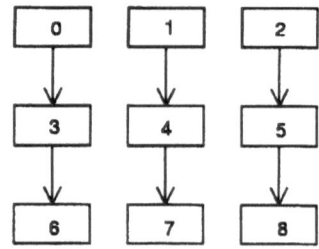

Figure 6.2.   Relational graph for nine widgets. Arrows indicate the below relationship.

While simple widgets and minimal container widgets have similar behavior in various toolkits, constraint widgets differ significantly, so we treat each toolkit separately. There is a Form widget in Athena, Motif, and OLIT, but these are quite different in functionality. For simple programs using OLIT, the Rubber tile widget is most appropriate. In the following sections we discuss implementing the drawing area with the menu program in Sec. 6.3.2, so that when the window is resized, the menu keeps its size and only the drawing area is changed.

6.1.2. Constraint Widget of the Athena Toolkit The Athena Form widget of class `formWidgetClass` (definitions in `Xaw/Form.h`) can be used as a container in applications to adjust internal windows in response to resizing the main application window. We describe the widget after presenting an example. Listing 6.1 is the same application as Listing 6.5 with one box container widget replaced by a Form widget. Parts that were changed are shown in bold. The only difference in the behavior of the two programs is that when the main window is resized, both internal windows are also resized. Note: We do not provide a layout order for the `frame` widget. Instead we specify that the menu widget is below the Canvas widget. The specification is done with a resource of `menu`, but it is interpreted by the frame widget.

To force the menu to have a fixed size, we must use the resources of the Form widget. The Form has only one regular resource of its own (besides those inherited from composite); `XtNdefaultDistance` takes as a value the number of pixels in the margins between widgets (default value 4). Additional constraint resources of the Form widget's children include

`XtNfromHoriz` takes as a value the widget to the right of which the child is placed.

`XtNbottom`, `XtNtop`, `XtNleft`, and `XtNright` refer to the relative distance of the respective edge from one of the edges of the Form. They take as values symbolic constants of the form `XawChainEDGE`, where `EDGE` can be `Bottom`, `Top`, `Left`, and `Right`. This means that the child widget edge in the resource name keeps a fixed distance from the form widget edge in the value. For example the following piece of code means that the left edge of the child keeps a fixed distance from the right edge of the container:

`XtNleft, XawChainRight`

There is another value for these resources, `XawRubber` (the default), which requires child edges to keep their proportional values from the parent edges. Additional constraint resources include margin values for specific orientations.

We illustrate the use of the resource by modifying Listing 6.1. As the program stands now, when the user enlarges the main application window, *both* the canvas

Listing 6.1. Menu and Drawing Program for Athena

```
#include <X11/StringDefs.h>
#include <X11/Intrinsic.h>
#include <X11/Xaw/Box.h>
#include <X11/Xaw/Form.h>
#include <Paper.h>

void start(),pause(), restart(), quit();
void paint();
Widget make_button(); /* From Listing 5.4 */

main (int arc, char **arv)
{
    Widget toplevel, frame, menu, canvas;
    Widget start_button, pause_button, restart_button,
      exit_button;
    XtAppContext app;

    toplevel = XtAppInitialize( &app, "Play",
        NULL, 0, &arc, arv, NULL, NULL, 0);

    frame = XtVaCreateManagedWidget("Frame",
        formWidgetClass, toplevel,
        NULL;

    canvas = XtVaCreateManagedWidget("Canvas",
        paperWidgetClass, frame,
        XtNwidth, 300, XtNheight, 200,
        NULL);
    XtAddCallback(canvas, XtNredrawCallback, paint, NULL);

    menu = XtVaCreateManagedWidget("Menu",
        boxWidgetClass, frame,
        XtNfromVert, canvas,
        XtNorientation, XtorientHorizontal,
        NULL);

    /* rest of the code from Listing 5.6 */
    /* (button creation, etc) */
}
```

and the menu widget increase. This is probably not what the user wants: There is no
point in changing the menu size, since button sizes remain the same. We add the
following statements so that only the canvas increases when the window is
enlarged:

```
XtVaSetValues(canvas,
    XtNbottom, XawChainBottom, /*  1  */
NULL);
XtVaSetValues(menu,
    XtNtop, XawChainBottom       /*  2  */
    XtNbottom, XawChainBottom, /*  3  */
    XtNright, XawChainLeft,  /*  4  */
NULL);
```

Specification 1 fixes the distance of the bottom edge of canvas from the bottom
edge of the container, so that the canvas widget absorbs all increases in height.
Specifications 2 and 3 fix the vertical size of the menu widget by fixing the distance
of its top and bottom edges from the container's bottom edge. This may seem
redundant, but if we do not use them, the menu increases in height, overlapping
with the canvas as we resize the window. Specification 4 keeps the horizontal menu
size fixed. Ideally we should provide specifications for all sides of each widget to
keep all margins fixed, but the preceding specifications ensure that the canvas that is
affected most by resizing.

Changing the menu layout requires more programming changes with the Form
widget than when using the Box widget. The following code produces a vertically
aligned menu to the left of the canvas:

```
XtVaSetValues(canvas,
    XtNfromHoriz, menu,
    XtNleft, XawChainLeft,
NULL);

XtVaSetValues(menu,
    XtNleft, XawChainLeft,
    XtNbottom, XawChainTop,
    XtNright, XawChainLeft,
    XtNorientation, XtorientVertical,
NULL);
```

The main weakness of the Form widget design is not allowing specifications
for overall widget size but only for edge positions. This makes things easier for the
widget writer but more difficult for the application programmer, a typical feature of

Xt. Letting programmers specify widget sizes as scalable or not requires a nontrivial tiling algorithm inside the widget, which was not provided.

6.1.3. Constraint Widget of the Motif Toolkit   The Motif XmForm widget of class xmFormWidget (definitions in Xm/Form.h) operates in the same basic ways as the Athena Form widget: By specifying pairwise relations between children. Thus to force the canvas to be above the menu, we need the statement:

```
XtVaSetValues(canvas,
    XmNbottomWidget, menu,
    XmNbottomAttachment, XmATTACH_WIDGET,
NULL);
```

There are 16 resources whose names are described generically by the expression Xm*NedgeKind*, where *edge* can be anyone of the four strings left, right, bottom, or top; and *Kind* anyone of the four strings Attachment, Offset, Position, or Widget. The attachment resource refers to the four sides of a widget, and it specifies how the side is positioned. It can have the values given in Table 6.1, with the corresponding interpretation. The values XmATTACH_OPPO-SITE_FORM and XmATTACH_OPPOSITE_-WIDGET refer to opposite sides of the form or the neighbor widget.

To keep a child widget from being resized if the parent is resized, we must attach at least some of its edges to those of the form widget. Leaving an edge unattached while attaching the opposite edge to a form edge maintains that dimension unchanged during resizing. The situation in Motif is the opposite of Athena; in Athena (and OLIT) the default maintains relative distance sizes; in Motif the default maintains the absolute distance from the edges. Therefore in Motif by default, a widget maintains its size when the top application window is resized. Listing 6.2 shows Motif code fragments for the same menu and drawing widget program in Listing 6.1 for the Athena toolkit.

Table 6.1.   Values of Attachment Resources for the Motif Form Widget

XmATTACH_NONE	No constraints on the side (default); on resizing it keeps it original distance from the respective edge of the parent
XmATTACH_FORM	Attach to corresponding side of the form widget
XmATTACH_WIDGET	Attach to widget specified by an Xm*Nedge*Widget resource
XmATTACH_POSITION	Attach to a certain distance from the corresponding side of the form widget (specified by Xm*Nedge*Position)
XmATTACH_SELF	Similar to the previous except that the initial layout is determined by the parent widget

The canvas is created after the menu because its resources refer to the menu widget. The canvas is attached to the frame by three sides while its bottom side is attached to the menu. When the main application window is resized by the user, the frame window is resized in the same way (since it is the top window of the application in this example). Because left and right sides of the canvas are attached to the frame, the canvas width changes to match frame width. The canvas is also attached to the frame at the top while the menu is attached at the bottom; therefore after resizing there is no empty space at either the top or bottom. What happens in the middle? Because the canvas is attached to the menu, there is no empty space left (if the frame increases) or overlaps (if the frame decreases). Therefore one or both of these widgets must have a different window size to accommodate an overall change in the vertical direction. Note: *If a widget is attached to no more than one side in each direction, then its size does not change.* In this case the menu has only one attachment (bottom), so its size remains fixed. Therefore canvas size changes.

Listing 6.2. Menu and Drawing for Motif

```
/*...*/
#include <Xm/RowColumn.h>
#include <Xm/Form.h>
/*...*/
    frame = XtVaCreateManagedWidget("frame",
        xmFormWidgetClass, toplevel, NULL);

    menu = XtVaCreateManagedWidget("menu",
        xmRowColumnWidgetClass, frame,
        XmNorientation, XmHORIZONTAL,
        XmNbottomAttachment, XmATTACH_FORM,
        NULL);

    canvas = XtVaCreateManagedWidget("canvas",
        paperWidgetClass, frame,
        XtNwidth, 300, XtNheight, 200,
        XmNleftAttachment, XmATTACH_FORM,
        XmNrightAttachment, XmATTACH_FORM,
        XmNtopAttachment, XmATTACH_FORM,
        XmNbottonAttachment, XmATTACH_WIDGET,
        XmNbottomWidget, menu,
        NULL);
```

The following code produces a vertically aligned menu to the left of the canvas. Menu size stays fixed when resized, and all size changes are absorbed by the canvas:

```
menu = XtVaCreateManagedWidget("menu",
    xmRowColumnWidgetClass, frame,
    XmNorientation, XmVERTICAL,
    XmNleftAttachment, XmATTACH_FORM,
    NULL);

canvas = XtVaCreateManagedWidget("canvas",
    paperWidgetClass, frame,
    XtNwidth, 300, XtNheight, 200,
    XmNrightAttachment, XmATTACH_FORM,
    XmNtopAttachment, XmATTACH_FORM,
    XmNbottonAttachment, XmATTACH_FORM,
    XmNleftAttachment, XmATTACH_WIDGET,
    XmNleftWidget, menu,
    NULL);
```

Another example is an application with four canvas windows stacked vertically. During resizing we want all of these to change in proportion; here is the code:

```
#define N 4
    /*...*/
    frame = XtVaCreateManagedWidget("frame",
        xmFormWidgetClass, toplevel,
        XmNorientation, XmVERTICAL,
        XmNfractionBase, N,
        NULL);

    for(i=0; i<N; i++) {
        canvas[i] = XtVaCreateManagedWidget (/*...*/, frame,
            XmNleftAttachment, XmATTACH_FORM,
            XmNrightAttachment, XmATTACH_FORM,
            /*...*/
            NULL);
    }
    XtVaSetValues(canvas[0], XmNtopAttachment,
      XmATTACH_FORM, NULL);
```

```
for(i=1; i<N; i++) XtVaSetValues(canvas[i],
        XmNtopAttachment, XmATTACH_POSITION,
        XmNtopPosition, i,
        NULL);

for(i=0; i<N-1; i++) XtVaSetValues(canvas[i],
        XmNbottomAttachment, XmATTACH_WIDGET,
        XmNbottomWidget, canvas [i+1],
        NULL);

XtVaSetValues(canvas[N-1],
        XmNbottomAttachment, XmATTACH_FORM, NULL);
```

Specifying the widget attachment relationship is not sufficient. We must also specify the position of the top edge of each but the first widget from the top edge of the frame. Distances are given as fractions whose numerators are obtained from the resource XmNtopPosition and the common denominator from the parent resource XmNfractionBase.

6.1.4. Constraint Widgets of the OLIT   The OLIT widget class most appropriate for our problem is the Rubber Tile class, rubberTileWidget-Class (definitions in Ol/RubberTile.h). It has a resource XtNorienta-tion, whose values include OL_HORIZONTAL and OL_VERTICAL (the default). Its widgets are stacked in the order they are created. In this respect it is quite similar to the control area widget. It also has a constraint resource, XtNweight, which is an integer specifying the decimal fraction of extra space allocated to the widget during resizing. Thus to keep the menu at fixed size, we need only the following statement:

```
XtVaSetValues(menu, XtNweight, 0, NULL);
```

No other relational specifications are needed.

Things are even simpler for the example with the four canvas windows—the desired behavior is the default.

6.2. COMPOUND WIDGETS

6.2.1. Overview   A compound widget is a composite widget with children created by the XtCreateWidget() call at the same time the parent is created. The most common example are pop-up menu widgets. Both the pop-up shell and a container widget are created with one call. Depending on the toolkit, the return can be the container (as in Motif) or the shell (as in OLIT).

In addition the widget provides functionality for interaction with children added by the application, thus greatly simplifying the overall task. For example a pop-up menu can include child button widgets normally activated by pressing a mouse button. The compound pop-up menu widget arranges for the button-pressing event in the widget event handler to be replaced by the enter window event, since a button-pressing event was already used to display the menu.

Scrolled window widgets are another (and simpler) example. Such widgets consist of a container, of two scrollbars, and a clipping widget that has the *content* widget as a child. (This is the Motif and OLIT arrangement; in Athena the scrolled widget is a sibling of the clipping widget.) The compound widget deals with scrollbar callbacks, and shifts the relative position of clipping and content windows.

Note: If the reader completed the Project 6.1, the result can be used to explore the structure of compound widgets—and to understand material in Sec. 6.2.

We describe scrolled windows in Sec. 6.2.2 and transient menus in Sec. 6.3.

6.2.2. Scrolled Windows   A large text file or a large image cannot be completely shown on a normal display. It is possible to create a virtual window with all the data, the *content* window but display only part of the text in a *scrolled window*. Listing 6.3 shows a program that displays a (presumably) large image in a scrolled window. The code is written is terms of variables (in capital letters) with different definitions in each widget set; the definitions are given later.

The program is very simple (excluding parts dealing with reading the image and color allocation). The calls TOOLKIT_INIT() and INTERMEDIATE() are needed only for OLIT; these are empty strings in Motif and Athena. We explicitly create only two widgets—the compound scrolled window widget scroll and its child, the content widget pix. Definitions of SCROLL_CLASS, PARENT, and

Listing 6.3.   Scrolled Window—File uv.c
_____

```
/*  Image Display with a Scrolled Window Widget  */

#include <X11/StringDefs.h>
#include <X11/Intrinsic.h>
#include <X11/Shell.h>

#include "uv_head.h" /*  See Listing 6.4  */

#include <Paper.h>
#include <Stdef.h>

void quit()
{
    exit (0);
```

```
}

void show_pix(Widget w, /*  Image Structure  */ *imgp)
{
    /*  Display Image Structure pointed by imgp  */
    /*  on window of widget w  */
}

main(int arc, char **arv)
{
    XtAppContext app;
    Widget toplevel, bb, scroll, pix;
    /*  Image Structure  */ Im;

    /*...read image and store in structure Im...*/

    TOOLKIT_INIT();
    toplevel = XtAppInitialize( &app, "viewer",
        NULL, 0, &arc, arv, NULL, NULL, 0);

    INTERMEDIATE();
    scroll = XtVaCreateManagedWidget("scroll",
        SCROLL_CLASS, PARENT, SCROLL_RESOURCES
        /*  no comma  */
        XtNwidth, 200, XtNheight, 200,
        NULL);

    pix = XtVaCreateManagedWidget("pix",
        paperWidgetClass, scroll,
        XtNx, 2, XtNy, 2,
        XtNwidth, Im.width, XtNheight, Im.height,
        XtNborderWidth, 1,
        NULL);
    XtAddCallback(pix, XtNredrawCallback, show_pix, &Im);

    /*  ...Perform operations needed for establishing   */
    /*  color correspondence between image and display  */
    /*  device, storing image in the server, etc        */
    /*  (see Chapter 9)...                               */

    XtRealizeWidget(toplevel);
    XtAppMainLoop(app);
}
```

SCROLL_RESOURCES are given in Listing 6.4. Only a few comments are necessary for each case. The Motif scrolled window widget has many resources, but for simple programs we need set only the scrolling policy to automatic and we are done! The scrolled window in OLIT must be parented by a nonshell container; hence the code is a bit more complex.

Note: Any time the window is scrolled, an expose event is generated for the canvas. Therefore the repainting function (show_pix in this case) is called quite

Listing 6.4.   Definitions for Scrolled Windows—File uv_head.h

```
#ifdef MOTIF
#include <Xm/ScrolledW.h>
#define TOOLKIT_INIT()
#define INTERMEDIATE()
#define SCROLL_CLASS xmScrolledWindowWidgetClass
#define PARENT toplevel
#define SCROLL_RESOURCES XmNscrollingPolicy, XmAUTOMATIC,
#endif

#ifdef ATHENA
#include <X11/Xaw/Viewport.h>
#define TOOLKIT_INIT()
#define INTERMEDIATE()
#define SCROLL_CLASS viewportWidgetClass
#define PARENT toplevel
#define SCROLL_RESOURCES XtNallowHoriz, True, XtNallowVert, \
   True,
#endif

#ifdef OLIT
#include<Xol/OpenLook.h>
#include <Xol/ScrolledWi.h>
#include <Xol/BulletinBo.h>
#define TOOLKIT_INIT() OlToolkitInitialize(\
(XtPointer) NULL )

#define INTERMEDIATE() bb = XtVaCreateManagedWidget
   ("frame",bulletinBoardWidgetClass, toplevel, NULL)
#define SCROLL_CLASS scrolledWindowWidgetClass
#define PARENT bb
#define SCROLL_RESOURCES
#endif
```

frequently, so it worth while to have an efficient implementation for it; for example store the image in the server (see Sec. 9.5.2).

If we look at the widget tree of a scrolled window (using, for example, the program of Project 6.1) we see that it consists of a container widget that contains three other widgets: two scrollbars and yet another container widget (Bulletin Board for OLIT, Drawing Area for Motif.) The latter is the widget returned by the function that creates the scrolled window; it is used as the parent for the window to be scrolled. Therefore the widget tree has the form shown in Fig. 6.3.

An obvious question is how to stop the intermediate container widget from growing to enclose the canvas window in its entirety. (Remember: The canvas widget is the item too large to fit on the screen.) It is possible to prevent that with resource values of the Bulletin Board widget. In OLIT we set the value of XtNlayout to OL_IGNORE; in Motif we achieve the same result by setting zero margins for the Drawing Area widget.

A potential complication exists in using scrolled windows for images because of the way X handles color. As we explained in Sec. 1.4.1, a colormap is a table describing the correspondence between image bits and actual colors. (Color and images are discussed thoroughly in Chap. 9, but for the issue at hand, we need not be concerned with the details.) If the image to be displayed uses the default color map, everything works fine. But if the image needs its own colormap, we have a bit of a problem. First, for the window manager to load the colormap reliably requires us to assign it to the top shell. This can easily be done with the code:

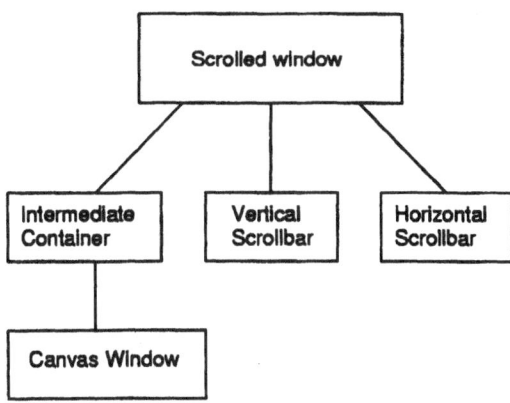

Figure 6.3.   Widget tree for a scrolled window.

```
Colormap cmap;
Widget wtop = pix;
while (XtParent (wtop)) {
    wtop = XtParent(wtop);
    XtVaSetValues(wtop, XtNcolormap, cmap, NULL);
}
```

Now the image appears with the correct colors, but the scrollbars may not; they may even be barely visible. The most general solution is to assign color resources to the scrollbar from colors we know have a high contrast. To do this we must find their widget IDs by using the XtNchildren resource of the scroll widget followed by calls for each of the children found.

```
XtIsSubclass(..., xmScrollBarWidgetClass);
```

In Motif these are determined from resources XmNhorizontalScroll-Bar and XmNverticalScrollBar, and in OLIT with XtNhScrollbar and XtNvScrollbar. After scrollbars are identified, we can assign high contrast colors to them from those used for the image.

6.3.   TRANSIENT MENUS

6.3.1.   Overview   Two types of menus appear temporarily in response to user action and disappear after a selection is made: *pop-up menus and pull-down menus*. Pop-up menus appear in any part of the screen, typically where the user presses the mouse button that activates the menu. Pull-down menus appear in a specific location, usually adjacent to the button of a menu already being displayed. The term *cascade button* is used for a menu entry that causes a pull-down menu to appear. The term *menu bar* denotes a permanently displayed menu with cascade buttons.

Building menus from scratch can be a challenge, so it is best to rely on existing compound widgets. Functions creating such widgets create both a pop-up shell and a container widget but return only the latter. A pop-up menu can have a widget of any class as its parent—the parent need not be composite. Theoretically this is true for pull-down menus as well, but some toolkits impose constraints (see Sec. 6.3.4).

In all toolkits the application provides only the means for popping up the menu. After that toolkit routines take over handling events. When a menu is popped up or pulled down it is usually spring loaded, so the menu stays up as long as the button that caused the action remains pressed. (See toolkit documentation for exceptions to such a policy.)

6.3.2. Athena Pop-up Menus   Athena has a simple menu class (definitions in Xaw/SimpleMenu.h) that requires children of a particular class—smeBSBObjectClass (definitions in Xaw/SmeBSB.h). The menu is created with:

```
menu = XtVaCreatePopupShell("menu_name",
    simpleMenuWidgetClass, parent,
    XtNlabel, "Menu title", NULL);
```

The title is optional. Buttons can be created with the function in Listing 6.4 provided we define their class as:

```
#define BUTTON_CLASS smeBSBObjectClass
```

Separators between buttons or between title and buttons can be added with a similar class using such code as:

```
#include <X11/Xaw/SmeLine.h>
    /*...*/
    XtVaCreateManagedWidget("line",
        smeLineObjectClass, menu,
        XtNlineWidth, 4, /* optional */
    NULL);
```

The proper way of activating such a menu is through the action procedure mechanism, using convenience functions provided by the Intrinsics:

```
static char internal_trans[] = "#augment \n\
    <Btn3Down>: XawPositionSimpleMenu( menu_name ) \
            XtMenuPopup( menu_name ) ";

    /*...later in another widget's function...*/
        XtNtranslations,
        XtParseTranslationTable(internal_transl),
    /*...*/
```

Highlighted variables in the definition refer to the widget name on the menu. There is no need for code to pop-down the menu.

6.3.3. Motif Pop-up Menus   A pop-up in Motif is created by such a call as:

```
Widget menu = XmCreatePopupMenu(parent,"menu", NULL, 0);
```

where `parent` need not be a container widget. Buttons can be created with the function in Listing 6.4. They can also be cascade buttons governing pull-down menus, as described in the following section.

We give the menu a title by using such code as:

```
XtVaCreateManagedWidget("title", xmLabelWidgetClass, menu,
    XmNlabelString,
    XmStringCreateLocalized("Actual Title"),
NULL);
```

as well as separators with such code as:

```
XtVaCreateManagedWidget("line", xmSeparatorGadgetClass,
  menu, XmNseparatorType, XmDOUBLE_LINE,
NULL);
```

Consult a motif manual for other types of separators.

While constructing a pop-up menu is routine, we need an event handler to activate it. The following code provides that:

```
void mpop(Widget w, Widget mw, XEvent *ep, Boolean
  *dispatch)
{
    if(ep->type==ButtonPress && ep->xbutton.button==3) {
        XmMenuPosition(mw, ep);
        XtManageChild(mw);
    }
}

main () {
    /*...*/
    menu = /*...*/
    /*...*/
    XtAddEventHandler(parent, ButtonPressMask,
            False, mpop, (XtPointer)menu);
    /*...*/
}
```

Note: There is no need to provide for closing the menu when the button is released; it is handled by Motif routines.

6.3.4. Motif Pull-down Menus   A pull-down menu in Motif is created by such a call as:

```
Widget pmenu = XmCreatePulldownMenu(parent, "widget_name",
  NULL, 0);
```

To use such a menu requires a cascade button to cause the menu to appear and ordinary buttons inside the pull-down menu.

The Motif widget (or gadget) class is xmCascadeButton (definitions in Xm/CascadeB.h and Xm/CascadeBG.h). It is created with such a call as:

```
XtVaCreateManagedWidget("button_widget_name",
   xmCascadeButtonWidgetClass, parent,
   XmNlabelString, XmStringCreateLocalized("label"),
   XmNsubMenuId, pmenu,
NULL);
```

Note: Both the pull-down menu and the cascade button must have the same parent.

Cascade buttons have two callback lists; XmNcascadeCallback functions are invoked just before the pull-down menu is mapped, and, XmNactivate-Callback functions are invoked when a mouse button is clicked on the cascade button, but no pull-down menu is attached. In such a case a cascade button functions as an ordinary button. Why would we do that instead of using the simple push-button? Some Motif container widgets insist on having all their children from the same class, so we may be forced to use a cascade button even for a single choice.

A convenient container for cascade buttons is a menu bar, in reality a row column widget created with the following call:

```
mbar = XmCreateMenuBar(frame, "mbar", NULL, 0);
XtManagedChild(mbar);
```

or more directly with:

```
mbar = XtVaCreateManagedWidget("mbar",
      xmRowColumnWidgetClass, frame,
      xmNrowColumnType, XmMENU_BAR,
    NULL);
```

We can modify the program in Listing 6.2 to allow pull-down menus from the selections, while placing the menu at the top:

```
menu = XtVaCreateManagedWidget("menu",
      xmRowColumnWidgetClass, frame,
      XmNrowColumnType, XmMENU_BAR,
```

```
    XmNorientation, XmHORIZONTAL,
    XmNtopAttachment, XmATTACH_FORM,
NULL);
```

Next we create all buttons with the function in Listing 6.4, while defining BUTTON_CLASS as xmCascadeButtonWidgetClass. The CALLBACK for exit and pause buttons can still be an XmNactivateCallback, but for those two buttons, we can select XmNcascadingCallback with the same functions as before. We provide the same pull-down menu for the start and restart that allows the user to select animation speed. We can have buttons with fast, medium, and slow labels and callback argument that is used to control animation speed. The code should resemble the following fragment:

```
static int animation_speed;
animate( /*...*/ )
{
    /*  uses animation_speed  */
}
/*  cascading callback of start button  */
start( /*...*/ )
}     animation_id = XtAppAddWorkProc( /*...animate...*/ );
}
/*  callback from the pulldown menu buttons  */
set_speed(Widget w, int speed)
}
    animation_speed = speed;
}
```

We may appear to start animation before selecting the speed parameter but this is not the case. The function start() does *not* actually start the animation—it only adds the work procedure. That function is called by the intrinsics only when there are no events in the queue, namely, only after all user selection actions are finished!

6.3.5. OLIT Pop-up and Pull-down Menus   OLIT has a compound pop-up menu widget, but the creation process returns the shell, not the container. The container widget must be obtained through the resource mechanism. The following code fragment illustrates its use:

```
#include <Xol/OpenLook.h>
#include <Xol/Menu.h>
#include < Xol/OblongButt.h>
```

```
main() {
   /*...*/
   menu_shell = XtVaCreatePopupShell("menu",
      menuShellWidgetClass,
      canvas, NULL);
   XtVaGetValues(menu_shell, XtNmenuPane, &menu, NULL);
   button1 = make_button(parent, "grid", /*...*/);
   /*...*/
}
```

There is *no need to add an event handler*: Open Look routines automatically add such a handler to the parent of the menu shell widget; in this case it is canvas. Pull-down menus are obtained through the menu button class. An example of the code follows:

```
#include <Xol/MenuButton.h>
   /*...*/
   m_button1 = XtVaCreateManagedWidget("m_button1",
      menuButtonWidgetClass, menu,
      XtNlabel, "color", NULL);
   XtVaGetValues(m_button1, XtNmenuPane, &sub_menu,
      NULL);
   m_button1[0] = make_button(sub_menu, "green", /*...*/);
   m_button[1] = make_button(sub_menu, "yellow", /*...*/);
   /*...*/
```

Menu buttons have the same appearance as oblong buttons except for a small triangle where moving the pointer invokes the pull-down menu.

The menu button widget does not have a cascading callback, but we can achieve the same effect (albeit less efficiently) by adding the common function to each of the submenu buttons. (See Sec. 6.3.6.)

6.3.6.   Another Note on Sensitivity   If we want to make a menu or cascade button insensitive, we must be more careful than in the case of Sec. 5.4.3 because pull-down menu buttons are not children of the menu or cascade button. The simplest solution is to pass widgets whose sensitivity will be changed as client data in the callback or have a separate callback. We illustrate this for the program with a menu and a drawing area with animation introduced in Sec. 5.4.2. let start_button and restart_button be menu (cascade) buttons and pause and exit ordinary selection buttons. Let bstart[] and brestart [] be widget arrays representing the respective submenu buttons. We then add callbacks in two loops (in addition to the callback that sets the speed for each button):

```
for(i=0; i<3; i++) {
    XtAddCallback(bstart[i], XtNselect, start, canvas);
    XtAddCallback(bstart[i], XtNselect, sensitize,
        start_button);
}
```

We proceed similarly for brestart[]. (Note: We use the OLIT callback name.)
The following is a possible implementation of the second callback:

```
sensitize(Widget w, Widget caller)
{
    disable( caller);
    if(strcmp(XtName(caller), "start"))
        disable( XtNameToWidget(XtParent(caller),
        "start") );
    else disable( XtNameToWidget(XtParent(caller),
      "restart") );
    enable( XtNameToWidget(XtParent(caller), "pause") );
}
```

6.4. CONCLUSIONS

The concluding comments in Chap. 5 are also valid here. As the number of parameters increases and their mutual interactions grow more obscure, it becomes less attractive to use a library of functions. Customizing by writing new code may be the right solution. For example, we may subclass a constraint widget, such as the Form class in Motif by having resources provide simpler (but less general) rules for the layout. It is necessary to write only the code that translates the simpler rules into the rules for the form widget.

Of course it may not even be necessary to create a new widget. For example suppose we want a vertical layout such that when a window is resized only one of the widgets increases or decreases and all other retain their size. This is trivial with the OLIT Rubber Tile widget (see Sec. 6.1.4), but not with Motif. We can write a function to generate these constraints. The code in Listing 6.5 shows a method that works for the layout of simple widgets. (For simplicity error-checking statements are omitted.) The main program does not have to deal with widget constraints—it has to call only the function fix_size_except() just before widgets are realized.

Listing 6.5.   Indirect Size Management—File fixsize.c

```
/*  Make widget w be the only one whose size is changed  */
/*  during window resizing  */
fix_size_except(Widget w)
{
   Widget parent = XtParent(w);
   Widget *kids;
   int nk, distance, i, j,

   XtVaGetValues(parent, XtNnumChildren, &nk, NULL);
   XtVaGetValues(parent, XtNchildren, &kids, NULL);
   /*  deal with widgets before w  */
   distance = MARGIN; /*  MARGIN is defined elsewhere  */
   for(i=0; i<nk, i++) {
      if(kids[i]==w) break;
      XtVaSetValues(kids[i],
         XmNtopAttachment, XmATTACH_FORM,
         XmNtopOffset, distance, XmNleftAttachment,
         XmATTACH_FORM,
         NULL);
      XtVaGetValues(kids[i], XtNheight,&height, NULL);
      distance += height+MARGIN;
   }
   /*  make sure that the w widget follows the size of the
   parent  */
   XtVaSetValues(kids[i],
         XmNleftAttachment, XmATTACH_FORM,
         XmNrightAttachment, XmATTACH_FORM, NULL);
   if(i>0) XtVaSetValues(kids[i], XmNtopWidget, kids[i-1],
         XmNtopAttachment, XmATTACH_WIDGET, NULL);
   else XtVaSetValues(kids[i], XmNtopAttachment,
     XmATTACH_FORM, NULL);
   if(i<nk-1) XtVaSetValues(kids[i], XmNbottomWidget,
     kids[i+1], XmNbottomAttachment, XmATTACH_WIDGET, NULL);
   else XtVaSetValues(kids[i], XmNbottomAttachment,
 XmATTACH_FORM, NULL);
   /*  deal with the rest  */
   distance = MARGIN;
   for(j=nk-1; j>i,j--) {
      XtVaSetValues(kids[j],
      XmNtopAttachment, XmATTACH_NONE,
         XmNbottomAttachment, XmATTACH_FORM,
         XmNbottomOffset, distance,
```

```
            NULL);
         XtVaGetValues(kids[j], XtNheight, &height, NULL);
         distance += height + MARGIN;
      }
   }
```

All major toolkits provide a widget class that allows the user to resize directly its children. Such widgets are called *paned*, and these provide means (grips or sashes) to support direct resizing of a child (pane). However it requires considerable user effort to achieve a desired layout, so indirect methods tend to be more convenient for the application user.

6.5. PROJECTS

1. Implement the suggestion in Sec. 6.2.2 for keeping the scrollbars visible when a special colormap is loaded.
2. Listing 6.5 provides a solution for fixing the size of all but one of the children when the parent is resized. Will this program work when the children are composite widgets? Why?
3. Implement a pop-up menu that has as entries the files of the directory the program is running. If a file is a directory, the button should provide a pull-out menu with the files of that directory. (If the reader is not sufficiently familiar with the Unix directory access functions, such as `opendir()`, `readerdir()`, etc, invoke your program with arguments * */* to obtain the information from the command line argument list.)

7

Text and Dialog Widgets

7.1. TEXT WIDGETS

7.1.1. Overview—Input Focus   Text widgets provide full text-editing abilities, and they allow extensive use of selections. They also make extensive use of action procedures that bind keystrokes to editing actions. Text widgets can be used for a range of text-related operations from entering a single word in a form to editing large documents. A text widget may support many operations besides entering text: Reading files, finding and substituting string patterns, cutting and pasting blocks of text, etc. Many of these operations have nothing to do with the window system the widget is implemented on (for example reading files). To keep our focus on window system issues, we limit discussion to entering and editing multiline strings, as opposed to editing files.

If the main purpose of a widget is to accept text, we must pay some attention to the issue of *input focus*, namely, the widget that accepts the keyboard output. In many applications (and all the examples discussed so far in this text), we ask the window manager to assign the focus to the widget that contains the pointer. This is not the best solution for an application whose main purpose is text entry. A better policy is to direct keyboard input to a text widget whenever the pointer is *within the application*, not necessarily within a text window. Suppose an application, such as an entry form, has N text widgets and the user is expected to enter text into these in a sequence. Instead of expecting the user to move the pointer with the mouse, we use a function with the following prototype:

```
XtSetKeyboardFocus(Widget toplevel, Widget destination)
```

where destination is a descendant of toplevel in the widget tree (i.e., its window is a subwindow of the window of toplevel) and the effect of the call is that whenever toplevel receives the input focus, it passes it to destination. Figure 7.1 illustrates this arrangement.

Initially we assign the focus to the first text widget:

```
static Widget toplevel;  /* top shell */
static Widget text[N];  /* a set of N text widgets */
/* ... */
   XtSetKeyboardFocus(toplevel, text[0]);
```

Let entry_done() be a callback invoked when the user indicates that she/he finished entering a particular item (usually by pressing a return key). The following is a possible code fragment for such a callback that has as client data the index of the widget in the array text[]:

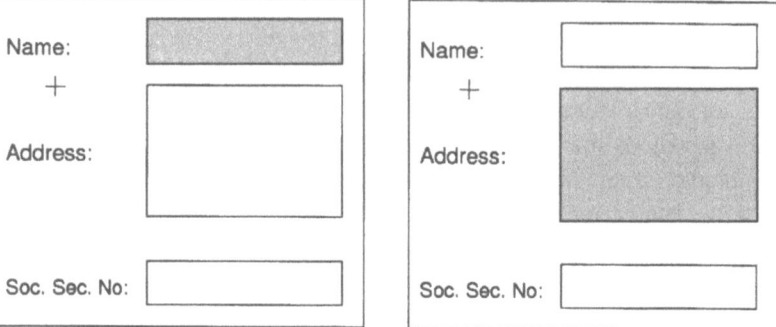

Figure 7.1.   Two views of a text-entry application containing three text-entry widgets. The cursor is denoted by crosshairs, and the widget that has the focus is gray.

```
/*   ...   */
int i = (int)client_data;
if (i<N-1) {  /* set focus to the next text widget  */
    XtSetKeyboardFocus(toplevel, text[i+1]);
}
else {  /* back to the first text widget  */
    XtSetKeyboardFocus(toplevel, text[0]);
}
```

This code assumes that `toplevel` and the array `text[]` are external variables. An alternative is to pass these as part of the client data. Note: The first argument of `XtSetKeyboardFocus()` must be the same in each call to make sure we achieve the focus transfer. In Fig. 7.1 after the user finishes entering his/her name (by pressing return for example), the focus moves to the next widget because of the callback action.

To provide visual feedback, we also make text widgets that lack focus insensitive. *Warning:* If we vary the sensitivity of widgets, we must call `XtSetKeyboardFocus()` *after* a widget has become sensitive.

In the rest of this section, we review text widgets from three major toolkits, and in Sec. 7.2 we present detailed examples using the Motif toolkit. One example involves entering single lines of text in a form and the other editing a given string.

7.1.2.   Athena Text Widgets   The Athena text-editing widget class is `asciiTextWidgetClass` (definitions in `Xaw/AsciiText.h`). Such a widget is created with the call:

```
text = XtVaCreateManagedWidget(
        "text", asciiTextWidgetClass, parent,
        XtNeditType, XawtextEdit, XtNtype, XawAsciiString,
        NULL);
```

We provide values for two resources specifying that our strings are ASCII and themselves the subject of editing (rather than being file names).

If data are stored in the ASCII string buffer, we provide these to the widget with the statement:

```
XtVaSetValues(text, XtNstring, buffer, NULL);
```

After finishing editing, we retrieve the edited string with the statement:

```
XtVaGetValues(text, XtNstring, &buffer, NULL);
```

7.1.3.   Motif Text Widgets   The basic Motif text-editing widget class is xmTextWidgetClass (definitions in Xm/Text.h). Text widgets of this class can handle multiline strings, but it is possible to confine them to one-line text through the resource mechanism. However Motif has a special widget class for editing single-line text, xmTextFieldWidgetClass (definitions in Xm/TextF.h). It is more efficient to use that class for single-line strings. Most resources of TextField have the same names as resources of Text, so the code for using either type is nearly identical. The following statements create, respectively, multiline, single-line, and efficient single-line text widgets.

```
/*  Multiline text widget  */
text_ML = XtVaCreateManagedWidget("text_ML",
        xmTextWidgetClass, parent,
        XmNeditMode, XmMULTI_LINE_EDIT, NULL);
/*  Single line text widget  */
text_SL = XtVaCreateManagedWidget("text_SL",
        xmTextWidgetClass,
        parent, NULL);
/*  Efficient single line text widget  */
text_ESL = XtVaCreateManagedWidget("text_ESL",
        xmTextFieldWidgetClass,
        parent, NULL);
```

The default value of the resource

```
XmNeditMode
```

is

```
XmSINGLE_LINE_EDIT;
```

therefore it need not be specified in the second statement. In all cases values are assigned and received by the calls:

```
XtVaSetValues (widget, XmNvalue, buffer, NULL);
/*  ...  */
XtVaGetValues(widget, XmNvalue, &buffer, NULL);
```

where `buffer` has type `String` (which is really `char *`). In the case of the `XtVaGetValues()`, call the memory allocation is done by the text entry widget. Note: Buffer contents are regular strings, *not* `XmStrings`.

7.1.4. OLIT Text Widgets   There are two text-editing widget classes in OLIT: `textEditWidgetClass` (definitions in `Xol/TextEdit.h`) and `textFieldWidgetClass` (definitions in `Xol/Textfield.h`). The first can handle text with any number of lines, the second only one-line text. `TextEdit` has more capabilities than `TextField`. A widget of that class is created with the call:

```
text = XtVaCreateManagedWidget("text",
        textEditWidgetClass, parent, NULL);
```

Default resource values are for multiline text and interpreting given text as something to be edited rather than a file name. Loading and unloading are achieved with:

```
XtVaSetValues(text, XtNsource, buffer, NULL);
/*  ...  */
XtVaGetValues(text, XtNsource, &buffer, NULL);
```

Warning: The OLIT resource `XtNsource` is different from the Athena resource with the same name and the Motif resource with a similar name (`XmNsource`). Both of the latter resources take a text widget value whose buffer holds the text to be edited.

7.2.   TEXT WIDGET APPLICATIONS

7.2.1.   Entry Form Application   In this section we describe an entry form application using the Text Field Motif widgets. We select a Form widget as a parent, then make it contain pairs of Label and Text Field widgets. The following code fragment creates the parent and such a pair:

```
#include <Xm/Form.h>
#include <Xm/Label.h>
```

```
#include <Xm/TextF.h>
/*  ...  */
    frame = XtVaCreateManagedWidget("frame",
        xmFormWidgetClass, toplevel,
        XmNfractionBase, 100, NULL);
    label[0] = XtVaCreateManagedWidget("label_0",
        xmLabelWidgetClass, frame,
        XmNlabelString, XmStringCreateLocalized("Name:"),
        NULL);
    text[0] = XtVaCreateManagedWidget("text_0",
        xmTextFieldWidgetClass, frame,
        XmNleftAttachment, XmATTACH_POSITION,
        XmNleftPosition, 25, NULL);
```

We specify that the text entry area occupies three-fourths of the parent widget width. Additional entries are created in the same way with only one change: To achieve uniform vertical spacing, we must specify for each one of these (both the label and text field widgets) the resources XmNtopAttachment with value XmATTACH_POSITION and XmNtopPosition with value the proper fraction of the total height. For example if we have five lines, it must be 20 for the second, 40 for the third, etc. To force a particular order of entry, we allow only one sensitive widget at a time.

To move from one text-entry location to another, we use the callback XmNactivateCallback, which is invoked when the user types the return character:

```
XtAddCallback(text[0], XmNactivateCallback, next_entry,
    text[1]);
```

Client data for the last widget may be either NULL or the first widget (to allow the user to repeat the process). We must also specify what to do with the data entered. One solution is to provide a different callback for each text-entry widget. Another is to provide the same callback but with instructions about further disposition of data. Instead of using client data for that purpose, we use the Motif resource XmNuserData to pass a pointer to a character string. Here is the code for the ith entry:

```
String data[N]; /*  N is the number of text entry
                 widgets */
XtVaSetValues(text [i], XmNuserData,
    (XtPointer) (&(data[i])), NULL);
```

Listing 7.1. Text Field Entry Callback

```
/*  Text Field Entry Callback  */
static Widget toplevel;
void next_entry(Widget w, XtPointer client_data)
{
    Widget sibling;
    String buffer;
    String *result;
    XtVaGetValues(w, XmNvalue, &buffer, XmNuserData,
        &result, NULL);
    /*  Copy the entered text to a permanent location  */
    *result = strdup(buffer);
    if(!client_data) {
        /*  ...  wrap up things up  ...  */
        /*  ...  exit or restart  ...  */
        return;
    }
    /*  Make the current widget insensitive and also  */
    /*  show the cursor position  */
    XtVaSetValues(w, XtNsensitive, False,
            XmNcursorPositionVisible, False, NULL);
    /*  Make the next widget sensitive with visible
    cursor  */
    sibling = (Widget)client_data;
    XtVaSetValues(sibling, XtNsensitive, True,
            XmNcursorPositionVisible, True, NULL);
    /*  redirect the focus  */
    XtSetKeyboardFocus(toplevel, sibling);
}
```

Listing 7.1 is a possible implementation of the callback that moves from field to field.

The XtVaGetValues() returns not only entered text but also the address of the permanent location to which it must be copied. As discussed in Sec. 7.1.1, it is necessary to use the top shell widget to reassign keyboard-input focus reliably, and the call must be made after the widget is made sensitive.

We can specify the size of the text-entry field (measured in number of characters) through the resource XmNcolumns. The result is accurate only if the font in effect has fixed width; otherwise, the text entry field accommodates *at least* as many characters. The font itself can be defined with the XmNfontList resource, which is an array of XFontStruct pointers. (See Sec. 8.3.4 for details on how X deals with fonts.)

7.2.2. Placing Text Labels in a Drawing If we wish to create an illustration that contains both text and line drawings, we cannot use a text widget because we cannot draw on it. If we use a drawing widget, then we must deal with the keyboard. As discussed in Sec. 4.4, that is not a simple process. The code in Listing 4.13 provides a minimal text-editing facility that allows erasing by backspacing. An alternative method involves using a pop-up text widget to enter text, then transferring it to the main widget.

We have two choices: Use the function collect_text() in Listing 4.13 for initial entry, then invoke the text edit widget only for modifying entries or always enter text through the text widget. Listing 7.2 (Part 1) shows the creation of the text widget and other initializations. The widget_set structure stores the

Listing 7.2. Pop-Up Text Widget (Part 1)—File mfed.c

```
#include <X11/Intrinsic.h>
#include <X11/StringDefs.h>
#include <X11/Shell.h>
#include <Xm/Text.h>
#include <Xm/DrawingA.h>
/*  structure for the objects of the drawing program  */
typedef struct {
    /*  ...  */
    String text_string;
    /*  ...  */
} App_object;
/*  structure for communication between widgets groups  */
typedef struct {
    Widget canvas, text, main_shell, text_shell;
    App_object *found;
} widget_set;
main(int arc, char **arv)
{
    Widget toplevel, frame, canvas,  /*  ...  */;
    Widget notepad, text;
    widget_set group;
    /* create toplevel and frame (container) widgets, etc. */
    /*  Create main drawing widget  */
    canvas = XtVaCreateManagedWidget("canvas",
        xmDrawingAreaWidgetClass, frame, NULL);
```

```
/*  ...  add callbacks for canvas, etc  ...  */
notepad = XtVaCreatePopupShell("notepad",
    transientShellWidgetClass, toplevel,
    XtNtitle, "Edit Text Here (CTRL/RTN to end)", NULL);
text = XtVaCreateManagedWidget("text",
    xmTextWidgetClass, notepad,
    XmNeditMode, XmMULTI_LINE_EDIT,
    XmNcolumns, 40, XmNrows, 10, NULL);
group.canvas = canvas;
group.main_shell = toplevel;
group.text = text;
group.text_shell = notepad;
XtAddEventHandler(canvas, /*  ...  event mask  ...  */,
    False, text_entry, &group);
XtAddCallback(text, XmNactivateCallback,
    back_to_canvas, &group);
XtRealizeWidget(toplevel);
XtAppMainLoop(app);
}
```

four widgets involved: drawing, text entry, and their respective shells. A pointer to such a structure is passed as client data to two event-processing functions: The handler for the canvas and the callback for the text widget.

The function text_entry() is called in response to the event that selects text to be edited or a position to place text; it is shown in Listing 7.2 (Part 2). The first task is to find the dimensions of the main shell widget and the absolute coordinates of its position to place the pop-up shell. Figure 7.2 shows the layout. The line segment with two arrows show where the text label will appear once entry is completed.

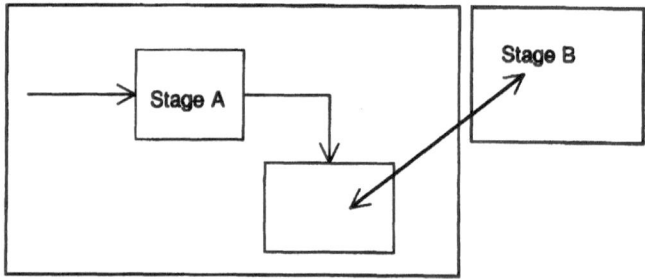

Figure 7.2.   Positioning a text-editing window with respect to the main drawing window.

Listing 7.2. Pop-up Text Widget (Part 2)—File mfed.c

```
/*  Event handler for canvas  */
void text_entry(Widget w, XtPointer client_data,
    XEvent *ep, Boolean *disp)
{
    Dimension pwidth, pheight;
    Position xpos, ypos;
    widget_set *group = (widget_set *)client_data;

    /*  Check that group is non zero and perform any
    unrelated event processing. We reach this point when
    text editing is needed.  */
    /*  First find dimensions of canvas to place popup  */
    XtVaGetValues(group->main_shell, XtNwidth, &pwidth,
        XtNheight, &pheight, NULL);
    XtTranslateCoords(group->main_shell, pwidth+4, 0,
        &xpos, &ypos);
    XtVaSetValues(group->text_shell, XtNx, xpos, XtNy,
        ypos, NULL);
    /*  search the list of canvas objects to see if the user
    has pointed to one of them. "group->found" points to
    one them or is NULL if the user did not point to any
    object  ...  */
    if(!group->found) {
        /*  create a new object, initialize its text to
        "", and, possibly, mark the position on the screen
        group->found points now to the new object  */
    }
    XtVaSetValues(group->text, XmNvalue,
        group->found->text_string, NULL);
    XtPopup(group->text_shell, XtGrabExclusive);
}
```

The rest of the code (outlined only in comments) searches the list of objects to find whether the application user has pointed to an existing object or to an empty space. In the latter case a new object is created with a null string as text. In either case the text (possibly a null string) to be edited is in group->found->text_string. This is then passed to the widget by the next XtVaSetValues() statement, then the text-editing window pops up.

The callback XmNactivateCallback is invoked when the Motif symbolic key KActivate is pressed. That key is *normally* bound to

Listing 7.2.   Pop-up Text Widget (Part 3)—File mfed.c

```
/*  Callback when text entry is finished  */
void back_to_canvas(Widget w, XtPointer client_data,
    XtPointer call_data)
{
    widget_set *group = (widget_set *)client_data;
    String buffer;
    /*  copy edited text in buffer  */
    XtVaGetValues(group->text, XmNvalue, &buffer, NULL);
    /*  erase old object and free any space not needed  */
    group->found->text_string = strdup(buffer);
    /*  ... draw new/modified object  ...  */
    /*  clean up  */
    XtVaSetValues(group->text, XmNvalue, "", NULL);
    XtPopdown(group->text_shell);
}
```

control/return. It terminates text entry, then calls the function back_to_ canvas() to resume normal operation. Listing 7.2 (Part 3) shows this function.

The call XtVaSetValues(... XmNvalue, ...) copies text into an internal buffer, so after completing text editing, we must copy the processed text to its original location: found->text_string.

7.3.   DIALOG WIDGETS

7.3.1.   The Basics   Dialog widgets are pop-up windows that open when there is a need for user input other than that already provided for by the application. For example if the user selects the exit button, the application may ask for confirmation. A more elaborate exchange is needed if data must be saved. The application may ask what to do with the data; if the user opts to save them, the application may ask for a file name. The text entry widget in the example in Sec. 7.2.2 is a special case of a dialog widget.

The term *dialog box* is almost synonymous with dialog widget except that the former does not imply that the dialog window is part of a specific widget. It is easy to build a dialog box based on the text entry form in Sec. 7.2.1. The frame widget of that example must be parented by a pop-up shell, as described in Sec. 5.5.4. The Athena toolkit provides a dialog widget that is in essence a one-line entry form.

Motif has many varieties of dialog widgets, all of which use a pop-up shell around a constraint or composite widget. It is beyond our scope to discuss all of these. Instead we focus on one built around the message box widget (class pointer xmMessageBoxWidgetClass, definitions in <Xm/MessageB.h>.) The widget is created through the following convenience function:

```
message = XmCreateMessageDialog(parent, "widget_name",
          args, nargs);
```

where args is the resource argument vector described in Sec. 3.1.3 and nargs is the number of its components. The dialog pops up (or down) by managing (or unmanaging) the returned widget, for example:

```
XtManageChild(message);
```

The message box is a composite widget built based on a bulletin board widget, and it can be used in other places besides dialog boxes. In its default configuration, it displays a message (possibly with a pixmap to its left) and three buttons labeled by default "Ok", "Cancel", and "Help".

The text message is assigned through the resource XmNmessageString, for example:

```
XtVaSetValues(message, XmNmessageString,
    XmStringCreateLtoR(
    "You asked to erase all files.\nDo you really mean \
it?",
    XmFONTLIST_DEFAULT_TAG), NULL);
```

If there are no new lines in the string, we may use the simpler function XmStringCreateLocalized(), which takes only one argument. Besides the text message, we must specify button callbacks by using the XtAddCallback() function and resources XmNokCallback, XmNcancelCallback, and XmNhelpCallback. The call data argument of the callback includes the reason, so that we can write simpler code by specifying a single callback function with a switch argument inside it, for example:

```
/* XmAnyCallbackStruct has an integer member, reason */
/* and an XEvent pointer member, event */
void dialog_callback(Widget w, XtPointer client_data,
    XtPointer call_data)
{
    XmAnyCallbackStruct
    *d = (XmAnyCallbackStruct *) call_data;
    switch(d->reason){
```

```
case XmCR_OK:
  /*  ... proceed with action  ...  */
  break;
case XmCR_CANCEL:
  /*  ... cancel action  ...  */
  break;
case XmCR_HELP:
  /*  ... display documentation  ...  */
  break;
  }
}
```

An interesting question is how to force the application to wait for the response to the dialog widget and to take into account the reply provided through that widget. The first objective can be achieved by making the pop-up window modal (see Sec. 5.5.4). However that does not solve the second requirement, so we need another approach. Let clean_up() be a function whose invocation requires user confirmation. Let us also assume we have a button labeled "Clean Up" that invokes it. The function clean_up() *should not be* the callback for that button. Instead the callback should be a trivial function that causes the dialog box to pop up; the function clean_up() should be the callback of the "OK" button. If we use a common callback, as in the earlier example, that function must be called in the XmCR_OK case. The callback for the "Cancel" button (or the code in the XmCR_CANCEL case) can be a message-confirming cancellation.

It is possible to add widgets to the message box as well as modify button labels. Additional buttons are placed after the button (originally) labeled "OK", other widgets are placed above the button row. For example we can add a text-entry widget with the statement:

```
text_entry = XtVaCreateManagedWidget("entry",
  xmTextFieldWidgetClass, message, NULL);
```

There is no need to add a callback, since the message widget provides one automatically.

The default children of the message box are *gadgets* rather than widgets. Thus we cannot assign individual background color to these, among other restrictions. On the other hand we can add new children that are widgets, as the preceding example shows.

7.3.2. Details of the Motif Dialog Message Box   Many resources can be used to refine the behavior of the dialog message box; we describe some of these here.

The resource XmDialogType takes one of several symbolic values, such as XmDIALOG_WORKING, XmDIALOG_QUESTION, etc. The only effect of the type is to specify the icon appearing next to the message. For example the working type displays an hourglass icon, the question type displays a question mark icon, etc. Default icons can be overridden by assigning an icon explicitly through the XmNsymbolPixmap resource. For example to request confirmation on erasing all files, we may enhance the seriousness of the message with a skull and bones icon. Assuming that such an icon exists in the file skull.icon, the following code fragment accomplishes the task:

```
#include <skull.icon>
/*  ...  */
    symbol = XCreatePixmapFromBitmapData(
        XtDisplay (message),
        DefaultRootWindow(XtDisplay(message)),
        skull_bits, skull_width, skull_height,
        /*foreground*/ 1, /*background*/ 0, /*depth*/ 8);
    XtVaSetValues(message, XmNsymbolPixmap, symbol, NULL);
```

Dialog type should not be confused with dialog *style*, which refers to pop-up modality. The following code fragment blocks all input to the application until the dialog window is poped down:

```
XtVaSetValues(message, XmNdialogStyle,
            XmDIALOG_FULL_APPLICATION_MODAL, NULL);
```

The default setting is nonmodal.

It is possible to modify button labels through resources XmNokLabel-String, XmNcancelLabelString, and XmNhelpLabelString. Their values are of XmString type.

A more serious issue is the fact that when a button (or text entry) is activated, the dialog window pops down. This is fine for many simple tasks, but there are cases when we may want the window to stay up, for example after entering text. Setting the resource XmNautoUnmanage to FALSE does the trick. However this resource must be set during the creation of the widget [not with SetValues()], which means that it must be passed as an argument to XmCreateMessage-Dialog(). Because there is no VarArg version of this function, we must use the method in Sec. 3.1.3. The following code fragment accomplishes this:

```
XtSetArg(args[nargs], XmNautoUnmanage, FALSE);  nargs++;
XtSetArg(args[nargs], XmNhelpLabelString,
        XmStringCreateLocalized("Done"));  nargs++;
```

We also relabel the help button in this case to provide an alternative means of terminating the dialog session. When we force to dialog to stay open, we have an opportunity for an *extended* dialog. After the user types a message, we can add a callback that changes the displayed message through the set value function, for example:

```
XtVaSetValues(message, XmNmessageString,
    XmStringCreateLtoR(
    "Thanks for responding to our inquiry.",
    XmFONTLIST_DEFAULT_TAG), NULL);
```

The new message immediately replaces the old one.

7.4. CONCLUSIONS

Text-editing widgets of the major toolkits provide extensive facilities, so we should use these as much as possible in applications instead of trying to create new ones. A challenging application involves combining text with other types of data, such as drawings or images. Listing 7.2 (Parts 1–3) provides a simple solution. This is sufficient when there is room for the text, but not when text labels must be inserted around other displays. One solution is to use a minimal special text-entry function (for example the one in Listing 4.13) for the initial placement, then a regular text edit widget whenever text must be modified. Another solution is to create an entry form with each field corresponding to a line of text whose width is computed from available space in the drawing.

Dialog widgets can be adapted to many tasks: They provide a basic pop-up/pop-down mechanism, a container widget, and a set of standard buttons and callbacks. There is virtually no limit to the functionality that can be added to these.

7.5. PROJECTS

1. Modify the code in Listing 7.2 (Parts 1–2) by using a dialog widget instead of the custom-made pop-up widget.
2. The implementation of the extended dialog suggested in Sec. 7.2.2 has the disadvantage that only one message and one reply are visible at a time. Create an implementation where past messages and replies remain visible to the user.

Hint: Plan in advance for messages and space for replies. It is convenient to have an array of structures, each consisting of a string and a function pointer for example:

```
typedef struct {
char  *  label;
void (*fun) ();
} pairs;
```

Then associate each to a pair of widgets—label for the message and callback for the text entry.

8

Drawing Operations

8.1. Basics of Drawing

8.1.1. Overview All drawing in X is done by Xlib functions. There is support for line drawing and text display, but not for drawing with curves other than circles or ellipses with axes parallel to the coordinate axes. There are two broad families of functions: Those that draw in a single color (monochrome) and those that can mix colors. Most of the functions discussed in Chap. 8 belong to the former category. Color and functions that use it are discussed in Chap. 9.

A monochrome function can draw with any single color that the display supports. Normally we distinguish a *foreground* color that is given to bits that are 1 and a *background* color given to bits that are 0. In X their values are part of the graphics context (see Sec. 8.1.3). For example to draw a green dashed line, we set the foreground to green, specify line style as dashed, then call the line-drawing function. If we want spaces between dashes to be red, we must first draw a solid red line, then draw a green dashed line on top of it (using replacement).

We discuss the following important drawing concepts specific to X as well as icons, fonts, and filling polygons with texture:

- Drawables: Server resources where drawing operations occur.
- Graphics context: Structure containing parameters used in drawing, such as color and line style.
- Regions: Unions of rectangles and polygons; useful for clipping operations.

The first three arguments of all drawing Xlib functions are a pointer to the display (server), a drawable (see Sec. 8.1.2), which is often a window XID, and the graphics context (see Sec. 8.1.3). Note: To keep our example code reasonably short, we do not include window creation operations.

In most examples we assume that the following statements are present earlier in the program:

```
static Display  *Dpy;
static Window   window;
static GC       gc;
```

In programs using Xt and toolkits based on it, we can obtain the first two from a widget by using such code as:

```
Dpy    = XtDisplay(w);
window = XtWindow(w);
```

(We already used such statements in the function paint() in Listing 2.4, Part 2.) The graphics context must be created by methods in Sec. 8.1.3. A simple way of testing Xlib drawing programs involves creating a drawing window with the Starter toolkit by using the following code:

```
/*  Template for testing Xlib drawing code  */
#include <X11/Xlib.h>
#include <Stdef.h>
void paint()
{
    Display  *Dpy;
    Window   window;
    GC       gc;
    St_get_default_args(&Dpy, &window, &gc);
    /*  Xlib code for drawing  */
}
main()
{
    St_vis_window(paint, 400, 400);
}
```

The function St_vis_window() establishes a connection to the server, creates and maps a window, then enters the event-waiting loop. When an expose event occurs, the function paint() is called. This use of the Starter toolkit complements its use in earlier chapters (with the exception of the spy program in Sec. 2.5), where we focused on window creation and event handling but did not bother with details of the drawing operation. Here however we leave window creation to the Starter toolkit to focus on drawing operations.

8.1.2. Drawables and Pixmaps   A server resource that can be the destination for graphics output is defined by X as a Drawable. A drawable can be either a Pixmap or a Window. The distinction is somewhat misleading. A graphics output may go into any piece of memory that can store such information. The X type Pixmap is an XID that provides access to such a region. A window must include such a piece of memory, and X offers the option that when the XID of a window is passed as a function argument, the server uses that to access the corresponding pixmap. The major difference from an application programmer's perspective is that the contents of a window pixmap are under the control of the window manager (in the absence of server backup), while the contents of a directly accessed pixmap are under the control of the application.

Given the availability of large amounts of memory in modern computers, it is a good general practice to draw on pixmaps rather than windows. In that case a

pixmap-to-window copying operation can be used to show the display. This not
only saves time when windows are refreshed (a time versus space trade-off), but it
also avoids showing half-finished drawings to the application user.

The following is a typical call for obtaining a handle to a pixmap:

```
Pixmap pxmp = XCreatePixmap(Dpy, DefaultRootWindow(Dpy),
   width, height, DefaultDepth(Dpy, DefaultScreen(Dpy))  );
```

The Dpy, width, and height arguments are self-explanatory. The second
and last arguments are needed to obtain information about the type of memory we
want to use. Such information cannot be obtained directly from the server
information pointer Dpy because X must account for the possibility of servers with
many screens (recall Sec. 2.1.2). If creating the pixmap fails, the server issues an
error message of the kind we saw in Sec. 1.4.3. Possible diagnostics are
BadAlloc (not enough resources), BadDrawbale (second argument was not a
drawable), and BadValue (zero dimensions or depth not supported by the screen).

Memory accessed through the pixmap XID is not cleared automatically, so it
must be cleared by the application. The following code fragment achieves that:

```
XSetFunction(Dpy, gc, GXclear);
XFillRectangle(Dpy, pxmp, gc, 0, 0, width, height);
```

where gc is a graphics context (see Sec. 8.1.3). The GXclear flag causes all
locations of the destination to have values of 0. (Normally XFillRectangle
assigns foreground values.)

After a pixmap is created, it can be copied in whole or in part into another
pixmap or a window by the function XCopyArea() that has the following
prototype:

```
XCopyArea(Display *Dpy,
   Drawable source, Drawable destination,
   GC gc, int x_source, int y_source,
   int width, int height, int x_dest, int y_dest)
```

The function copies a rectangle of width width and height height with upper
left corner at x_source, y_source in drawable source into a rectangle with
similar dimensions and upper left corner at x_dest, y_dest in drawable
destination. This is the same as the function *bitblt()* used in many other
window systems.

Pixmaps are destroyed and their space freed by the function:

```
XFreePixmap(Display *, Pixmap)
```

8.1.3.   Graphics Context   A drawing may contain lines of different color, thickness, and style. (The word style refers to whether the line is solid, dashed, dotted, etc.) Similarly text may be displayed with characters of different sizes and typeface styles. Passing all these parameters as part of line-drawing or text-display routines is not practical because there are so many of them and only a few are pertinent at a time. The X Window System uses a data structure in the server where the values of such pertinent parameters (more than 20 of them) are stored; it is called the *graphics context* (GC).

The choice of parameters that are members the GC is rather arbitrary, and it is an odd assortment. Section 8.1.4 gives a complete list; here we explain the use of the structure.

An Xlib function creates a GC structure for a given drawable, then returns a pointer to a structure that contains an XID number and a cache of the server structure. However the drawable does not acquire ownership of the structure, so it can also be used with other drawables, *provided all of these correspond to a refresh memory with the same number of bits per pixel as the original*.

The following code fragment illustrates use of the function:

```
GC gc;
XGCValues values;
static unsigned long valuemask = GCForeground |
                                 GCBackground;
values.foreground = BlackPixel(Dpy, DefaultScreen(Dpy));
values.background = WhitePixel(Dpy, DefaultScreen(Dpy));
gc = XCreateGC(Dpy, DefaultRootWindow(Dpy), valuemask,
     &values);
```

The structure with type XGCValues contains all graphics context information on the client side. The variable valuemask is used to specify which members of the structure values are read (see Sec. 1.4.2). In this example BlackPixel and WhitePixel yield values used by the particular server. The preceding code creates a GC appropriate for the display, with default values for all its members except foreground and background colors. Instead of returning an XID, XCreateGC() returns a pointer to an application structure whose members include an XID called gid and an XGCValues structure called values. This structure serves as a *cache* on the client side of values stored in the server. Sec. 8.1.4 discusses the role of the cache. The type GC is a pointer to an _XGC structure; the arrangement is shown in Fig. 8.1. Members of the structure contain the same values as the server structure and thus serve as a cache. (We discuss exceptions in Sec. 8.1.4.)

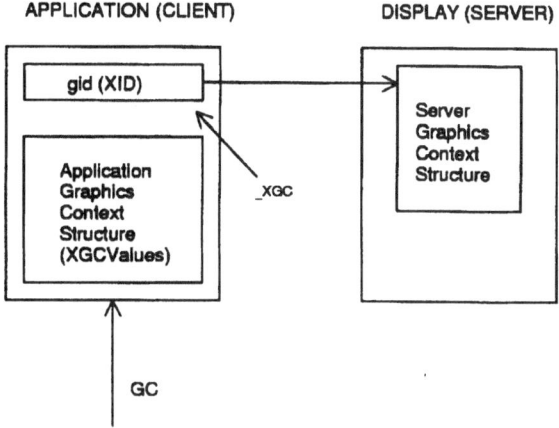

Figure 8.1.   The GC arrangement between client and server.

In summary XCreateGC() performs the following tasks:

- Creates (silently) the _XGC type structure
- Copies appropriate values from the XGCValues structure that was its fourth argument according to the third argument, valuemask
- Sends structure values to the server
- Receives an XID for the server structure from the server
- Stores that XID in a member of the _XGC type structure
- Returns a pointer to the latter structure (gc)

It is possible to obtain a GC by the following code, which relies on a macro that extracts information from the display structure:

```
GC gc = DefaultGC(Dpy, DefaultScreen(Dpy));
```

Such a GC might be shared among applications, so its usefulness is limited.
A GC is destroyed by:

```
void XFreeGC( Display *, GC)
```

For reasons just stated, *the default GC should never be destroyed.*
The prototype of a function that copies one GC onto another follows:

```
XCopyGC(Display *Dpy, GC source, unsigned long mask, GC
    destination)
```

The mask determines which members are copied.

Caution

It is necessary to create a GC before copying another onto it.

For example the following sequence creates a GC g2 that is an identical copy of the
GC g1:

```
g2 = XCreateGC(Dpy, window, 0, NULL);  /* use default values */
XCopyGC(Dpy, g1, 0xFFFF, g2);      /* copy all values */
```

Members of the _XGC structure are not directly accessible, but various
functions can access them, most generally through the function XChangeGC(),
which has the following prototype:

```
XChangeGC( Display *Dpy, GC gc,
        unsigned long valuemask, XGCValues *values);
```

When a change is made on the client side, the same change is also made at the
server. Listing 8.1 shows examples of using this function.

Listing 8.1.   Graphics Context Functions

```
XGCValues gcvalues;
/*  Set line width to n pixels  */
gcvalues.line_width = n;
XChangeGC(Dpy, gc, GCLineWidth, &gcvalues);
/*  ...  */
/*  Make lines dashed  */
gcvalues.line_style = LineOnOffDash;
XChangeGC(Dpy, gc, GCLineStyle, &gcvalues);
/*  ...  */
/*  Make lines solid and set width to m  */
gcvalues.line_style = LineSolid;
gcvalues.line_width = m;
XChangeGC(Dpy, gc, GCLineStyle | GCLineWidth, &gcvalues);
```

Arguments GCLineStyle and GCLineWidth are bit patterns that determine which of the values of the gcvalues structure will be looked at. (See Sec. 8.1.1 for arguments Dpy and gc.)

Besides the general function XChangeGC(), there is a set of convenience functions that can be used to change values of members of the GC. Listing 8.2 illustrates how to use some of these.

The last piece of code merits some comments. Exclusive OR (XOR) may give incorrect results when the background is not zero. The correct way of drawing on a nonzero background with XOR is to replace the value of the foreground color with a new value obtained by an XOR between the old foreground color and the background color, thus:

```
new_frgr = frgr XOR bcgr
```

Then, if we draw, we have

```
result = new_frgr XOR bcgr = (frgr XOR bcgr) XOR bcgr = frgr
```

Listing 8.2. Graphics Context Convenience Functions

```
/*   ...   */
XGCValues gcvalues;
/*   ...   */
/*  Set foreground value to n   */
XSetForeground(Dpy, gc, c);
/*   ...   */
/*  Use copy (replacement) mode for drawing operations   */
XSetFunction(Dpy, gc, GXcopy);
/*   ...   */
/*  Set exclusive OR (XOR) mode for drawing operations   */
XGetGCValues(Dpy, gc, GCForeground | GCBackground |
    GCFunction, &gcvalues);
if(gcvalues.function != GXxor) { /*  we need the change   */
    if(gcvalues.background != 0)
        XSetForeground(Dpy, gc,
            gcvalues.foreground^gcvalues.background);
    XSetFunction(Dpy, gc, GXxor);
}
/*   ...   */
```

Table 8.1. Graphics Context Members

| Type and name | GC Members with a client cache | |
	Comments	Default
int function	Symbolic values as in Listing 8.2	Gxcopy
unsigned long foreground	Foreground color	0
unsigned long background	Background color	1
int line_width	Line width in pixels	0
int line_style	Symbolic values as in Listing 8.1	LineSolid
int cap_style	Symbolic values for the precise shape of line ends*	CapButt
int join_style	Symbolic values for the precise shape of corners*	JoinMiter
int fill_style	Symbolic values, see Sec. 8.2.1	FillSolid
int fill_rule	Symbolic values, see Sec. 8.2.2	EvenOddRule
int arcmode	Symbolic values, see Sec. 8.2.1	ArcPieSlice
unsigned long plane_mask	Used in overlays. see Sec. 9.6.2	0xFFFFFFFF
int ts_x_origin, ts_y_origin	Offset for tile or stipple operations, see Sec. 8.2.1	0, 0
int clip_x_origin, clip_y_origin	Origin for clipping, see Sec. 8.4	0, 0
int subwindow_mode	Specifies whether subwindows clip*	
Bool graphics_exposures	see Sec. 2.3.1	True
int dash_offset	Parameter used in dashed-line drawing*	0
	GC Members without a reliable client cache	
Pixmap tile	Full-depth pixmap for tiling, see Sec. 8.2.1	All foreground pixel
Pixmap stipple	Bitmap for stippling, see Sec. 8.2.1	All 1s
Font font	Font for text, see Sec. 8.3.4	Mystery
Pixmap clip_mask	Mask for clipping, see Sec. 8.4	No mask
char dashes	Description of dashed-line pattern*	4 (4 on, 4 off)

* Items not discussed in this text.

This is what we want. Therefore we use the function XGetGCValues() (which has the same prototype as XChangeGC()) to determine background and foreground values. (We also determine whether the XOR mode is already in use to avoid unnecessary work.)

Note: It is probably a good idea to use XOR only in one-bit screens and to avoid it altogether in all other screens. While XOR lets us erase with the same function as drawing, such a convenience is probably not worth the complexities just discussed. (Apparently some modern graphics systems do not offer that mode at all.)

8.1.4. Members of the Graphics Context and Their Cache   Table 8.1 divides members of the GC into two groups: Members cached in the client and those that are not. Actually some of the members in the second group are cached under some conditions, but it is best for beginning X applications programmers to be conservative. In practical terms caching means that values provided with a call to XGetGCValues() are valid.

The values returned by a call to XGetGCValues() are not reliable for GC members listed in the second group. Unfortunately there are no diagnostics. Thus we can call the following without problems except that vv.clip_mask may contain garbage:

```
XGetGCValues(Dpy, gc, GCClipMask, &vv);
```

To retrieve the existing value of one of the members in the second part of the table we must maintain our own cache. Of course this is impossible with the initial values. Fortunately the defaults for all of these except for font are well-defined. We discuss how to find the default font in Sec. 8.3.4.

8.2.   DRAWING FUNCTIONS

8.2.1.   Lines, Arcs, and Filled Areas   Here we present examples of simple drawing operations. We can clear a rectangular area in a window with the call:

```
XClearArea(Dpy, window, x, y, width, height, False);
```

To draw a straight line segment from (x1,y1) to (x2,y2) requires the call:

```
XDrawLine(Dpy, window, gc, x1, y1, x2, y2);
```

Drawing a circular (or elliptic) arc requires a bit more work because the arc-drawing function of Xlib, XDrawArc(), accepts somewhat unusual arguments.

It draws an arc within a rectangle of width w and height h; with upper left corner at x, y; and the extent specified by two angles, start_angle and duration_angle. The function prototype is

```
XDrawArc(Display *dp, Drawable dr, GC gc, int x, int y,
    unsigned int w, unsigned int h,
    int start_angle, int direction_angle);
```

If w equals h, the drawn arc is circular; otherwise it is elliptical. Figure 8.2 shows the definition of angles measured in sixty-fourths of a degree, so that 90° is passed as 90*64, or 5760. The following code draws an arc starting with more intuitive values: Its center (cx, cy), radii rx and ry, and angles expressed in degrees:

```
x = cx - rx; y = cy - ry;
w = rx + rx; h = ry + ry;
start_a *= 64;
length_a *= 64;
XDrawArc(Dpy, window, gc, x, y, w, h, start_a, length_a);
```

A filled arc drawn by the function XFillArc() which takes exactly the same arguments as XDrawArc(). The shape of the filled area is determined by the GC. If we call the following, filled arcs resemble a pie slice:

```
XSetArcMode(Dpy, gc, ArcPieSlice)
```

If we call the following, the filled area is bounded by the arc and its chord:

```
XSetArcMode(Dpy, gc, ArcChord)
```

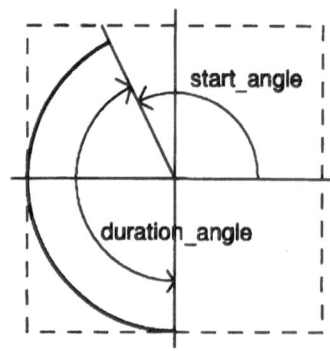

Figure 8.2.   Definition of an arc in Xlib.

The form of the filled area is also specified by the GC. To obtain a solid color, we must call

```
XSetFillStyle(Dpy, gc, FillSolid);
```

The foreground color is then used to fill the area. To obtain a pattern that is a bitmap (1-bit pixmap) requires the following pair of calls:

```
XSetStipple(Dpy, gc, some_bit_map);
XSetFillStyle(Dpy, gc, FillStippled);
```

In this case foreground and background colors are used.

To fill with an arbitrary image (pixmap) requires the following pair of calls:

```
XSetTile(Dpy, gc, some_pix_map);
XSetFillStyle(Dpy, gc, FillTiled);
```

In this case foreground and background colors have no effect.

It is possible to tile the entire area of a window with a pixmap with the call:

```
XSetWindowBackgroundPixmap(Dpy, window, pix);
```

where `window` and `pix` are the XIDs of the window and the pixmap, respectively. The following call uses the same pixmap as the parent window of `window`, which produces a *transparent* window:

```
XSetWindowBackgroundPixmap(Dpy, window, ParentRelative);
```

However if the window is moved or resized, the illusion of transparency is lost, since the original pixmap is still used. The transparent appearance is reinstated if we force an expose event (by closing and reopening the window for example). The window is never entirely invisible because the frame of the window created by the window manager during reparenting remains.

8.2.2. Polygons and Filled Polygons   Some Xlib functions (including those for drawing polygons) rely on the type `XPoint`, defined as follows:

```
typedef struct {
    short x, y;
} XPoint;
```

The Xlib function for polygon plotting is `XDrawLines()`, which has the following prototype:

```
XDrawLines(Display *dp, Drawable dr, GC gc,
        XPoint *v, int n, int mode);
```

where the first three arguments are the standard ones; the fourth argument points to an array of the polygon vertices, and the fifth argument, n, is the size of the array. *It must be no greater than 2046 to guarantee that the call will work on all X servers.* The mode argument indicates how coordinates will be interpreted. It can have one of two (predefined constant) values: CoordModeOrigin, or CoordModePre-vious. The former specifies that all coordinates are absolute (i.e., with respect to the origin of the drawable); the latter specifies that all coordinates (except the first) are relative (i.e., with respect to the previous point).

Listing 8.3 illustrates plotting a polygon on a pixmap just large enough to contain it. The code in Listing 8.3 assumes that all polygon points have the same color, so it is drawn on a pixmap of depth one. We start with a structure bit_map that contains a pointer to a pixmap, its dimensions, and a pair of coordinates. The function bounding_box() computes the smallest right rectangle containing the polygon P, and it computes a new polygon Q by moving the origin of the coordinates to the top-left corner of the bounding rectangle. These coordinates are stored in p->xoff and p->yoff. We omit listing the function bounding_-box(), since it is a simple routine. (See Sec. 8.4.1 for some suggestions.) The next statement creates a pixmap just large enough to allow us to plot Q. Then we create a GC *with the same depth as the pixmap.* Because we may have to draw many polygons, the GC is stored in a static variable, and it is created only once in each execution of the application.

When the drawing mode is GXClear, all drawn pixels are given the value 0; when the drawing mode is GXset, all drawn pixels are given the value 1. Therefore the next group of statements first stores 0 in all pixels of the pixmap, then it stores 1 in all pixels that belong to the polygon.

To actually draw the polygon on the screen, we call the function bit_plot(), which is a wrapper for XCopyPlane(), which copies the pixmap to a window. The function XCopyPlane() is similar to XCopyArea(), discussed in Sec. 8.1.2, but it takes one extra argument that indicates the plane we copy. In this case we copy into the lowest bit of the memory. The color of the polygon is determined by the foreground and the color of the surrounding by the background.

Caution

Pixmaps are *not transparent.* When a plane is copied, both foreground and background pixels are copied, so the background may obscure other drawn figures. Transparency can be achieved only by using XOR. The background color is kept constant.

Listing 8.3.   Drawing a Polygon on a Bitmap—File pxpol.c

```c
#include <X11/Xlib.h>
typedef struct {
    Pixmap pxm;
    int width, height, xoff, yoff;
} bit_map;
static Display  *Dpy;
static Window    window;
static GC        gc;
bit_map *  prepare_polygon(XPoint P[], int n)
{
    static GC pxm_gc = NULL;
    XPoint *Q;
    bit_map *p = (bit_map *)malloc(sizeof(bit_map));
    bounding_box(P, n, &(p->xoff), &(p->yoff), &(p->width),
        &(p->height), &Q);
    /*  Create and clear pixmap. The first time also create a
    GC  */
    p->pxm = XCreatePixmap(Dpy, DefaultRootWindow(Dpy),
    p->width, p->height, 1);
    if(pxm_gc == NULL)
        pxm_gc = XCreateGC(Dpy, p->pxm, 0, 0);
    XSetFunction(Dpy, pxm_gc, GXclear);
    XFillRectangle(Dpy, p->pxm, pxm_gc, 0, 0, p->width,
        p->height);
    /*  Draw the Polygon on the Pixmap  */
    XSetFunction(Dpy, pxm_gc, GXset);
    XDrawLines(Dpy, p->pxm, pxm_gc, Q, n, CoordModeOrigin);
    return p;
}
bit_plot(p, dx, dy)
    bit_map  *p; int dx, dy;
{
    XCopyPlane(Dpy, p->pxm, window, gc, 0, 0, p->width,
        p->height, p->xoff + dx, p->yoff + dy, 1);
}
```

A filled polygon can be drawn by calling XFillPolygon(), which has the same arguments as XDrawLines() with one exception: The sixth argument of XDrawLines() (indicating relative or absolute coordinates) is the seventh argument of XFillPolygon(). The sixth argument of XFillPolygon() is used to indicate whether the polygon is convex or self-intersecting. The predefined constant Complex is a safe choice, and it should not cause a significant reduction in speed. Thus to draw the filled polygon in Listing 8.3, we replace the XDrawLines() call by:

```
XFillPolygon(Dpy, p→pxm, pxm_gc, Q, n, Complex,
    CoordModeOrigin);
```

The appearance of the filled area is determined by the graphics context as in the case of filled arcs, described in Sec. 8.2.1. If a polygon is *self-intersecting*, there is an ambiguity in the definition of its interior, so Xlib allows the application programmer to select the appropriate definition through the graphics context. This is illustrated in Fig. 8.3. The original polygon is shown on the left; a polygon filled after the following call is shown in the center:

```
XSetFillRule(Dpy, gc, EvenOddRule);
```

A polygon filled after the following call is shown on the right:

```
XSetFillRule(Dpy, gc, WindingRule);
```

(See [Pa96], Chap. 12 for a discussion of the two algorithms used.)

The function XFillPolygon() draws part but not all of the boundary; therefore for better quality results, we should use an intermediate pixmap, and also

Input Polygon   EvenOddRule   WindingRule

Figure 8.3.   Ambiguity in the definition of the interior of a self-intersecting polygon.

call XDrawLines() for the boundary. The function has no way of handling polygons with holes.

8.3.   ICONS, CURSORS, AND FONTS

8.3.1.   Definitions and the Icon File Format   Icons and fonts are bit maps (pixmaps of depth 1), and cursors are pixmaps constructed from bit maps. The term *icon* is often reserved for the bit map displayed on a window when it is reduced to a small size by the window manager (iconified), but it is also used for any bit map stored in a file in a particular format, the *icon file format*. The same format is often called the bit map format, but we prefer the term icon because bit map has a broader meaning in other window systems. Bit maps obtained from such files can be used for any purpose: Marking selection buttons in menus, representing characters in video games, etc. A *font* is a set of bit maps stored in another special format, and their most common (but not only) use is for alphanumeric character images. *Cursors* are pixmaps used to mark the position of the pointer; these are normally constructed from bit maps, either icons or fonts.

Data in icon files are represented by printable characters, so that data can be included in a C program. In particular pixel values are expressed by *hexadecimal numbers*, for example 0x0E. Each hexadecimal digit has 4 bits, so its value represents a particular bit arrangement. Thus 0x0E represents the bit array:

0000 1110

0xCB represents

1100 1011

Such values can be stored in a char array. Earlier systems used short arrays with each element holding 16 pixels. However the current X standard requires an 8-bit pattern. The Unix utility program bitmap always requires an argument; it is used to produce a file that can be included in a C program; for example if we invoke bitmap cat.icon, draw an icon, then save it, the file cat.icon contains data of the form:

```
#define cat_width 16
#define cat_height 16
static char cat_bits[] = {
    0x01, 0x80, 0x03, 0xc0, 0x03, 0xc0, 0xf7, 0xef,
    0xfe, 0x7f, 0xfe, 0x7f, 0x9f, 0xf9, 0x9f, 0xf9,
```

```
0xff, 0xff, 0xfe, 0x7f, 0x7e, 0x7e, 0x7c, 0x3e,
0xc3, 0xc3, 0xf8, 0x1f, 0xce, 0x73, 0xc0, 0x03};
```

Then the image can be included in a C program with the statement:

```
#include <cat.icon>
```

Figure 8.4 shows the icon represented by the preceding bits. (This is the icon used for the grab cursor of the spy program described in Sec. 2.6.)

Converting this format into a pixel array and vice versa is a straightforward process, but it requires us carefully to writing the code. The X Window System has functions that create bit maps directly from icon descriptions, which we discuss next.

8.3.2.   Creating Bit Maps from Icon Files   The X Window System does not have a separate data type for bit maps, but the word Bitmap is used in the names of functions instead of the word Pixmap if the result is always a pixmap of depth 1. There are two pertinent Xlib functions:

```
XCreateBitmapFromData(),
```

used when an icon file has been included with the C code; and

```
XReadBitmapFile(),
```

which reads the icon file. The function

```
XCreateBitmapFromData()
```

Figure 8.4.   Form of icon contained in file cat.icon.

creates a pixmap of depth 1, where the bit pattern corresponds to that of an icon file with the format described in the previous section. The function has the following prototype:

```
Pixmap XCreateBitmapFromData( Display *Dpy, Drawable dr,
    char * iconbits, int width, int height )
```

All arguments except iconbits have the same meaning as arguments for XCreatePixmap() (see Sec. 8.1.2); in particular the role of dr is exactly the same. The member iconbits is a pointer to a char array where icon data are stored, as described in Sec. 8.3.1. If the program contains the statement:

```
#include <cat.icon>
```

Then the call is

```
Pixmap cat_icon;
cat_icon = XCreateBitmapFromData(Dpy,
        DefaultRootWindow(Dpy),
        cat_bits, cat_width, cat_height);
```

We can use the structure bit_map in Sec. 8.2.2 to store all information about bit maps created by a function prepare_bitmap(), then have the bit map drawn in different locations with the function bit_plot(), as shown in Listing 8.4. The coordinates cx and cy define the relative position of the bit map with respect to arguments of this function. In Listing 8.4 the bit map is always centered with respect to coordinates passed to the plotting function.

The function XReadBitmapFile has the following prototype:

```
Boolean XReadBitmapFile( Display  Dpy, Drawable dr,
    char * file_name, int *width, int *height, Pixmap
*px,
    int *xpos, int *ypos )
```

The last two arguments are important only for cursor icons (see Sec. 8.3.3), so we ignore them for the time being. If we use the bit_map type defined in Listing 8.3, the following code is appropriate:

```
bit_map *p;
XReadBitmapFile(Dpy, DefaultRootWindow(Dpy), &(p->width),
&(p->height), &(p->pxm, &(p->xoff), &(p->yoff));
```

Listing 8.4.   Creation of Bit Maps from Icons

```
bit_map *  prepare_bitmap(char iconbits[],int w,  int h,
    int cx,  int cy)
{
    bit_map *p = (bit_map *)malloc(sizeof(bit_map));
    p->pxm = XCreateBitmapFromData(Dpy,
            DefaultRootWindow(Dpy),  iconbits,  w,  h);
    p->width = w;
    p->height = h;
    p->xoff = -cx;
    p->yoff = -cy;
    return p;
}
/*  Program using the above function  */
    /*  ...  */
    static bit_map *pi;
    /*  ...  */
    pi = prepare_bitmap(cat_bits, cat_width, cat_height,
            cat_width/2, cat_height/2);
    /*  ...  */
    bit_plot(pi, 100, 200);/*  defined in Listing 8.3  */
```

Bit maps are always drawn with foreground (for bits that are 1) and background (for bits that are 0) colors and mode specified by the graphics context.

A collection of bit maps in icon file format resides in the X subdirectory include/X11/bitmaps.

8.3.3. Creating Cursors from Icons Cursors (also called pointers or sprites) are images used to mark a position on the screen that is controlled by the movement of the mouse. X has a special type Cursor for such objects, which are created by a function with prototype:

```
Cursor XCreatePixmapCursor( Display *Dpy,
    Pixmap Cursor_icon,
    Pixmap Cursor_mask, XColor *foreground,
    XColor *background, int hx, int hy )
```

Both Cursor_icon and Cursor_mask (if present) must be bit maps (pixmaps of depth 1), and these must have the same size; otherwise an error occurs (server message BadMatch). Bit maps are usually created through the XCreateBitmapFromData() function; these can be freed by using the

XFreePixmap() after creating the cursor object. The shape formed by nonzero pixels of the mask bit map is usually slightly larger than that of the cursor icon, so the cursor can be outlined when displayed against an area similar in color to its icon. If we decide not to use a cursor mask, the value None is passed. Arguments foreground and background point to structures containing color information for the cursor icon and the mask, respectively. (For type Xcolor, see Sec. 9.2.1.)

Important Point

Icons are bit maps, so these are always drawn in the foreground color. Cursors are full-depth pixmaps, so their colors must be specified when they are created. Colors can be changed later by a call to the function XRecolorCursor() (see Sec. 8.3.5).

The last two arguments (hx and hy) specify the *hot spot* of the cursor (the point whose coordinates are controlled by the mouse) relative to the upper left corner of the pixmap. The size of the cursor is specified by the system, so there is no information about dimensions in the call to XCreatePixmapCursor().

It is possible to create a mask automatically for a given icon by using image-processing techniques: For each bit that is one in the original icon, we set any neighboring bits that are zero to one. This produces a slightly enlarged version of the icon figure. (See [Pa96], Sec. 3.2.2 for an example of such a mask creation program.) Listing 8.5 shows the creation of a red cursor using the cat icon in Fig. 8.4 and assuming availability of a mask-generating function.

We chose the hot spot of the cursor to be its center—a reasonable choice for a cat, but not an arrow. Creating a cursor does not necessarily mean that it will be used. It appears on the screen only after a call to XDefineCursor(), which has following argument structure:

XDefineCursor(Display *Dpy, Window w, Cursor cursor_xid)

The first two arguments are self-explanatory; the third argument is the XID returned by a call to XCreatePixmapCursor(). The third argument may also have the value None; in that case the cursor used for the window is the same as the parent window cursor.

8.3.4. **Text and Fonts**   Most windowing systems display text by means of a set of bit maps, each of which contains the image of a character. A collection of such bit maps and a header structure is called a font. Because bit maps cannot be scaled, a font encapsulates both typeface style and size. This definition is the same

Listing 8.5.   Cursor Creation

```
#include <cat.icon>
static Cursor red_cat_cursor;
void creation_of_cursor(void)
{
    XColor Cursor, Cmask;
    unsigned char mask_bits[32];
    Pixmap Cursor_icon;
    Pixmap Cursor_mask;
    int hot_x = 8, hot_y = 8;
    make_cursor_mask(cat_bits, mask_bits, 16, 16);
    Cursor_icon = XCreateBitmapFromData(Dpy,
        window, cat_bits, 16, 16);
    Cursor_mask = XCreateBitmapFromData(Dpy,
        window, mask_bits, 16, 16);
    /* Assignment of colors - see Chapter 9 */
    Ccursor.red = 0xFFFF; Ccursor.blue = Ccursor.green = 0;
    /* red */
    Cmask.red = Cmask.blue = Cmask.green = 0xFFFF;
    /* white */
    red_cat_cursor = XCreatePixmapCursor(Dpy,
        Cursor_icon, Cursor_mask, &Ccursor, &Cmask,
        hot_x, hot_y);
}
```

as that used in traditional typography, but it differs from that used in some text-formatting system (such as *troff*), where the word font refers only to typeface style. X uses a naming convention for fonts that includes all relevant information (in addition to style and size). Since this results in cumbersome names, most systems maintain simple font name aliases, for example timesroman, helvetica, etc. We discuss naming conventions and font file location in Sec. 8.3.6.

Fonts are always kept on the server; which one is used is specified by the GC. On the other hand the client may need precise information about the size of text labels (for example to enclose these by rectangles with a given margin between lines and text, as in the case of menu buttons). For this purpose X provides the client with an *information structure* containing data that can be used to compute the height and width of character strings.

Determining the default font used by the server is a major headache in X. The default font is implementation-dependent, so we cannot rely on a known value. The following function queries the server about a font:

```
XFontStruct  *font_info = XQueryFont( Display  *Dpy,
                                      XID font_id);
```

Unfortunately we must provide a font XID to call it! Since font is part of the GC, we may try to find its XID by the sequence:

```
XGCValues v;
XGetGCValues(Dpy, gc, GCFont, &v);
font_info = XQueryFont(Dpy, v.font);
```

However this does *not* work because XGetGCValues() looks only at the client GC cache; as mentioned in Sec. 8.1.4, font is one of the values that are not cached. There is a tortuous way around this problem by using the call:

```
font_info = XQueryFont( Dpy,
            (GContext) XGContextFromGC(gc)  );
```

The function XGContextFromGC() returns the XID of the server GC structure from the client cache (in effect gc->gid), then we rely on the fact that the second argument of the function XQueryFont() can be an XID of the server GC structure.

Things are much easier if we load a new font, for example Helvetica. We can call a function with the font name as second argument and not only obtain information about it, but also load it on the server:

```
font_info = XLoadQueryFont( Dpy, "Helvetica");
```

If the font is not found, the function returns a NULL value. This happens either because the font itself does not exist or because we have used a nonexisting alias. The latter is a likely event when we port a program across different systems; Sec. 8.3.6 discusses how to deal with these issues. The X utility xlsfonts lists all font names that are available on the system.

After a font is loaded, we set it in the GC by the call:

```
XSetFont(Dpy, gc, font_info->fid);
```

If we plan to use a mixture of fonts in an application, it is best to create an array of XFontStruct pointers, fill it using one call to XLoadQueryFont() per font, then select the current font through XSetFont().

Once we have a pointer to an XFontStruct, we can lay out text carefully. The width of a text string in pixels is given by a function with prototype:

```
XTextWidth(XFontStruct  *font_info, char  *s, int number);
```

where number refers to the number of characters in the string s (which can be obtained with the strlen() function). For example:

```
XTextWidth(font_info, "Hello", strlen("Hello"));
```

The function XQueryTextExtents() returns detailed information about the displayed text, but it is rather complex to use. A simple way of estimating the line height of text printed with a given font is from the expression:

```
font_info->ascent + font_info->descent
```

To display a character string text with its lower left corner at (x, y), we can use the following Xlib call:

```
XDrawString(Dpy, window, gc, x, y, text, strlen(text) );
```

Positions x and y can be updated by the following code:

```
static XFontStruct *font_info;
    x += XTextWidth(font_info, text, strlen(text));
```

or

```
    y += font_info->ascent + font_info->descent;
```

Xlib has many other functions for displaying text, including

```
XDrawImageString(),
```

which takes exactly the same arguments as XDrawString(), but it has a slightly different behavior. Both functions display the text in the foreground color, but they do other things differently:

- XDrawString() ignores background color and uses whatever mode is effective in the GC (XOR, replacement, etc).
- XDrawImageString() ignores the GC mode (it always uses replacement), but it uses the background color to fill a tight rectangle around the text.

8.3.5. Font Cursors   X maintains a *cursor font*, and it provides a simple call to construct a cursor from one of these predefined shapes. The function prototype is

```
#include <X11/cursorfont.h>
Cursor XCreateFontCursor(Display *Dpy, unsigned int name)
```

where `name` can be chosen from a list of symbolic names, for example `XC_leftbutton` (shows a mouse with left button pressed), `XC_middlebutton` (shows a mouse with middle button pressed), `XC_clock` (shows a rather cryptic rendition of a grandfather clock), etc. Once we create a cursor, we must call `XDefineCursor()` to make the new cursor actually appear.

The cursor created by these calls is black and white. We reassign colors with a function that has the following prototype:

```
XRecolorCursor(Display  *Dpy, Cursor cursor,
    XColor *foreground, XColor *background);
```

The first two arguments are self-explanatory; the last two are the same as in the function `XCreatePixmapCursor()`, discussed in Sec. 8.3.3. (Of course we also can recolor a cursor created by the latter function.)

8.3.6.   Font Names and Font Libraries   The full X name of a font has 13 parts (fields), as in the following examples:

```
-adobe-helvetica-bold-r-normal--14-140-75-75-p-82-
iso8859-1
-adobe-new century schoolbook-bold-i-normal--10-100-75-
75-p-66-iso8859-1
-adobe-symbol-medium-r-normal--18-180-75-75-p-107-adobe-
fontspecific
-linotype-helvetica-bold-r-narrow-sans-10-100-72-72-
p-46-iso8859-1
-schumacher-clean-medium-r-normal--8-80-75-75-c-50-
iso8859-1
```

Dashes serve as field delimiters, and fields themselves may contain blanks. In one system the first three fonts have the following aliases:

```
Adobe-Helvetica-Bold
NewCenturySchlbk-BoldItalic
Symbol
```

These aliases can be used as arguments to XLoadQueryFont() instead of the full names (at the risk of compromising portability). Wildcarding with * (for strings) and ? (for single characters) is also allowed but with somewhat unpredictable results. The meaning of the fields follow:

- Foundry: Name of the font supplier (adobe, linotype, or schumacher in the examples); foundry is a historical throwback to the days when typefaces were cast in lead.
- Typeface or font family: Name describing a particular character style, for example helvetica, new century schoolbook, symbol, etc.; some typefaces may have nonalphanumeric characters. Thus the symbol family contains bit maps representing mathematical symbols and Greek letters used in equations. Not all foundries have all typefaces.
- Weight: Usually bold, medium, or light. Not all typefaces have all weights; the light category is rather rare.
- Slant: r (roman), i (italic), or o (oblique); the first represents upright characters, the other two slanted.
- Set width: Usually normal; there a few narrow fonts, which give words a crowded appearance.
- Style variations: Often omitted (with two successive dashes). The expression sans (as in the fourth example) implies no serifs.
- Pixels: Actual point size in pixels (see the following bulleted item).
- Point size times 10: Point size is the height of the tallest character in a font (usually {) measured in one-seventy-second of an inch. This is the measure of size used in typesetting languages. Most book text is printed in 10-point size. This field contains the point size times 10. The previous field depends on the resolution; For 75 dpi it is approximately the same as the true point size.
- Vertical and Horizontal Resolution (two fields): Dots per inch used in the font design.
- Spacing: Proportional (p) or monospace (m) are the two most common values.
- Average width (in tenths of pixels).
- Character Set (two fields).

Key parameters for display purposes are point size (determines the size of the labels), weight, and slant (the last two for emphasis).

There is a function lets us find the available fonts in a system. (The utility xlsfonts [see Sec. 8.3.4] is built around it.) It has the following prototype:

```
char **  XListFonts(Display *Dpy, char *pattern,
    int maximum_count, int *returned_count);
```

It returns an array of font names that match the given pattern, but no more than maximum_count. The pattern "*" returns all fonts. The actual number of fonts found is returned in returned_count. The following simple program lists all fonts that match a pattern given as a command line argument:

```
#include <X11/Xlib.h>
int main(int arc, char **arv)
{
    char **cp, **cp0;
    int i, kount;
    Display *Dpy = XOpenDisplay ("");
    if(Dpy==NULL) return(-1);
    cp = cp0 =
        XListFonts(Dpy, arc>1? arv[1]: "*", 256, &kount);
    printf("%d fonts found\n", kount);
    for(i=0; i<kount; i++, cp++) printf("%s\n", *cp);
    if(kount) XFreeFontNames(cp0);
    XCloseDisplay(Dpy);
    return(0);
}
```

For example, to list all Adobe fonts we must run

```
a.out "*adobe*"
```

Note: Quotes on the argument are essential to avoid having the shell interpret wildcard characters. To find all 10-pointsize fonts (and possibly a few others) run

```
a.out "*100*"
```

8.4. REGIONS

8.4.1. Concept   X has a facility for creating in effect bit maps on the client side. The type Region is a handle to a collection of points, the only limitations on its shape are those imposed by Xlib functions that may be used to build and manipulate regions. These limit the shape to unions and intersections of rectangles and/or polygons. The basic region creation function has the following prototype:

```
#include <X11/Xutil.h>
Region XPolygonRegion(XPoint P[], int nPoints,
                      int filling_rule);
```

where argument nPoints is the number of points in the array P[]. The filling_rule is the same as the argument used in GC functions that specify how a polygon is filled (Sec. 8.2.2). The Region type is not defined in X11/Xlib.h but in X11/Xutil.h, which must be included in any files using regions. Since the region handle refers to a client structure, there is no reference to the server or a drawable. As a matter of fact we can create and manipulate regions without a call (explicit or implicit) to XOpen Display().

The most common use of regions is to specify *clip masks*, a member of the GC that specifies which pixels can be drawn on a drawable (See [Pa96], Chap. 16 for the theory of clipping.) It can be specified through either a 1-bit pixmap by the function:

```
XSetClipMask(Display  *  Dpy, GC gc, Pixmap mask)
```

or through a region by the function:

```
XSetRegion(Display  *  Dpy, GC gc, Region mask);
```

The use of region clip masks makes various graphics operations possible that are not directly supported by Xlib, such as filling polygons with holes. Listing 8.6 provides an example of such code. The function XSubtractRegion() performs a logical operation on Regions A and B, then stores the result on C.

Because regions are opaque handles, the region where we store the results of logical operations must have been created previously by the statement:

```
C = XCreateRegion();
```

The following statement frees the memory associated with Region R:

```
XDestroyRegion(R)
```

Additional region logical operations include unions, intersections, and exclusive OR:

```
/*  C = A union B  */
XUnionRegion(Region A, Region B, Region C)
/*  C = A intersection B  */
XIntersectRegion(Region A, Region B, Region C)
/*  C = A XOR B  */
XXorRegion(Region A, Region B, Region C)
```

In this case Region C must have been created earlier by a call to XCreateRegion(). All these functions also have a limitation. Since regions

Listing 8.6.   Filling the Space between Polygons

```
/*  Fill the space between polygons P and Q  */
fill_non_simple_polygon(XPoint *P, int n, XPoint *Q, int m)
{
    Region A, B, C;
    /*  construct regions A and B from polygons P and Q  */
    A = XPolygonRegion(P, n, EvenOddRule);
    B = XPolygonRegion(Q, m, EvenOddRule);
    /*  create an empty region handle  */
    C = XCreateRegion();
    /*  make region C have the points of A that are not in
    B  */
    XSubtractRegion(A, B, C);
    /*  we no longer need A and B  */
    XDestroyRegion(A); XDestroyRegion(B);
    /*  set clip mask to C  */
    XSetRegion(Dpy, gc, C);
    /*  free C as well, it has been recreated in the
    server  */
    XDestroyRegion(C);
    /*  fill a large rectangle, only C will show  */
    XFillRectangle(Dpy, window, gc, 0, 0, 1000, 1000);
}
```

are in effect bit maps, we cannot use them to find the vertices of the polygon that results from these operations.

Regions are useful for various geometric operations besides creating clipping. For example to find whether a point is within a polygon, we can simply call a function available for the purpose, thus:

```
if( XPointInRegion(poly_region, x, y) == True)
    printf("Point %d %d is inside\n", x, y);
```

The following function finds the smallest rectangle that encloses the given region:

```
XClipBox(Region A, XRectangle  *G)
```

Such a function can be used to find the bounding box of a polygon by constructing the region from the polygon through the XPolygonRegion() function. In this way we can implement the function bounding_box() in Listing 8.3.

There are many other functions that manipulate regions, but these should be used with caution. In particular avoid using `XShrinkRegion()`. This function attempts to scale regions, a task that cannot be done properly for most scale values because bit maps cannot be scaled properly (See [Pa96], Sec. 13.1.1); since regions are stored as bit maps, these cannot be scaled either.

8.4.2.   Nonrectangular Windows   Regions can be used to create non-rectangular windows. This feature is supported only by the SHAPE extension of Xlib, but that seems to be available in most servers. We make sure that it exists with the code:

```
int major_v, minor_v;
/*  ...  */
if(XShapeQueryVersion(Dpy, &major_v, &minor_v)==0)
    printf("No SHAPE extension on this server");
else {  /*  build non rectangular window  */  }
```

To access it, we need the following line in our program and the `-lXext` flag in the object-linking line of the makefile:

```
#include <X11/extensions/shape.h>
```

The simplest way of creating a top window that is not rectangular is by creating a region, say, `FunnyShape`, with the appropriate shape, then call

```
XShapeCombineRegion(Dpy, XtWindow(toplevel),
    ShapeBounding, 0, 0, FunnyShape, ShapeSet);
```

where `toplevel` is the top shell in the application. Listing 8.7 shows a minimal program that creates a window that is a rhomb. The shape of the shell widget is set to a rhomb; this in turn clips the canvas. Only widgets from Xt are used; the window color and dimensions can be changed through the resource mechanism. A further discussion of nonrectangular windows is beyond our scope. See [JR94], Chap. 18, for more on this topic.

8.5.   CONCLUSIONS

In Chap. 8 we cover the basic drawing operations of X. While the operations described in Chap. 2 can be implemented in a simpler way by using Xt, there is no such possibility for drawing functions discussed here: We must deal directly with Xlib, although in simpler cases we can use the Starter toolkit.

Listing 8.7.   Creating a nonrectangular Window—File `rhomb.c`

```
/*  Nonrectangular window using the X shape extension  */
#include <stdio.h>
#include <X11/StringDefs.h>
#include <X11/Intrinsic.h>
#include <X11/Shell.h>
#include <X11/extensions/shape.h>
void paint();
String fallbacks[] = {
   "*canvas.width: 200", "*canvas.height: 200",
   "*canvas.background: red",
   NULL};
main(int arc, char **arv)
{
   XtAppContext app;
   Widget toplevel, canvas;
   toplevel = XtVaAppInitialize( &app, "Rhomb",
         (XrmOptionDescList)NULL, 0, &arc, arv,
         fallbacks, NULL);
   canvas = XtVaCreateManagedWidget("canvas",
      coreWidgetClass, toplevel, NULL);
   XtAddEventHandler(canvas,
                     ExposureMask |
                     StructureNotifyMask,
                     False, paint, NULL);
   XtRealizeWidget(toplevel);
   set_clip_mask(canvas);
   XtAppMainLoop(app);
}
/*  Function that specifies the window shape  */
set_clip_mask(Widget w)
{
   XPoint P[4];
   Dimension width, height;
   Region  Rhomb;
   /*  Compute a rhomb shape based on the window
   dimensions  */
   XtVaGetValues(w, XtNwidth, &width, XtNheight, &height,
      NULL);
   P[0].x = 0;          P[0].y = height/2;
   P[1].x = width/2;    P[1].y = 0;
   P[2].x = width;      P[2].y = height/2;
   P[3].x = width/2;    P[3].y = height;
```

```
    Rhomb = XPolygonRegion(P, 4, EvenOddRule);
    XShapeCombineRegion(XtDisplay(w),
        XtWindow(XtParent(w)), ShapeBounding, 0, 0,
        Rhomb, ShapeSet);
}
/*  Function called on Expose and Resize events  */
void paint(
    Widget w,
    XtPointer client_data,
    XEvent *ep,
    Boolean *disp)
{
    static Dimension old_width = 0, old_height = 0;
    Dimension width, height;
    /*  If the window size has changed recompute the rhomb
    shape  */
    XtVaGetValues(w, XtNwidth, &width, XtNheight, &height,
        NULL);
    if( old_width>0 && old_height>0 &&
        (old_width != width || old_height != height) )
        set_clip_mask(w);
        old_width = width; old_height = height;
}
```

Here we have used Starter toolkit functions for window creation and event handling because we focus on drawing functions. In contrast in Chaps. 3 and 4 we used Starter toolkit functions for drawing, since our emphasis there was on events and window creation. Of course we may avoid using the Starter toolkit altogether, as we saw in Listing 8.7. Listing 8.8 shows an additional example that uses action procedures instead of an event handler. The program draws black slices of $30°$ separated by $30°$ gaps. The canvas is a Core class widget; because it does not have an exposure callback list, the painting function is made an action procedure.

8.6. PROJECTS

1. Write a program to draw concentric rings of different colors (a real rainbow!).

2. (a) Modify Listing 8.3 to create a program for constructing an icon bit map from a polygon or a polyline. (b) Create a sequence of animation frames from the following process: Start with a simple line figure, compute its form in a sequence of positions, then convert the line figures into icons using the program in Part a.

Listing 8.8. Pie Slices—File zpie.c

```c
/*  Show six pie slices  */
#include <X11/StringDefs.h>
#include <X11/Intrinsic.h>
static Display *Dpy;
static Window   win;
static GC       gc;
void paint(void)
{
    int i;
    for(i=0; i<6; i++)
        XFillArc(Dpy, win, gc, 60, 55, 200, 200, 3840*i,
        1920);
}
/*  Make paint() an action procedure  */
static XtActionsRec act[] = {  {"paint", paint} };
static char  trans[] = "<Expose>: paint()";
int main(int arc, char **arv)
{
    XtAppContext app;
    Widget top, canvas;
    top = XtAppInitialize( &app, "Pie",
        NULL, 0, &arc, arv, NULL, NULL, 0);
    XtAppAddActions( app, act, XtNumber(act) );
    /*  Create a canvas widget  */
    canvas = XtVaCreateManagedWidget("canvas",
        widgetClass, top,
        XtNwidth, 300,    XtNheight, 300,
        XtNtranslations, XtParseTranslationTable(trans),
        NULL);
    XtRealizeWidget(top);
    Dpy = XtDisplay(canvas);
    win = XtWindow(canvas);
    /*  Create a Graphics Context  */
    {
        XGCValues values;
        int Scr = DefaultScreen(Dpy);
        values.foreground = BlackPixel(Dpy, Scr);
        values.background = WhitePixel(Dpy, Scr);
        gc = XCreateGC(Dpy, win,
            GCBackground | GCForeground, &values);
        XSetArcMode(Dpy, gc, ArcPieSlice);
    }
    XtAppMainLoop(app);
}
```

3. Starting with the code of the short program in Sec. 8.3.6, write a program that not only prints font names but also displays them on a window. (You may choose to display a name in its own font.)

4. Reimplemenmt a program from Chaps. 5–7 by replacing the Paper Class widget with a Core class widget (as done in Listings 8.7 and 8.8) and using Xlib functions instead of Starter toolkit functions.

9

Color and Images

9.1. OVERVIEW

There are two basic reasons for using color in computer system application. The first is for *labeling* items (two curves in a graph, menu buttons, etc); the other is for color *image display*. In all graphics devices based on television technology, a color is defined by a triplet of red, green, and blue (RGB) values. The difference between two application types is seen in how RGB values must be specified.

• In an image display RGB values are *given* for each point in the image. If the device is incapable of displaying such values, then we must find a *close approximation* to them. For example a full-color image is usually given with 24 bits per pixel (8 bits per color). We can display an approximation to it in an 8-bit device by using the most significant bits of each color with adjustments to preserve the true average color of areas. Such transformations are known as *color halftoning*. (See [Pa96], Chap. 21, for a description of the process.) Other times we may want to adjust RGB values to compensate for a too bright or too dim color in a particular display. In all these cases RGB values are determined by factors beyond control of the window system. We must also specify a large number of these—many images contain thousands of values, so that even a rough approximation may contain over 100 colors. For labeling we have more flexibility in the choice of RGB values. We need *distinct* colors without caring too much about the exact hue; we also typically do not need many colors. Using more than 10 labeling colors in a GUI is likely to overload the user.

Color display is not a challenge if we have a display device with 24 bits per pixel (16,777,216 possible colors) or even with 16 bits per pixel (65,536 possible colors). If we insist that our applications run only on machines with at least 16 bits per pixel, we do not need most of the material in this chapter. Color displays become a challenge with the (quite common) 8-bit-per-pixel displays.

As discussed in Sec. 1.4.1, pixel values are mapped into colors (RGB values) through the video lookup table, or hardware colormap. The exact correspondence is determined by a (logical) colormap loaded into the video lookup table. To display a particular color, we place the index of the colormap that points to the RGB values of the color in refresh memory, and the video lookup table takes care of the rest. Therefore creating color displays is straightforward, *once* we know the correspondence between real colors and colormap index values.

The easiest way to deal with color is to let each application create its own colormap. Unfortunately this has some undesirable side effects. Since the video lookup table is a unique resource, the colormap of only one application at a time can be loaded in that table. Normally loading is done by the window manager in response to the pointer position. This ensures that the active application appears with the correct colors, but there is no guarantee about the others. A different color-map for each application causes significant distortions in the appearance of the screen as well as flashing when we move the pointer over different application windows.

Another solution is to use a single colormap for all applications. This keeps a consistent screen appearance and avoids flashing. Such a solution presents only a minor challenge to labeling applications—these have to find the common table, see if there is space, then add their own color definitions. In an 8-bit-per-pixel device, the colormap has 256 places, so we can accommodate 25 different applications even if each uses ten *distinct* labeling colors. (Labeling colors are most likely shared, so the number of applications may be even greater.)

Unfortunately the single colormap solution presents serious difficulties for image displays when an application requires hundreds of colors. One compromise solution is to reduce the number of RGB values for an image so they fit in the common colormap if the appearance of the image is not significantly changed. A good example are gray scale images that contain many intensities but no color. In this case RGB values are identical, so we need only 256 places in the colormap. If this is still too many, we can drop the least significant bit of each pixel without visibly changing the image. Then we are left with only 128 values to fit in the common colormap.

This solution presents no problems if we run only one copy of the application, but if we run a second copy, it can add another 128 values to the common colormap. Therefore we must provide code that checks whether desired values are already in the common colormap. This solves the problem of running many copies of the same application, or groups of similar applications, but it leaves the problem of simultaneously running two applications with different colormaps, as illustrated in Fig. 9.1, where Application *A* may be a web browser and Application *B* a video

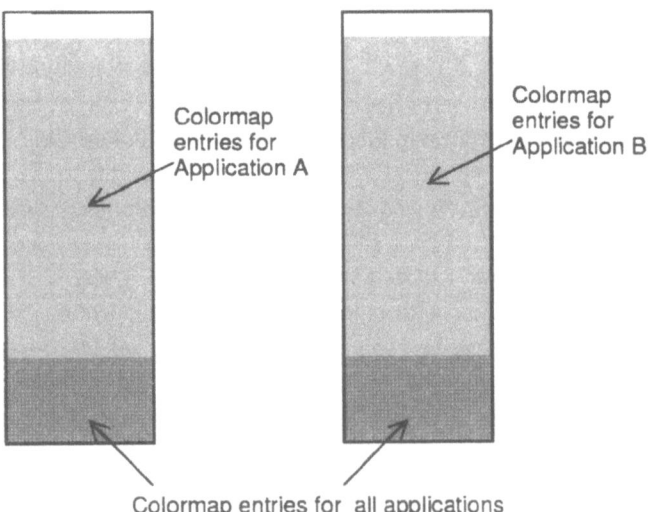

Colormap entries for Application A

Colormap entries for Application B

Colormap entries for all applications

Figure 9.1.   Possible colormap entries for two applications that display images.

game. (One of the two colormaps may be the default colormap but with most of its entries taken by one of the applications.)

The situation in Fig. 9.1 requires at least one of the applications to create its own colormap. It is possible to minimize variations in the display appearance if while assigning values to elements of a new colormap, we reserve space for some (if not all) of the common colors (the dark gray part in Fig. 9.1). We describe how to implement such a strategy in Sec. 9.4. However before dealing with new colormaps, we discuss how to use existing colormaps in Sec. 9.2.

Dealing with colormaps in X is complex due to the simple design of the X server. Decisions about color allocation naturally belong to the server, so trying to do the task from the client side is a little like providing instruction over the phone for repairing a piece of equipment.

9.2.   USING EXISTING COLORMAPS

9.2.1.   Using Color in X and the X Toolkit   Note: The `Colormap` type is
an XID that refers to a server structure containing the actual colormap table. All X servers have a *default colormap* that can be accessed with the following code fragment:

```
Display *Dpy;
Colormap cmap;
/* ... */
cmap = DefaultColormap(Dpy, DefaultScreen ( Dpy) );
```

The macro `DefaultColormap()` obtains the information from the `Display` structure.

Each widget also has a colormap that may or not be the same as the default colormap. In applications using Xt the colormap can be found through the resource mechanism:

```
Colormap cmap;
Widget w;
/* ... */
XtVaGetValues(w, XtNcolormap, &cmap, NULL);
```

A colormap consists of an array of *color cells*. X provides a client-side structure with the color cell information. The structure is called `XColor`, and it has the following declaration:

```
typedef struct {
    unsigned long pixel;
```

```
    unsigned short red, green, blue;
    char flags;  /*  whether to ignore some of the colors  */
    char pad;    /*  to provide an even number of bytes  */
} XColor;
```

The `pixel` member is the bit pattern corresponding to color composed of the three given values `red`, `green`, and `blue`. The member `flags` is used to allow colors to be selectively reset. To change all colors, `flags` must have the value `DoRed | DoGreen | DoBlue`.

The space allocated for elements of the `XColor` structure is generous—it allows 8 bits per color and an extra 8 bits to be used for a transparency factor. Since color display becomes a challenge only in devices with 8 bits per pixel (256 entries in their colormap), we construct all of our examples for such a case. X allows an application to query a server about its color-handling abilities (see Sec. 9.3), and it makes sense to have different code for handling color according to display device capability.

Assumption

In all the *examples* in this chapter we assume that there are no more than 8 bits per pixel in the images to be displayed and the colormaps of the devices used have no more than 256 entries, so that indices can be safely stored as `int` (rather than insisting on `unsigned long`).

Two functions can be used to create a colormap entry from an `XColor` structure: `XAllocColor()` and `XStoreColor()`. Both functions have the same prototype:

```
Boolean XAllocColor(Display *Dpy, Colormap cmap,
         XColor *color_cell_ptr)
Boolean XStoreColor(Display *Dpy, Colormap cmap,
         XColor *color_cell_ptr)
```

Another pair of functions creates entry groups: `XAllocColors()` and `XStoreColors()`, which take the same arguments and a fourth, the number of entries to be created.

The arguments are self-explanatory, but there is a major difference in how the `pixel` member of `color_cell_ptr` is treated. The function `XAllocColor()` ignores the `pixel` value given to look for an existing color cell with the given RGB values. Then it assigns the value from that cell to `pixel` and returns. If it does not find one, it attempts to create a new cell; if successful, it places the value corresponding to the first available place in `pixel`. The value assigned by this function must be used for all subsequent references to that particular RGB color. This function also *ignores the values of the given flags*. Since applications cannot modify the contents of color cells after the initial assignment, we say that such cells are *read-only*.

The function `XStoreColor()` creates a color cell with the *given* pixel value and changes colors according to given flags. However pixel values cannot be arbitrary, and these must be obtained by another function call that returns *read/write* color cells. That process is described in Sec. 9.2.3.

Both functions return `False(0)` if they fail to accomplish their task, usually because of a lack of space in the colormap.

9.2.2. Color Specification by Name   While other window systems allow applications to refer to a few selected colors by name, X has a data base of hundreds of color names for which it provides RGB values. This feature is particularly useful in applications that use color for labeling (rather than for image display). The data base can be queried with a function that has the following prototype:

```
Boolean XParseColor( Display *Dpy, Colormap cmap,
    char  *  color_name, XColor *color_cell_ptr )
```

The first two arguments are self-explanatory, `color_name` is the given name and `color_cell_ptr` is a pointer to the structure where the RGB values are copied from the data base. If the color cannot be found, the function returns `False`. Color names can be composite, and these can contain spaces (which are ignored). If the return of `XParseColor()` is `True`, the function `XAllocColor()` can be called with the pointer `color_cell_ptr` as its third argument. Such a sequence of calls is used for example in the color resource conversion routine, `color_convert()`, described in Sec. 3.3.5. Because Xt resource conversion routines hash, their string arguments are better to use than Xlib calls. Thus to use the color `blue` to draw in the window of widget w, we need only execute the code:

```
Pixel brush;
color_convert(w, "blue", &brush);
/*  assumes short pixel values  */
if(brush >=0) XSetForeground(Dpy, gc, brush);
```

The code is efficient because the resource conversion function caches color names, and it does not need to check the color data base in each call. Because `brush` need not be a widget resource, we avoid the problems discussed in Sec. 3.4 while taking advantage of the resource conversion mechanism.

9.2.3. Color Specification by RGB Values If we already have RGB values, the task is quite easy for one color, as shown in Listing 9.1. The code assumes that colors are given as 8-bit values; therefore these must be shifted left to make a 16-bit value as expected in the XColor structure col_def. The latter serves both to provide values (red, green, and blue) and also to receive values (pixel) when used as argument to XAllocColor().

Certain complications arise if we want to assign an array of RGB values. Application programs that deal with full pictures are usually simpler if we allocate *contiguous* colors. That is, if two pixels have values that differ by an amount k, the corresponding colormap indices also differ by k. We may also not want to give up so easily if color allocation fails because colors may already be loaded, possibly by another copy of the same application. The function XQueryColors() reads the contents of a colormap, then determines whether what we are looking for already exists. Listing 9.2 provides an example of appropriate code. The function fit_RGB_colors does three things: It tries to allocate colors in the existing colormap. If that fails, it checks whether the colors are already loaded; if so, it returns the pixel value of the colormap where the colors are loaded. If the colors are not found, then it tries to create a new colormap using the location passed by the last argument, newmap. If the last argument in null, then no attempt is made to create a new colormap.

Listing 9.1. Storing RGB values—File addRGB.c

```
/*  Assumes no more than 8 bits per color and a short
colormap  */
typedef unsigned char *pPixel;
static Display *Dpy;
static Colormap cmap;
int add_RGB_color(pPixel red, pPixel green, pPixel blue)
{
    XColor col_def;
    col_def.red = red  << 8;
    col_def.green = green  << 8;
    col_def.blue = blue  << 8;
    if( XAllocColor(Dpy, cmap, &col_def)
        return (int)col_def.pixel;
    else return -1; /*  allocation failed  */
}
```

Listing 9.2. Storing an Array of RGB Values—File `fitRGB.c`

```c
/*  Assumes no more than 8 bits per color and a short
colormap  */
typedef unsigned char *pPixel;
#define CMAP_SIZE 256
int fit_RGB_colors(Widget w,
   pPixel red_pix[], ppixel green_pix[],
   pPixel blue_pix[],
   int RGB_length, Colormap *newmap)
{
   int i, j;
   Display *Dpy = XtDisplay(w);
   Colormap cmap;
   XColor ccell[CMAP_SIZE];
   unsigned long plane_masks[2];
   Pixel pixels[CMAP_SIZE];
   int cstat, nr, ng, nb; /*  auxiliary variables  */
   int red[CMAP_SIZE], green[CMAP_SIZE], blue[CMAP_SIZE];
   /*  Obtain colormap of widget (error checking
   omitted)  */
   XtVaGetValues(w, XtNcolormap, &cmap, NULL);
   for(i=0; i<RGB_length; i++) {
      red[i] = red_pix[i]  << 8;
      green[i] = green_pix[i]  << 8;
      blue[i] = blue_pix[i]  << 8;
   }
   /*  Ask for enough read/write color cells to fit the
      given colors  */
   cstat = XAllocColorCells(Dpy, cmap, True, plane_masks,
      0, pixels, RGB_length);
   if(cstat) {  /*  Successful allocation  */
      /*  Assign proper color values to the color
      cells  */
      for(i=0; i<RGB_length; i++) {
         ccell[i].pixel = pixels[i];
         ccell[i].red = red[i];
         ccell[i].green = green[i];
         ccell[i].blue = blue[i];
         ccell[i].flags = DoRed | DoGreen | DoBlue;
      }
      XStoreColors(Dpy, cmap, ccell, RGB_length);
      return (int)pixels[0];  /*  ccell[0].pixel  */
   }
```

```
      else {  /*  Allocation failed  */
          /*  Read colormap contents and check whether  */
          /*  the colors we want are already there  */
          for(i=0; i<CMAP_SIZE; i++) ccell[i].pixel = i;
          XQueryColors(Dpy, cmap, ccell, CMAP_SIZE);
          /*  we guess matching colormap entry starts at j  */
          for(j=0; j<CMAP_SIZE-RGB_length; j++) {
              /*  try to confirm guess  */
              for(i=0; i<RGB_length; i++) {
                  nr = ccell[j+i].red&0177400;   /*  red, etc
                                            are unsigned!  */
                  ng = ccell[j+i].green&0177400;
                  nb = ccell[j+i].blue&0177400;
                  if( nr != red[i] || ng != green[i] ||
                  nb != blue[i]) break;
              }
              if(i == RGB_length)
                  return (int)ccell[j].pixel; /*  success! all
                                            colors found  */
          }
          /*  Colors were not found  */
          if(newmap) {
              /*  Try for a new colormap - See Section 9.4  */
          }
          else return -1;   /*  failure  */
      }
  }
```

The first few statements of the function fit_RGB_colors() are equivalent to those of add_RGB_color(). The call to function XAllocColorCells() is the first new operation. This function has the following prototype:

```
int XAllocColorCells(Display *Dpy, Colormap cmap,
    Boolean contiguous,
    unsigned long plane_masks[], int nplanes,
    unsigned long pixels[], int RGB_length)
```

The first two arguments are self-explanatory; the third is set to True for contiguous color cells. The functions offers the option of allocating read/write colormap entries in two forms, either as planes (see Sec. 1.4.1) or pixels. The plane feature is useful for overlays; and it is discussed in Sec. 9.6.2. In Listing 9.2 we ignore the planes by setting the fifth argument to zero and requesting the allocation of RGB_length pixels. The array pixels[] contains *returned* values.

If allocation succeeded, i.e., we find room for all colors, we proceed to create colormap entries. First we copy the returned pixel values and the given RGB values into the XColor array of ccell[], then we call XStoreColors() to load the pixel and RGB values into the colormap. Finally the function returns the value of the first pixel. This is an *offset* used to modify values during the creation of displays. Thus to see the color described by:

```
red[n], green[n], blue[n]
```

we must put in refresh memory not n but n+offset, where offset is the value returned by fit_RGB_colors().

If cell allocation by XAllocColorCells() fails, we read the values of all colormap cells using the function XQueryColors(). (The arguments of this function are self-explanatory.) Then we look for a match between the RGB values returned in the array ccell[] and the given color arrays. The variable j in Listing 9.2 refers to the presumed start in the colormap of the block of colors we are looking for. In general the first few entries in the colormap are likely to correspond to colors other than those of an image. Therefore we would have saved time by starting with a nonzero value of j. Because comparing unsigned variables may not work, we copy members of structures in the ccell[] into int variables.

If we are unable to find a match, then we have the option of creating a new colormap. That process is discussed in Sec. 9.4.

9.2.4.   Economizing on Colors   It is possible to save on colormap entries by observing that not all entries of the red, blue, and green arrays are used in a given image. Assume that we deal with an 8-bit image and let u[] be an array of type int and size 256 initialized to all 0. We can examine all pixels of the image and set u[z] equal to 1 if the 8-bit value z occurs in the image. Then we run the code:

```
for(z=0; z<256; z++) {
    if(u[z]) u[z] = add_RGB_color(red[z], green[z],
                                  blue[z]);
}
```

This allocates *noncontiguous* color cells and only when they are actually needed.

To display the image, we must replace each value z by u[z], which is where problems can occur. If we are going to display only one image, this is an acceptable solution. If we are going to display a group of images, then it is likely that each image will have colors not seen in others; so if we need new colormap entries, we may run out of colors anyway. The same is true if we start with one image but perform various operations on it: New versions are likely to have new colors.

An aggressive color-economizing technique may replace colors in an image by similar colors if entries for the latter exist in the colormap. Again this may be acceptable for decorative displays but not for serious image-processing applications where slight differences in color may be quite significant in the application.

X supports certain standard colormaps and encourages their use (so images can share the same colormap), but this is of little help in practice. If we use colors for labeling or displaying simple images, then the default colormap is likely to suffice. Problems occur when we need to display images for nondecorative purposes. An image may come with a colormap that is quite distinct for good reason (for example conventions used by physicians to label medical images.)

An even more aggressive color-economizing technique looks for the *nearest* available color if there is no space on the colormap to allocate a new color. This can be accomplished with the following code:

```
/*  Find nearest color to given RGB values  */
/*  Find the values of the existing colormap  */
XColor existing_cells[256];
XQueryColors(Dpy, cmap, existing_cells, 256);
{
    long i, d, d0, i0;
/*  initialize d0 to the distance between pure white and
pure black  */
    d0 = 65536*3;
/*  initialize i0 to a value indicating failure  */
    i0 = -1;
    for(i=0; i<256; i++) {
        d = abs(red - existing_cells[i].red) +
            abs(green - existing_cells[i].green) +
            abs(blue - existing_cells[i].blue);
        if(d<d0} { d0 = d; i0 = i; }
    }
/*  i0 is the index of the nearest color  */
}
```

The preceding technique is appropriate *only for decorative displays* because the actual displayed colors may be quite far from the original colors. In addition the resulting image may have contouring artifacts because too many different original colors were mapped on the same color. Halftoning (see [Pa96], Chap. 21) may be used to remove those artifacts.

9.2.5. X Colormap Odds and Ends   There are many subtle differences in the effects of various colormap related functions we used so far, so it is worth revisiting them. X distinguishes between *read-only* color cells that cannot be modified by any application and *read/write* color cells that can be modified by the allocating application. (They are read-only for other applications.) If we use an existing colormap (as we do throughout Sec. 9.2), the only way of obtaining read/write color cells is by calling XAllocColorCells(), as described in Listing 9.2. (There is another function that provides read/write color planes, but its discussion is beyond our scope.) The function XStoreColors() can be used to write on such cells. The function XAllocColors() can be used to access color cells in a read-only mode. In this way we allow applications to share information about a colormap. Thus if Application *A* uses XAllocColorCells() and XStoreColor() to create an entry with RGB values (200, 180, 20), then Application *B* can find the colormap index (pixel value) to this RGB triplet by calling XAllocColor().

Because of such color cell sharing, freeing color cells is a bit complex. The function FreeColors() frees an array of color cells only if it is called by the same application that called XAllocColorCells() to obtain that array. Otherwise cells are actually freed only if the calling application is the only one running that called XAllocColors(). The prototype for this function is:

```
void FreeColors(Display  *  Dpy, Colormap cmap, unsigned
long pixels[], int npixels, unsigned long planes)
```

The last argument is 0 unless we want to free whole planes.

Caution

When a color description is loaded in the video lookup table (hardware color-map), it stays there even after the application exits or color cells are free. X does not clean up entries in the hardware table. This may cause a discrepancy between screen appearance and information obtained by querying a colormap.

9.3.   VISUALS

How we deal with color depends a lot on the capability of the device. If a device has 24 bits per pixel, life is much easier than with a device with 8 bits per pixel. Also not all displays have writable video lookup tables, so if we plan to create a new colormap, we must first determine whether the server supports colormaps. This information is contained in a structure of type Visual. A pointer to a visual is also needed by certain Xlib routines, so we need to know about them even if we do not plan to create a new colormap.

The server has a default visual that is returned by the macro Default-Visual(), as shown in the following code fragment:

```
Display  *Dpy;
Visual   *visual;
/*  ...  */
visual = DefaultVisual( Dpy, DefaultScreen(Dpy) )
```

Applications using Xt can find the visual used through the following code:

```
Visual  *visual;
Widget  w;
/*  ...  */
XtVaGetValues(w, XtNvisual, &visual, NULL);
```

The visual so obtained can be passed to the functions that need it without further analysis.

Attention

If you are writing an application to run only on platforms that are certain to have a programmable colormap and in addition you are not interested in adjusting the program to take full advantage of the display device, then you can skip the rest of this section.

If you are creating a new colormap *and* you are concerned about *porting* the application to different platforms, then you need to know more about visuals. They tell you whether the platform supports the kind of colormap you want to create. However before checking the visuals, we must first check whether there is enough depth in the display. The following macro returns the number of bits per pixel in the refresh memory:

```
DefaultDepth(Display *Dpy)
```

If there are not enough bits per pixel to support the number of colors desired, we must drastically change display strategy. This typically means creating new images using halftoning (see [Pa96], Chap. 21, for a discussion of the process) and starting over again. If there are enough bits, then we must deal with visuals.

We cannot look directly at members of the Visual structure because it is opaque. Instead we look into the information structure XVisualInfo obtained by using the function XGetVisualInfo(). The first member of this structure is a pointer to a Visual structure; the rest include the number of colormap entries, the number of bits per colormap index (which should be the same as the number returned by DefaultDepth), and most important a class member referring directly to the capacity and programmability of the video lookup table. The six possible classes are referred to by symbolic names DirectColor, Pseudo-Color, GrayScale, TrueColor, StaticColor, and StaticGray. The first three imply a programmable video lookup table, the other three a fixed table. The names are not particularly informative; this is a place where the practice of using long descriptive names in X would have helped. Table 9.1 gives an explanation for the names.

The classes DirectColor and TrueColor imply that refresh memory can accommodate three *separate* indices for the red, green, and blue colors and of course three Digital-to-Analog (D/A) converters so that the full range of colors supported by the device can be displayed at the same time. TrueColor is usually found in color displays with 24 bits per pixels, where there is no real need for a programmable colormap. DirectColor is found in color displays with 16 bits per pixel. There we may use 5 bits per color and the colormap to decide the mapping of 8-bit image colors to the 5 bits of the display.

Classes PseudoColor and StaticColor imply that there is only one index for the colormap but three D/A converters. We can show color pictures on such a device but with a limited range of colors. (These classes are often found in color displays with 8 bits per pixel.)

The classes GrayScale and StaticGray imply that there is only one D/A converter and shades of only one color are shown. (It need not be actually gray—the color seen depends on the phosphorus of the display!)

Clearly there is a hierarchy among the three types of devices: If a device can support PseudoColor, it can also support GrayScale by setting values of the three basic colors equal to each other. Similarly if a device can support DirectColor, it can also support PseudoColor by setting the three color indices equal to each other.

Table 9.1.   Visual Types

D/A Converters	Typical Bits per Pixel	Programmable Video Lookup	Fixed Video Lookup
3	16 or 24	DirectColor	TrueColor
3	8	PseudoColor	StaticColor
1	8	GrayScale	StaticGray

Caution

Information provided by visuals is often not reliable, since (1) even if the
device supports a certain functionality, the server implementer may not have
provided proper visual support and (2) the visual may reflect what the
hardware *can do* rather than what it *actually does*.

A typical case of the second situation occurs when a color monitor on a
particular device is replaced by a monochrome monitor. This is easy to do; We need
connect it only to the output of the green D/A converter. There is no way of
ensuring that the server is aware of such an external wiring change, so interrogating
the visual structure provides the answer that the display supports color whereas in
reality it does not.

Suppose now that an application has two sets of label colors: One with real
color and the other with shades of gray. If the visual says there is no support for
color, the program selects the second set of labels. However if the visual says there
is color support, the program should also check a user-provided flag or
environmental variable before selecting the real color label set.

The simplest way of checking the visual structure is by using the function
XMatchVisualInfo() (instead of XGetVisualInfo()). Its use is
illustrated by the code in Listing 9.3 for the case when we want to determine if
it is possible to load a colormap for an 8-bit-per-pixel display.

Listing 9.3. Visual Checking

```
static Display *Dpy;
/*  ...  */
    Visual *v = find_visual(8, PseudoColor);
/*  ...  */
Visual *find_visual(int desired_depth, int desired_type)
{
    XVisualInfo vtemp;
    if( XMatchVisualInfo(Dpy, DefaultScreen(Dpy),
        desired_depth, desired_type, &vtemp) )
        return vtemp.visual;
    else return (Visual *)0;
}
```

9.4.   CREATING AND USING NEW COLORMAPS

Creating a new colormap is the simplest way of using color, but it is an antisocial act for other applications, as explained in Sec. 9.1. Therefore new colormaps should be created only when there is no other way of running an application.

The Xlib function that creates new colormaps has the following prototype:

```
Colormap XCreateColormap( Display *Dpy, Window win,
    Visual *visual, int allocation_policy)
```

The first and third arguments are self-explanatory. For window we may pass the root window—it need not be an application window, since it is used only to provide information about the display screen. The fourth argument specifies the color cell allocation policy. The symbolic value `AllocAll` specifies that all colormap entries are read/write; thus they are under the complete control of the application. The other possible value, `AllocNone`, allows colormap entries to be used as read-only by other applications, so it is the more sociable solution. (Clearly this is the case with the default colormap.) However if we create a colormap because we have an image with many colors, we are justified in being greedy. The following code is safe in most cases:

```
Display *Dpy;
Colormap cmap = XCreateColormap( Dpy,
                    DefaultRootWindow(Dpy),
                    DefaultVisual(Dpy, DefaultScreen
                    (Dpy)), AllocAll);
```

The call to `XCreateColormap()` initializes only a data structure, and neither assigns values to colormap entries nor loads it in the video lookup table. All such operations come later: Values are added by the `XAllocColors()` or `XStoreColors()` functions.

After creating a new colormap we must tell the window manager so that whenever the pointer is in the application window, the colormap is automatically loaded into the video lookup table. This is achieved with the code:

```
Widget toplevel;
Colormap cmap;
XtVaSetValues(toplevel, XtNcolormap, cmap, NULL);
```

While it is theoretically possible to have different colormaps in different application windows, some window managers cannot handle the situation.

Listing 9.4. Storing Colors—File `setRGB.c`

```
static Display *Dpy;
#define CMAP_SIZE 256
int set_RGB_colors(Colormap new_cmap, Colormap old_cmap,
    pPixel red[], pPixel green[], pPixel blue[], int n)
{
    int i, j, skip_cells;
    XColor ccell[CMAP_SIZE];
    if(new_cmap == NULL || n>=CMAP_SIZE) return -1;
    if(old_cmap != NULL) {
        skip_cells = CMAP_SIZE -n;
        if(skip_cells>0){  /* Copy some color cells from
                               old colormap */
            for(i=0; i<skip_cells; i++) {
                ccell[i].pixel = i;
                ccell[i].flags = DoRed | DoGreen | DoBlue:
            }
            /* Find the RGB values of these cells in the old
            colormap */
            XQueryColors(Dpy, old_cmap, ccell, skip_cells);
            /* Write the found RGB values in the new
            colormap */
            XStoreColors(Dpy, new_cmap, ccell, skip_cells);
        }
        else { /* no space in colormap, error */ }
    }
    else skip_cells = 0;
    /* Create array of color cells for additional
    colors starting at index (pixel value) skip_cells */
        for(j=0, i=skip_cells; j<n; i++, j++) {
            ccell[j].pixel = i;
            ccell[j].red = red[j]<<8;
            ccell[j].green = green[j]<<8;
            ccell[j].blue = blue[j]<<8;
            ccell[j].flags = DoRed | DoGreen | DoBlue;
        }
    /* Add new color cells in new colormap */
    XStoreColors(Dpy, cmap, ccell, n);
    return skip_cells; /* same as ccell[0].pixel */
}
```

Therefore a new map should be assigned to a *Shell* widget, normally the top widget of an application or a pop-up shell.

Listing 9.4 shows the code that fills the cells of a new colormap. First it tries to be sociable by copying colors from the common colormap, then it uses code similar to that in Listing 9.2.

The code can be modified so that not all available spaces (besides the n given) are filled from the old colormap. On the other hand if n equals CMAP_SIZE, we may have to take drastic measures. In such case the values 0 and 1 are likely to correspond to black and a very dark color. Since in most displays 0 and 1 are used for white and black (or vice versa), loading such a colormap makes most other applications disappear. We can choose to assign 0 (or 1) to white, but then we must modify the image so that pixels with that value are mapped into a neighboring one.

The name of the function in Listing 9.4, set_RGB_colors(), emphasizes that it ensures that such colors will be in the colormap; the function fit_RGB_colors() in Listing 9.2 tries only to place them.

9.5.   IMAGE STRUCTURES

9.5.1.   XImage Structure   Raster images (or simply images) are usually read from a file in one of the many common formats (plain raster file, GIF, etc). A description of image file formats is beyond our scope (see [MvR96] for detailed coverage). We assume that the image has been read and converted into a pixel array, so it is ready for display. Each image is also associated with a (logical) colormap that establishes correspondence between pixel bit patterns and colors. The color-map can be *explicit* (arrays of RGB values) or *implicit* (rules to connect pixel bit patterns and colors).

Before the image is actually displayed, we must (1) add the color correspondence (possibly modified) of the image colormap to the server color-map and (2) create the appropriate X structure for image display. We dealt with the first step in the first four sections of this chapter; here we focus on the second step. X provides two options for image storage: Keep the image on the server side in the form of a pixmap or keep the image on the client side in an XImage structure. Xlib has several functions for manipulating XImages, including copying them onto a (server) drawable. The choice between the two is a time–space trade-off. If we keep the image on the client, we must copy it to the server each time the window that displays it has to be redrawn in response to expose events. This copying generates substantial traffic between client and server. If we keep the image on the server, we avoid the traffic but double server memory requirements by keeping in effect a backup copy of all windows that display images.

There is an additional complication. Quite often the image read from a file must be modified before it can be displayed because of server limitations (refresh memory and/or colormap). As mentioned in the discussion of colormaps, we can drop the least significant bit in an 8-bit gray scale image, or we can perform a halftoning operation to display a 24-bit full-color image using an 8-bit refresh memory. In such cases we may have to keep a copy of the original image. Consider for example an image-editing program where the user selects a subimage from a display. What is usually needed is not a subimage of what is displayed, but the corresponding subimage of the original.

In all cases the first step is to create an XImage structure before doing anything else. This is the point where an approximation must be performed; part of the structure follows:

```
typedef struct _XImage {
    int width, height;       /*  size of image  */
    /*  ...  */
    int format;              /*  XYBitmap, XYPixmap,
                             ZPixmap  */
    char *data;              /*  pointer to image data  */
    int byte_order;          /*  data byte order, LSBFirst,
                             MSBFirst  */
    int bitmap_bit_order;    /*  bit order within bytes  */
    /*  ...  */
    int depth;               /*  depth of image  */
    /*  ...  */
} XImage;
```

The member data contain values to be copied to a drawable. The significance of many of the other members is obvious, but a few require special attention: format, which can assume the three symbolic values listed, specifies the connection between bits and pixel. In a ZPixmap each byte (or more) of the data array corresponds to a pixel; in the other two forms, there is more than 1 pixel per byte. Since we do not give full coverage of all details of Xlib, we focus on two common special cases: a ZPixmap with 1 byte per pixel and a XYBitmap where 8 pixels are packed in 1 byte. In both cases pixels are stored in scan line order in a byte array. Various Xlib functions manipulate members of XImage, so we never have to deal with them directly.

Note: Most image files also contain the appropriate colormap and this should be examined before attempting to create the XImage structure.

9.5.2. Creating XImages from Full-Depth Raster Images We assume here an 8-bit-per-pixel display, an image that is also 8 bits per pixel, that we already created appropriate colormap entries, and we know the values of the following variables:

```
char   *img_pstart      Start of pixel array
int    img_width        Image width
int    img_height       Image height
```

if color cells are contiguous:

```
int   img_pixel_offset      First colormap location
                            where pixel color is stored
```

If we do not use contiguous colormap entries, we assume we have already modified pixel values as described in Sec. 9.2.4. The value of img_pixel_offset can be obtained as the return of a function, such as set_RGB_colors() (Listing 9.4) or fit_RGB_colors() (Listing 9.2). Then the XImage can be created by the code in Listing 9.5.

The function XCreateImage() takes 10 arguments, the first two of which are self-explanatory. The next three arguments describe the arrangement of input data. The third argument is the number of bits per pixel (8 in this case). The fourth argument (ZPixmap) is discussed in Sec. 9.5.1. The fifth argument is an offset value that indicates how many pixels to ignore in the beginning of the data array; this value is usually 0.

The sixth argument must always be an array of bytes containing data. This array is *not copied*, so it should never be freed until we are ready to free the XImage. The function XCreateImage() stores only a pointer to it. The seventh (img_width) and eighth (img_height) arguments are self-explanatory.

The ninth argument is an integer that must be an integer submultiple of the scan line length: Only values 8, 16, and 32 are acceptable. If the actual scan line

Listing 9.5. Creating an XImage

```
Display *Dpy;
Visual *visual;
XImage *xi;
xi = XCreateImage(Dpy, visual,
    8, /*  bits per pixel  */
    ZPixmap,
    0, /*  bit/byte arrangement  */
    img_pstart, img_width, img_height,
    8, /*  scanline length is multiple of 8  */
    0  /*  bytes to skip at the end of a scanline  */
    );
/*  if contiguous color cells are used  */
XAddPixel(xi, (long)img_pixel_offset);
```

length is not a multiple of these numbers, data must be added to make the length such a multiple. The last argument has the value 0, indicating contiguous scan lines.

The last statement adds to all the pixels the pixel offset determined while assigning values to the colormap. As we saw earlier in this chapter, RGB values of 0 are not stored at the 0th position of the colormap but at the first free position. Therefore a 0 value of the image must be replaced by a value equal to the pixel offset. Because color cells are contiguous, the same offset must be added to all pixels. If we did not use contiguous color cells, pixel values should have been replaced already by the method in Sec. 9.2.4.

An XImage (or part of it) can be copied into a pixmap or displayed in a window with the function XPutImage() that has the following prototype:

```
void XPutImage(Display *Dpy, Drawable px, GC gc, XImage
    *xi, int x_src, int y_src, int x_dest, int y_dest,
    int width, int height)
```

This function copies only part of an image unless both x_src and y_src are zero and width and height equal the image dimensions.

Two functions can be used to copy from a drawable into an XImage: XGetImage() copies a new XImage and XGetSubImage() copies a preexisting XImage. Both return a pointer to an XImage. These functions perform the equivalent of a screen dump. Also they can ignore values in some refresh memory planes. The function XSubImage() is quite different from those two: It creates a new XImage from an existing one without looking at a drawable. It has the following prototype:

```
XImage *XSubImage(XImage *xi, int x, int y,
    int width, int height)
```

where x and y are coordinates of the top-left corner of the new image with respect to the old one, while width and height refer to the new image. Because data in an XImage may be quite different than data in an image file (see Sec. 9.5.1), this function is not as useful as it seems.

To save the image in the server, we must store it on a pixmap (created using methods in Secs. 8.1.2 and 8.2.2) by using the XPutImage() function with the pixmap as drawable. In this case we must free the XImage structure by calling:

```
XFree((caddr_t)xi);
```

To display the image, we must use the XCopyArea() function discussed in Sec. 8.1.

9.5.3. Creating XImages from 1-Bit-per-Pixel Images

One-bit-per-pixel images are usually stored as character sequences, as described in Sec. 8.3.1. In this case an `XImage` may be created with the code:

```
Display *Dpy;
Visual *visual;
XImage *xi;
unsigned char *bitmap_data;
int width, height;
xi = XCreateImage(Dpy, visual, 1, XYBitmap, 0,
    bitmap_data, width, height, 8, 0);
```

The array `bitmap_data` can be read from a file or included in the program code. The flag `XYBitmap` specifies that data are in 1-bit per-pixel format. The resulting `XImage` can be displayed with the `XPutImage()` function without changing the process described in Sec. 9.5.2. The function checks the format of the structure, then displays pixels correctly, provided that the order of bits and bytes is the same in system that created the image as in the system that displays the image. We do that by comparing the values of `xi->bitmap_bit_order` and `xi->byte_order` with the values returned by the macros `BitmapBitOrder(Dpy)` and `ImageByteOrder(Dpy)` respectively.

Usually when the data are in bit-per-pixel form we may bypass the `XImage` structure and create a pixmap *directly* from the bitmap by using the function `XCreatePixmapFromBitmapData()`. In this case we must select explicitly the two colors to be used. (The `XImage` solution relies on the colormap for that.) The following is a typical call:

```
int Scr = DefaultScreen(Dpy);
Pixmap pxm = XCreatePixmapFromBitmapData(Dpy,
    DefaultRootWindow(Dpy),
    bitmap_start, width, height,
    BlackPixel(Dpy, Scr), /* pixels with value 1 */
    WhitePixel(Dpy, Scr), /* pixels with value 0 */
    DefaultDepth(Dpy, Scr) );
```

Note: Motif widgets store icons for labeling menu buttons as pixmaps, while OLIT widgets store them as `XImages`.

9.6. OVERLAYS

9.6.1.   General Considerations   The term *overlay* refers to the display of two (or more) independently drawn images. For example in a video game, one image is the background, and another image is the set of moving characters. In this discussion we use the term basic display for a background image and overlay for the rest.

There are two ways of creating overlays in X. The first is based on the general technique, where some color planes are reserved for the basic display and some for the overlay. The second is based on a special facility of X, which allows the use of a pixmap rather than a fixed color for the color used in drawing; strictly speaking this technique only simulates an overlay.

The first technique reduces the number of available colors: If we use b bits for the background and v bits for the overlay, we have a total of $2^b + 2^v$ colors rather than 2^{b+v} colors.

The second technique has no effect on how many colors are available for the display, but it requires an extra copy of the background pixmap for each color. The amount of server memory used can be reduced if we create the pixmap for each overlay color dynamically; this amounts to a time versus space trade-off.

If we have a display with large depth compared to the depth of the background image and the overlays, allocating planes may be the preferred method because writing application programs is much simpler in this case (after the initial allocation). Dynamically updated pixmaps may be the preferred solution for displays with small depth. In such a case we trade some server memory and programming complexity for a larger number of colors. We discuss each technique in the next two sections.

9.6.2.   Allocating Planes   According to the graphics hardware description in Sec. 1.4.1 when writing in refresh memory, we can specify how new information is stored. For example new information can replace old information (copy mode) or the two can be combined by using a bitwise logical operation, such as exclusive OR (XOR). It is possible to refine the writing operation even further by specifying the bits in each pixel that are affected. For example we can change only the third and fourth bits of each pixel (in copy, XOR, or whatever mode is enabled). Section 1.4.1 introduces the term plane to refer to corresponding bits of pixels, so we can say that we are writing on the third and fourth plane if we change only the third and fourth bits of each pixel.

X allows us to select planes through the graphics context and the function XSetPlaneMask(). The following code selects the three planes corresponding to the most significant bits:

```
#define HIGH_BITS 0340
XSetPlaneMask(Dpy, gc, HIGH_BITS);
```

The value 0340 masks the 5 lower bits. To draw on the five least significant bits, we use

```
#define LOW_BITS 037
XSetPlaneMask(Dpy, gc, LOW_BITS);
```

Such selective writing is useful for overlays. For example in a video game, we may use the five least significant bits for the background image and the three most significant bits for moving objects. When an object is redrawn to another postition, we do not have to worry about restoring what was behind it in the previous position. Selecting planes is simple enough, but there is a complication: The video lookup table looks at all bits to determine color., so we must define a colormap that contains multiple color definitions. Suppose for example that the bit pattern 10001 corresponds to red color in the background. This should appear whenever there is no other object in front, so that we can assign pixel value 00010001 to red. (We do not worry for the moment about how to convince X to do that.) Let red now be represented by 001 in the overlay. Red must show on the screen *no matter what is in the background*; therefore all bit patterns 001xxxxx must correspond to red. This is where we waste colormap space (as mentioned in Sec. 9.6.1): We must use 32 values for red rather than just one value.

The colormap specification takes the following form:

```
000    xxxxx    xxxxx determines color (32 values)
001    xxxxx    001 determines color, same for all xxxxx
010    xxxxx    010 determines color, same for all xxxxx
 ⋮
111    xxxxx    111 determines color, same for all xxxxx
```

In this example the 3-bit overlay allows seven colors (rather than eight) because the 000 value is used to let the lower 5 bits specify the color. The colormap contains seven groups of 32 values, all mapped to a single color, and 32 additional values, each corresponding to a distinct color.

Such a colormap specification can be straightforward if we create a new colormap for an application, but it is not so if we are using a colormap shared with other applications. We must convince the X server to allocate the proper color cells by calling XAllocColorCells() with carefully selected arguments. We provide the code for the preceding example with one modification: We request only 4 bits for the background to allow for the possibility that some colormap entries are used by other applications. We still assume that the total of background colors and other application colors is no more than 32. We start with the call:

```
XAllocColorCells(Dpy, cmap, True, plane_masks, 0, pixels,
    16);
```

This is similar to the call of the same function in Listing 9.2. The next call is more interesting; we use symbolic constants for generality:

```
#define BACK_VALUES        32
#define BACK_VALUES_LOG     5
#define HIGH_VALUES         7
XAllocColorCells(Dpy, cmap, True, plane_masks,
    BACK_VALUES_LOG, pixels, HIGH_VALUES);
```

We ask for seven color cells *and* five planes. Strictly speaking *we do not obtain the whole planes, only values connected with returned color cells.* If we print plane masks values in octal (after the function returns), we see the following numbers:

001   002   004   010   020

If we print the pixel values in octal, we see the following numbers:

040   100   140   200   240   300   340

This means that we have color cells 040–077, 100–137, etc. However color cell 020 is not available, since the plane 020 is ours only in combination with returned pixel values.

Next we must assign color values to colormap entries. The part for the background image is straightforward, but for the sake of presenting a complete example, assume we want to display a 4-bit gray image. The following code does the job:

```
XColor ccell[256];
for(n=0; n<16; n++) {
    ccell[n].pixel = pixels[n];
    ccell[n].red   = n<<12;
    ccell[n].green = n<<12;
    ccell[n].blue  = n<<12;
}
```

We shift by 12 bits rather than 8 because our image data are only 4 bits deep. The image offset is `pixels[0]`.

The color assignment for the overlay is a bit more complex. Let `overlay_color[]` be an array of `Xcolor` type that has RGB values filled by, for example XParseColor(). We must fill not only the seven values, but also those that correspond to various combinations of the lower five bits. We create a mask array as follows:

```
unsigned char mask[BACK_VALUES];
for(i=0; i<BACK_VALUES; i++) mask[i] = i;
```

Then the color assignment code is

```
/*  start from the previous value of n  */
for(j=0; j<HIGH_VALUES; j++) {
    for(i=0; i<BACK_VALUES; i++, n++) {
        ccell[n].pixel = pixels[j] | mask[i];
        ccell[n].red   = overlay_color[j].red;
        ccell[n].green = overlay_color[j].green;
        ccell[n].blue  = overlay_color[j].blue;
    }
}
```

We can then store colors in the colormap by using the statement:

```
XStoreColors(Dpy, cmap, ccell, n);
```

While the overall code is rather short, it must be carefully written.

Once we have completed this arrangement, the rest of the program is rather simple. We select the planes to write by calls to XSetPlaneMask() and colors by calls to XSetForeground(). For example to draw in the color corresponding to overlay_color[3], we must set the foreground by the call:

```
XSetForeground(Dpy, gc, pixels[3]);
```

9.6.3. Simulating Overlays with Tiling Pixmaps We can simulate overlays using the fact that in X, the foreground need not be a fixed color; it can be a pixmap or a bit map. In such a case the color given to a pixel depends on its location. We already saw how to use pixmaps (Tiles) and bit maps (Stipples) to fill regions (Sec. 8.2.1). The function XSetFillStyle() selects not only how pixels are colored during filling, but also how they are colored during drawing. In particular pixels normally given the foreground color are now assigned a value from the stipple or tile pattern. As a result drawing with an exclusive OR operation on the filled area produces images whose color corresponds to the 0 value, usually white. Let pxm be a pixmap with a copy of the background display. The following code lets us draw a white line on top of the pixmap:

```
Display  *Dpy;
Window   w;
GC       gc;
Pixmap   pxm;
/* display pixmap */
   XCopyArea(Dpy, pxm, w, gc, 0, 0, width, height, 0, 0);
/* set drawing style and mode */
   XSetFillStyle(Dpy, gc, FillTiled);
   XSetFunction(Dpy, gc, GXxor);
/* make the pixmap itself the foreground*/
   XSetTile(Dpy, gc, pxm);
/* Draw a white line diagonally across the window*/
   XDrawLine(Dpy, w, gc, 0, 0, width, height);
```

To draw in a different color, we must pass a pixmap to the XSetTile() function that is the result of an exclusive OR between the original pixmap and the pixel value for the color. The following code fragment shows how to construct such a pixmap:

```
static Display  *Dpy;
static Window   w;
static GC       gc;
static Pixmap   pxm;
void use_color(char *s)
{
    XSetFunction(Dpy, gc, GXxor);
    /* erase old color */
    XFillRectangle(Dpy, pxm, gc, 0, 0, width, height);
    /* select new color */
    XSetForeground(Dpy, gc, add_named_color(s));
    /* give a new value to the pixmap */
    XFillRectangle(Dpy, pxm, gc, 0, 0, width, height);
}
```

There is no need to call XSetTile() again. We changed only the values of the pixmap, not the pixmap XID.

When using this method, we must be sure to have the background image cover the entire window because X assumes that the image is repeated over the entire window (hence the term tiling). Drawing in the tiling mode on empty areas results in incorrect displays. (Of course we could write code to look for the background image boundaries, then change mode when drawing outside.) Such problems do not arise when using separate planes for the overlay, as described in Sec. 9.6.2.

Things become more complex when overlay images are multicolor, for example an icon drawn on a rectangle of a different color. In this case we divide drawing and erasing operations into two parts.

1. To draw a filled rectangle, use `FillTiled`, `GXxor`, and XOR the pixmap with the rectangle color, then call `XFillRectangle()`.
2. To draw the icon, use `FillSolid`, `GXcopy`, set the foreground to the icon color, set the background to the rectangle color, then draw the icon bit map using `XCopyPlane()`.
3. To erase the icon on the rectangle, use `FillSolid`, `GXcopy`, set the foreground to the rectangle color, then call `XFillRectangle()`.
4. To erase the rectangle, use the same code as in Step 1.

The order of operation is important. The following code implements drawing an overlay that is an icon with a red figure on a yellow background with left corner at x, y:

```
static Display  *Dpy;
static Window    w;
static GC        gc;
static Pixmap    pxm;
static Pixmap icon_pixels;
/*  DRAW  */
/*  Draw a filled rectangle using the tiling mode  */
   XSetTile(Dpy, gc, pxm);
   XSetFunction(Dpy, gc, GXxor);
   use_color("yellow");
   XFillRectangle(Dpy, w, c, x, y, icon_width,
       icon_height);
/*  Draw using ordinary mode  */
   XSetFillStyle(Dpy, gc, FillSolid);
   XSetFunction(Dpy, gc, GXcopy);
   XSetForeground( Dpy, gc, add_named_color("red") );
   XSetBackground( Dpy, gc, add_named_color("yellow") );
   XCopyPlane(Dpy, icon_pixels, w, gc, 0, 0,
       icon_width, icon_height, x, y, 1);
```

The following code can be used for erasing:

```
/*  ERASE  */
/*  replace the icon by a solid rectangle  */
   XSetFillStyle(Dpy, gc, FillSolid);
```

```
    XSetFunction(Dpy, gc, GXcopy);
    XSetForeground( Dpy, gc, add_named_color("yellow") );
    XFillRectangle(Dpy, w, c, x, y, icon_width,
        icon_height);
/*  Draw a filled rectangle using the tiling mode, removing
it in effect   */
    XSetTile(Dpy, gc, pxm);
    XSetFunction(Dpy, gc, GXxor);
    use_color("yellow");
    XFillRectangle(Dpy, w, c, x, y, icon_width,
        icon_height);
```

Note: The first block of drawing code is the same as the second block in the erasing code. We use the exclusive OR tiling operation only for a solid overlay. Once the solid overlay is created, we can draw more complex images on it.

We can use many more colors than in regular overlays. If we use n colors for the background and other applications, we have $256 - n$ colors available for the overlay versus $\log_2 \lfloor 256 - n \rfloor$ according to Sec. 9.6.2. We pay a price by having to keep a copy of the window and the time needed to redraw the pixmap whenever we call the use_color() function. We may save some time at the expense of programming complexity by not changing the whole pixmap but only the part relevant to drawing. In that case the pixmap should be restored to its original value after each operation.

9.7   CONCLUSIONS

We discuss the Xlib facilities for creating and using colormaps and for displaying raster images, including the XImage structure. Full-color or gray-scale images are large consumers of memory, and these usually demand their own color-maps. Displaying full pictures in color (as opposed to using a gray scale) on 8-bit displays is a challenge, but it can be done with color halftoning.

Handling colormaps with the X Window System is more complicated than with many earlier graphics systems because X tries to preserve the proper appearance for all windows in a display, so it imposes various restrictions on using colormaps. This approach is reasonable for GUIs, but it creates complications for graphics- and image-processing applications where user attention may be focused only on one or two windows. The simple design of the X server causes additional difficulties. If a display with 24 or more bits per pixel is available, displaying full pictures in color at the same time as other applications presents no problem.

9.8. PROJECTS

1. Write a program to list *all* visuals supported by a display device. Use the function XGetVisualInfo().
2. Create a filled rectangle whose color varies smoothly along the horizontal axis from pure red to pure green.
3. Modify the code in Listing 9.2 to let the application create a new color-map if there is no space for image colors in the existing colormap. In particular when an address for a new map is given, create a new one by a call such as:

```
*newmap = XCreateColormap( ... );
```

   Then call the function set_RGB_colors() with arguments the new map, the old map, and the color arrays given.
4. Write a program that uses three overlays, each of 1 bit.

10

<hr>
<hr>
<hr>

Selections

10.1. INTERCLIENT COMMUNICATION

10.1.1. Introduction Communication between different application programs is desirable in many circumstances. Transferring a block of text from one text editor to another is one of the most obvious cases where communication between two running programs is useful. The cut-and-paste or drag-and-drop operations used in most desktop environments involve communication between applications.

There are many ways of transferring data between programs. One-way pipes where one application's output is another application's input are used extensively in Unix, and these are easily set up by the user. For example, the following command lists the five largest files of a directory sorted in order of size:

```
ls -1 | sort -nr +3 | head -5
```

Two-way pipes (see Sec. 4.3.3) are more useful, but these are more difficult to set up. In contrast to one-way pipes, the two-way pipe mechanism must be written explicitly in a program.

Because all X programs communicate with the server with a mechanism roughly equivalent to a two-way pipe, we can take advantage of that situation to allow communication between any two applications by using the server as an intermediary. So far we saw two methods of interclient communication: Window properties and client messages.

The spy program in Sec. 2.5 obtains information about other programs by looking at their window properties. For example, the WM_CLASS property provides the name of the application running in the window, and the WM_CLIENT-MACHINE provides the name of the machine on which the client is running. Clearly an application must plan in advance to assign a property to one of its windows that contains information to be made available to other programs.

The client message mechanism described in Sec. 2.4.2 is more general. We dealt with the case when the window manager sends a message to an application asking it to exit, but there is no theoretical limit on either the type of message or the sender. For practical reasons such messages have to be relatively short. An application composes an event, then places it in the event queue of the intended recipient. If the receiving application contains code that looks for client messages, it will eventually look at that event.

Both of these mechanisms require advanced planning, we also need another method that lets desktop users transfer data between any two programs whenever such a transfer makes sense. The X Window System provides such a mechanism, called *selection*. The user identifies data to be transferred in one application, then points to the application where the data must go. (Similar mechanisms are provided by most modern desktop systems.) There is not data transfer when a selection is made. The first application simply informs the server that it owns the selection data. When the user points to the second application, it requests data from the server; the server passes the request to the first application. Therefore *the first application must still be running.*

There is another mechanism, called clipboard selection, that makes it possible to transfer data even after the first application exits. In essence the clipboard is a process whose main purpose is to take the selection from the original owner and keep it for future requests. Rather than move data from Application *A* to Application *B* directly, we move data from *A* to the clipboard, and later from the clipboard to *B*. (Most other window systems support only clipboard selections.)

The ICCCM (Sec. 1.1.3) specifies how X programs should communicate with each other, and all X applications are supposed to follow it. The Xt provides a few high-level functions that implement these specifications; therefore application programmers do not have to refer to the ICCCM.

There are many variations in the user interface of selection. For example double clicking the mouse while the cursor is on a word in a text editor renders the characters of that word the selection data. Clicking the left button in one line and the right button in another results in the selection of a block of text. Visual feedback is provided by displaying the selected text in reverse video.

The common drag-and-drop mechanism is a user interface for identifying the recipient of data. Obviously selection data does *not* actually follow the cursor. When the mouse button is released over a window, the corresponding application requests selection data from the server.

While text is the most common type of selected data, it is relatively easy to establish a mechanism for data selections of any type, such as integers, pixmaps, etc. We need only agree on a common format for the data between the provider and the receiver of the selection, then implement two data conversion processes, one for each side. The reason that applications with nontext selection are not common is the reluctance of developers to invest effort for a feature that will find limited use rather than an inherent implementation difficulty. A new type of selection is not useful until it is available in more than one application.

10.1.2. Basic Selection Mechanism in X   We explain the basic selection mechanism in X in more detail than in Sec. 10.1.1 by listing the functions called in each step. We use the familiar example of transferring text between two text editing programs, *A* and *B*, each editing a different file. To transfer a block of text from *A* and *B*, follow steps 1–2.

- Step 1: Select the block of text by some means (for example, double clicking in a window of *A* to select a single word). The appropriate callback or event handler of Application *A* responds to that action by providing visual feedback and also calling the function XtOwnSelection(), (which informs the server that Application *A owns the selection.*) Arguments of this call include a pointer to a function that is called whenever the server wants data.

- Step 2: Indicate the intention to transfer data to recipient Application *B* (for example by a single mouse click in the area where data are to be inserted). The appropriate callback or event handler of Application *B* responds to that action by calling the function XtGetSelectionValue(). Once selected, data can be copied by other applications besides *B* by repeating the Step.

Functions XtOwnSelection() and XtGetSelectionValue() (see Sec. 10.2.1) do not perform data transfers—instead they register functions that do the actual work with the Intrinsics. Two pointers to functions, *SelectionToServer*() and *LoseSelection*(), are among the arguments of XtOwnSelection(). One of the arguments of the function XtGetSelectionValue() is a pointer to a callback *SelectionFromServer*(). (Names of the last three functions can be anything; they are provided by the applications.) The data transfer takes place as follows:

1. When XtGetSelectionValue() is called, the Intrinsics call *SelectionToServer*(... , &D, ...) in the application that *owns* the selection. (see Sec. 10.2.2 for a prototype of this function and a detailed discussion of its arguments) D is a place to store the selection data.

2. On return of *SelectionToServer*() the Intrinsics call *SelectionFromServer* (... D, &E ...) in the application that *wants* the selection (see Sec. 10.2.2.) This function copies data from D to E, (the intended location in Application *B*). The Intrinsics know about E because its address is passed through XtGetSelectionValue().

Figure 10.1 shows the process. Server location D is not permanent storage: If application *A* exits, the selection is lost.

The function *LoseSelection*() is called by the Intrinsics when an application requests selection ownership. Since the function was registered by the previous owner, it informs that application that it is no longer the owner. Normally this function removes selection markings (such as highlighting).

The preceeding outline *of the mechanism* needs some clarifications. Strictly speaking the selection owner is not an application but a widget, so we can use selection to transfer data within an application. However within an application, data transfer can be accomplished with a simpler mechanism than selections. This discussion assumes there is only one selection on the server, but we can have more

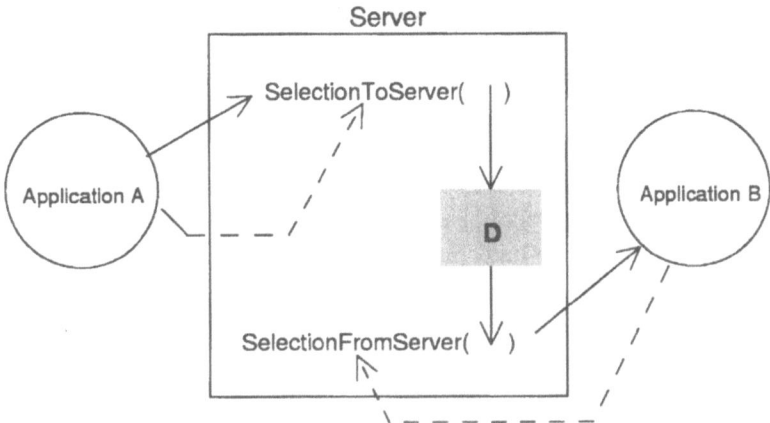

Figure 10.1.   Data flow (*solid lines*) during data transfer as a result of a selection. Dashed lines represent which application registers a function.

because selections must have distinctive names and relevant functions check them. We discuss this point when describing specifications of the X functions involved.

The application receiving a selection need not exist when a selection is made. Selections are commonly used to select a text string representing a file name and then to start an application that needs a file name. The new applications asks the server for the selection, if one exists, it uses the string for a file name. If no selection exists, it may ask the application user to provide the name.

The basic mechanism is the same regardless of the data form: To exchange pixmaps instead of text between applications, nothing changes in the preceeding discussion. Only functions that transfer data from the selection owner to the server and from the server to the selection requester deal with the precise data form.

10.2.   THE GORY DETAILS

10.2.1.   Function Specification   Here we provide prototypes for functions discussed informally in Sec. 10.1.2. First is the function that is called to make an application the owner of a selection:

```
XtOwnSelection ( Widget w, Atom selection_name, Time time,
    Boolean (*SelectionToServer)(),
    void (*LoseSelection) (),
    void (*Done) () );
```

where w is the widget that becomes the selection owner. This function is usually called by the event handler or an action procedure of the widget. The selection_name is an atom corresponding to a name that characterizes the selection; it is used by those requesting the selection. Predefined selection atoms include XA_PRIMARY and XA_SECONDARY. New atoms can be specified by code similar to that used in Sec. 2.4.2, for example:

```
XA_TRIANGLE = XinternAtom(XtdISPLAY (w),
                "TRIANGLE_SELECT", FALSE);
```

A good value for time is

```
XtLastTimestampProcessed(XtDisplay(w)).
```

The three function pointer arguments are registered with the Intrinsics, and *SelectionToServer*() does the important work of delivering, so these selection data, as described in Sec. 10.2.2. (Note: the three function names are variables, so these can be changed.) The role of the function *LoseSelection*() is explained in Sec. 10.1, its prototype is

```
void (*LoseSelection) (Widget w, Atom * selection_name)
```

The function *Done*() is called after the selection is delivered to the requester, its prototype follows:

```
void (*Done) (Widget w, Atom * selection_name, Atom * type)
```

This function can be used to free memory allocated for the data transfer. In both cases w is the selection owner; selection_name is a pointer to the name of the selection, such as XA_PRIMARY, and for the last function, type is the data type of the selection (see the following discussion).

While the first function, *SelectionToServer*(), is essential, the other two are optional, and the corresponding arguments may be NULL, especially for the *Done*() function.

The prototype for the function that requests the selection is

```
void XtGetSelectionValue ( Widget w, Atom selection_name,
    Atom type, void (*SelectionFromServer) (),
    XtPointer client_data, Time time)
```

where w is the widget making the request (it must be realized) and selection_name has the same meaning as in XtOwnSelection(). The type is an atom describing data type, for example as a character string (XA_STRING). The function *SelectionFromServer*() is registered as a callback. It is the one that does the actual work—XtGetSelectionValue() returns immediately. The `client_data` are provided for *SelectionFrom Server* (), `time` can be

```
XtLastTimestampProcessed(XtDisplay(w))).
```

10.2.2. Data Transfer   Here we discuss two functions essential for data transfer. Their names are defined by the application and registered with the Intrinsics as described in Sec. 10.2.1. The function that delivers the selection to the server has the following prototype:

```
Boolean SelectionToServer (Widget w, Atom *selection_name,
    Atom*target_type, Atom *type_r,
    XtPointer *value_r, unsigned long *length_r,
    int *format_r)
```

The first two arguments are self-explanatory. The `target_type` refers to the type of selection data; the remaining four arguments are assigned values that contain the selection and describe it as well. An example of such a function is shown in Listing 10.1. The application is a graphics editor (such as a computer-aided design [CAD] program). We assume two kinds of selection by the user: A block of text that is the primary selection (atom of name XA_PRIMARY) or a triangle that is a selection selection (atom of name XA_TRIANGLE). However information about the triangle is also transmitted in the form of text, so for this reason we need an extra step to convert integers into a string. The `*format_r` value specifies data are interpreted as bytes.

The code assumes that the text of the primary selection is pointed to by the variable `textp` and geometric data are in the array v. (Information is placed there when a selection is made.) The function *SelectionToServer* () is not called until there is a request for the selection.

Note: Even though the function in Listing 10.1 handles both of types of selections, the function `XtOwnSelection`() must be called twice, once for each selection name. For example:

```
XtOwnSelection(w, XA_PRIMARY,
    XtLastTimestampProcessed (Dpy),
    SelectionToServer, LoseSelection, NULL);
XtOwnSelection(w, XA_TRIANGLE,
    XtLastTimestampProcessed (Dpy),
    SelectionToServer, LoseSelection, NULL);
```

Listing 10.1. Example of a Function That Delivers a Selection to the Server—File sel.c

```
static char *textp;      /* Applications stores primary
                            selection there */
static Xpoint v[3];      /* Applications stores three points
                            there */

Boolean SelectionToServer(Widget w, Atom *selection,
        Atom *target,
        Atom *type_r, XtPointer *value_r,
        unsigned long *length_r, int *format_r)
{
    /*   code to be added later - Listing 10.3  */

    if (*target==XA_STRING) {
        *type_r = XA_STRING;
        if (*selection==XA_PRIMARY) {
            *value_r = XtNewString(textp);
            *length_r = strlen(textp);
        }
        else if (*selection==XA_TRIANGLE) {
            static char bf[128];
            sprint(bf, "%d %d %d %d %d %d",
                v[0].x, v[0].y, v[1].x, v[1].y,
                v[2].x, v[2].y);
            *value_r = XtNewString(bf);
            *length_r = strlen(bf);
        }
        else return (FALSE);
        format_r = 8;
        return (TRUE);
    }
    return (FALSE);
}
```

Listing 10.2 describes the function that receives the data; it is registered as callback by XtGetSelectionValue(). The last five arguments of this callback correspond to call data, but for this special case, these are given individually rather than lumped in a single structure. The client data argument holds a function that takes as argument selection data and was specified during the call of XtGetSelectionValue(). Again we must call this function twice, once for each type of selection:

Listing 10.2. Example of a Function That Receives a Selection from the Server—File sel.c

---

```
void SelectionFromServer (Widget w, XtPointer client_data,
        Atom *selection, Atom *type, XtPointer value,
        unsigned long *length, int *format)
{
    void (*use)() = (void (*)())client_data;

    /*  check if reasonable values  */
    if (*type==XA_STRING && *format==8 && value != NULL) {
        if(*selection==XA_PRIMARY) use (w, (char *) value);
        else if(*selection==XA_TRIANGLE)   {
                XPoint V[3];
                sscanf( (char *)value,
                    "%d %d %d %d %d %d",
                    &(V[0].x), &(V[0].y),
                    &(v[1].x), &(V[1].y),
                    &(V[2].x), &(V[2].y));
                use (w, V);
        }
    }
}
```

```
void use_text (Widget w, char *);
void use_triangle (Widget w, Xpoint *);
XtGetSelectionValue( w, XA_PRIMARY, XA_STRING,
    SelectionFromServer, (XtPointer)use_text,
    XtLastTimestampProcessed(XtDisplay(w)) );
XtGetSelectionValue( w, XA_TRIANGLE, XA_STRING,
    SelectionFromServer, (XtPointer)use_triangle,
    XtLastTimestampProcessed(XtDisplay(w)) );
```

Notice the symmetry between the code of functions *SelectionToServer*() and *SelectionFromServer*(). We are implementing a communication protocol. Only one thing is missing: The ICCCM requires a selection delivery function to respond to an inquiry about supported targets. Listing 10.3 does that and replaces the first comment in Listing 10.1.

In this case the reply is that only one type, text string, is supported. The format is set to 32 because atoms have values that are stored in full words. We discuss additional selection types in Sec. 10.3.

Listing 10.3.   Responding to a TARGETS inquiry—File sel.c

```
static Atom targets = 0;

if(targets==0)
    targets = XInternAtom(XtDisplay(w),
        "TARGETS", False);

if(*target==targets) {
    *type_r = XA_ATOM;
    *value_r = (XtPointer) XtNew(Atom);
    *(Atom *) *value_r = XA_STRING;
    *length_r = 1;
    *format_r = 32;
    return (TRUE);
}
```

10.3.   NONTEXT SELECTIONS

10.3.1.   Integers and XIDs   It is not difficult to introduce new types of selections: We define selection name, type, then provide appropriate code in the functions that interact with the server. Of course such a type can be used only between applications that know about it. We must also be more careful with conversions other than strings of text. We start with integer types. In the example in Sec. 10.2.2 we may prefer to send point coordinates directly without the additional work performed by sprintf() and sscanf(). Furthermore we can use an arbitrary polygon rather than a triangle. In this case we give the selection the more appropriate name POLY_SELECT. The needed code is shown in Listing 10.4. In the first function, we allocate memory for an integer array to hold data and pass the array address to the server by the assignment:

```
*vale_r = (XtPointer)v;
```

We can also do things differently by breaking the selection into parts and passing the number of points in the first part, then use the assignment for the second:

```
*value_r = (XtPointer)P;
```

(Similar considerations apply in the opposite direction.) However we must be careful with word length in such cases. Since members of the XPoint structure are shorts, we must declare the variable u as pointing to shorts rather than integers.

Listing 10.4. Integer Conversion—File sel.c

```
/*  Selection Owner Data  */
static Xpoint *P;
static int np;

    /*  code inside SelectionToServer()  */
    if(*selection==POLY_SELECT && *target==XA_INTEGER) {
        register i;
        *type_r =(XA_INTEGER;
        *format_r = 32;
        v = (int *)malloc((2*np+1)*sizeof(int));
        *value_r = (XtPointer)v;
        *v=np;
        for(i=0; i<np; I++) {
            *(v+2*i+1) = P[i].x;
            *(v+2*i+2) = P[i].y;
        }
        *length_r = 2*np+1;
        return (TRUE);
    }
  /* code inside SelectionFromServer()  */
    if(*selection==POLY_SELECT && *type++XA_INTEGER
    && &format==32
    && value !=NULL) {
      int *v;
      v=(int *)value;
      /* *v is the number of points, *(v+2*i+1) and
      *(v+2*i+2) are the x, y coordinates of the ith
      point */
    }
```

Listing 10.5. Pixmap—File sel.c

```
static Pixmap selPx; /* value assigned by user action */
    /* ... */
    /*code inside SelectionToServer() */
    if (*target==XA_PIXMAP {
        /* selection type is checked elsewhere */
        Pixmap *pxp = (Pixmap *)malloc(size of(Pixmap));
        *type_r = XA_PIXMAP;
        *format_r = 32;
        *value_r = (XtPointer)pxp;
```

```
        pxp = selpx}
        *length_r = 1; /* Only one Pixmap */
        return(TRUE);
    }
    /* code inside SelectionFromServer() */
    if*type==XA_PIXMAP && *format==32 && value !=NULL) {
        Pixmap *fpx = (Pixmap *)value;
        /* use the pixmap, for example */
        XSetFunction(Dpy, gc, GXcopy);
        XCopyArea(Dpy, *fpx, win, gc,
        0, 0, wsel, hsel, xt, yt);
    }
```

Another type of selections involve XIDs, the tags sent by the server to the client to identify server resources. As explained in Sec. 1.4.2, these implement the types Window, Pixmap, Colormap, etc. The code in Listing 10.5 shows how to implement pixmap selection. If we must do some photocomposition, we can cut, then paste parts of one picture to another by transferring only the pixmap XID. The atom XA_PIXMAP is predefined.

Variables Dpy, gc, etc., are assumed to be defined elsewhere. The received pixmap is copied in a window whose upper left corner is at xt and yt. It is easy to define these variables in the receiving program except for two: The width (w_sel) and height (h_sel) of the pixmap, which are determined during the selection process. Unless these are constant for all selections, they must become part of the selection as well.

Since it is possible to have a selection with more than one type, we show how to use the feature in that case. Assume the user selects a rectangle from a display pixmap. Then the program creates a new pixmap selPx, which contains the selection; static variables w_sel and h_sel store the dimensions. Then call:

```
XtOwnSelection(w, PIX_SELECT, /*  ...  */);
```

The type PIX_SELECT has been previously defined as

```
Atom PIX_SELECT = XInternAtom(XtDisplay(toplevel),
    "PIX_SELECT", False);
```

Listing 10.6 shows the delivery function.

To initiate a selection transfer, the receiving application must make two requests:

```
XtGetSelectionValue( w, PIX_SELECT, XA_Integer,
        grab_pix, (XtPointer) f,
        XtLastTimestampProcessed(XtDisplay(w)) );
```

Listing 10.6. Providing Pixmap Dimensions—File sel. C.

```
  /* code inside SelectionToServer() */
if(*selection == PIX_SELECT) {
   if(*target==XA_Interger) {
      int *u;
      *type_r = XA_INTEGER;
      *format_r = 32;
      u=(int *)malloc (2*sizeof (int));
      *value_r = (XtPointer)u;
      *u    = w_sell;
      *(u+1) = h_sell;
      *length_r = 2;
      return(TRUE);
   }
   if(*target==XA_PIXMAP) {
      /* ... code from Listing 10.5 ... */
   }
}
```

```
XtGetSelectionValue( w, PIX_SELECT, XA_PIXMAP,
        grab_pix, (XtPointer) f,
        XtLastTimestampProcessed(XtDisplay(w)) );
```

The function grab_pix() is the callback, with code given in Listing 10.7.

Since the callback order is not guaranteed, we store received values in static variables and keep a count. When we receive two selections, then we are ready to use the pixmap. The function use_pixmap() is provided by the application and passed to the callback as client data. Inside that function is code to cast its last argument into a pixmap, for example:

```
Pixmap *fpx = (Pixmap *)img_data;
```

Besides using the full-selection mechanism to copy pixmaps from one application to another, we can also use the window property mechanism as in the spy program in Sec. 2.5. Once a program grabs the pointer, then it can use it to identify a window and copy the window contents (or part of it) on a pixmap of its own (see Project 3).

10.3.2. Image Selections   Using pixmaps for selections is efficient, since we need to transfer only an XID, but it is not enough if we want to use original image data. In that case we must transfer *image pixel* values. Necessary modifications in the pixmap transfer code are:

Listing 10.7. Receiving Pixmap and Its Dimensions—File sel.c

```
void grab_pix(Widget w, XtPointer client_data,
Atom *selection, Atom*type, XtPointer value,
  unsigned long *length, int *format)
{
    static XRectangle rdim;
    static XtPointer img_data;
    static int kount = 0
    void (*use_pixmap)() = (void (*)())client_data;
    if (*selection !=PIX_SELECT) return;

      if(*type==XA_INTEGER && *format==32 && values !=NULL) {
        int *u;
        u = (int *)value;
        rdim.width = *u;
        rdim.height = *(u+1);
        kount++;
      }
      else
      if(*type==XA_PIXMAP && *format==32 && values !=NULL) {
        img_data = value;
        kount++;
      }
      if (kount==2) {
        use_pixmap (w, &rdim, img_data);
        kount = 0;
      }
}
```

```
/*  Establish Selection Name and Data Type - in main () */
XA_IMAGE = XInternAtom(XtDisplay(toplevel), "IMAGE",
  False);
/* ... */
static unsigned char *output_block; /* filled after selection */
    /* inside SelectionToServer() */
    if (*target==XA_IMAGE) {
        *type_r = XA_IMAGE;
        *value_r = (XtPointer)output_block;
        *length_r = w_sel*h_sel;
        *format_r = 8;
        return(TRUE);
    }
```

We need not change anything in the `SelectionFromServer()` function, since in Listing 10.7 we pass the value as an `XtPointer`. The receiving function must have code to do the unpacking:

```
for(y=0; y<r->height; y++) for (x=0; x<r->width; x++) {
    *cp++ = * (v+y*r->width+x);
}
```

where `cp` is a pointer to a pixel array.

For an application to use a selection type it must include all pertinent pieces of code. In practice this often means that the new selection is available only between copies of the same application. In such a case simpler solutions may be available.

If we allow a single application to have more than one image-editing widget, then we can transfer from one widget to another by copying data from an internal array to another internal array. In other words we need one copying operation rather than three. (The third is done by the Intrinsics.) Of course a program with many editing widgets is going to be more complex than a program with just one, so there is a trade-off between the simplicity of the data exchange mechanism and the complexity of the application.

10.3.3. Marking Selections   A common way of marking text selections is by reverse video. We can achieve a similar effect in line drawings by drawing polygons with larger width on top of the original while using the exclusive OR mode. An alternative method uses blinking, as described in Sec. 4.3.2. When a selection is made, we add a time-out process to invoke a function that draws with exclusive OR, successively drawing and erasing the chosen object. The code that follows shows a possible implementation that assumes a (private) object type `Own_Object`. The type is also assumed to have a method `plot` for plotting the object. It also advisable to include the widget ID, say, w, as part of the object. A pointer to the selected object is passed as client data to the time-out:

```
/* Mark a Selection by Flashing   - It assumes an object */
/* structure and a function for plotting it. */
static int has_selection;
    /*  ...  */
#define APP(B)  XtWidgetToApplicationContext(B)
#define T_SPAN 100 /* period of blinking in milliseconds */
static int erased = 0;
void time_out(Own_Object *sp)
{
    sp->plot(sp);
    erased = 1 - erased;
    if(has_selection) XtAppAddTimeOut(APP(sp->w), T_SPAN,
                    time_out, sp);
```

```
    else {
        if (erased) {
            sp->plot(sp);
            erased = 0;
        }
    }
}
mark_selection(Own_Object *S)
{
    if(has_selection) XtAppAddTimeOut(APP(w), T_SPAN,
                        time_out, S);
}
```

This works well if the selection moves from one application to another. In this case the flag has_selection is set to FALSE (0), and the time-out is not reinstalled. A few lines of code ensure that the object is not erased. Unfortunately it does not work if the selection moves within an application because has_selection will still be TRUE. We cannot explicitly remove the time-out because the Intrinsics do not keep proper track of them (see [AS90], pp. 299–300).

The correct solution is *not* to add the time-out for the new selection when it is made but to add the time-out at the next call of the time-out process. We can do this by using the fact that the application must keep a pointer to the selected object to be passed to other applications. (This may be either a static variable or better attached to the widget through the user data mechanism described in Sec.11.3.) Let S denote the pointer and diff() a function that takes as arguments two object pointers and returns TRUE if these are not the same. Then the preceding code can be modified as follows:

```
void time_out(Own_Object *sp)
{
    if(diff(sp, S)) {
        XtAppAddTimeOut (APP(S->w), T_SPAN, time_out, S);
        if(erased) {
            sp->plot (sp);
            erased = 0;
        }
    }
    else {
        /* time_out code from version above */
        sp->plot(sp);
        /* ... etc ... */
    }
}
```

While this method is far more complex than marking the selection with reverse video, it is applicable to any selected objects other than text or lines. If need be, instead of a blinking object, we can have a blinking outline.

10.4.   IMPLEMENTATION ISSUES

10.4.1   User Interface   Most systems accept the convention that the left mouse button (No. 1) is used to select, the middle button (No. 2) to transfer data, and the right button (No. 3) to activate pop-up menus. However, the term select has a broader meaning in this case. In a text editor we use the left button to select the place to insert new text and in a drawing program to color a pixel on the screen. In text editors text is selected (in the narrow sense) as the string between locations of successive clicks of the left and middle buttons. A double click of the left button selects the nearest *word*.

Successive clicks of the left and middle button can be used to select a rectangle of pixels or pixmaps, but there is no natural counterpart to words in the case of images. Things are a bit more complex in the case of polylines, where there is no natural order. The following description is possible for a drawing editor (or CAD programs in general) policy.

When the left button is clicked away from an object, we interpret the action as drawing. If it is clicked near an object, we set a flag and take no action until the next button click. If it is from the middle button, we check whether it is near the same object, then select that object or part of it. If it is again from the left button, we assume the user wishes to draw. Note: Double clicking has a different meaning here than in text editors.

We can also enclose objects (or parts thereof) in rectangles to select them. A complete coverage of this topic is beyond our scope.

Besides making a selection, we also need a means of inserting a selection. A drag-and-drop operation is a possibility, but it has limitation. For example we can select an object, then copy it in many locations—a drag-and-drop operation is quite cumbersome in this case. Another possibility is to apply the following rule: When the user's action indicates drawing (in general creation of an object), if there is a selection, then the selection is copied at that point. The code should invoke `XGetSelectionValue()` and provide a callback to copy the selection.

10.4.2.   Application-Programming Interface   Selections are usually supported by the widget code, but as we showed, they can be supported by an application as well. If an application provides selections, it needs a static storage for data; since there can be only one selection of each type at a time, this is not a problem. We need a library that supports selections by hiding some of the details from the application writer. Suggestions follow:

For text selection the library must provide a function `select_text (w, x, y, s)`, where w is a widget, x and y are coordinates of the top-left character, and s is a null terminated string. Coordinates are needed for the function marking the text. A possible implementation of the function follows:

```
#define  LATEST(A)     XtLastTimestampProcessed(XtDisplay(A))
static  Boolean has_text_selection = FALSE;
Boolean select_text(Widget w, int x, int y, char *s)
{
    if(has_text_selection) XtDisownSelection(w,
                                XA_PRIMARY, LATEST(w));
    /* copy x, y, and s in static storage, */
    /* compute length of s (needed for selection) */
    /* and dimensions of text block (needed for marking) */
    has_text_selection = XtOwnSelection(w, XA_PRIMARY,
        LATEST(w), SelectionToServer, LoseSelection, NULL);
    if (has_text_selection) mark_text_selection(w);
    return has_text_selection;
}
```

where the function `mark_text_selection ()` uses static data to highlight the selection. The highlight is removed by the function *LoseSelection* (). This function is called by the server when the application loses selection ownership, but it is not called when a different selection is made within the application—that is the purpose of calling `XtDisownSelection ()`, which forces the call of *LoseSelection* ().

A function `request_text (w, f)` (where w is a widget) can request the text selection to be passed as an argument to a function f with the prototype `void f (Widget w, char *s)`. A possible implementation follows:

```
void request_text(Widget w, void (*f)() )
{
    XtGetSelectionValue( w, XA_Primary, XA_STRING,
        SelectionFromServer, (XtPointer)f, LATEST (w) );
}
```

Similar pairs of functions, such as `select_polygon(w, P, n)` and `request_polygon(w, f1)` or `select_pixmap(w, rp, px)` and `request_pixmap(w, rp, f2)`, can be used for other selection types. The P may be an array of `XPoints`, rp a pointer to an `XRectangle` structure, and px a pixmap. Possible prototypes for f1 and f2 are

```
void f1(Widget w, Xpoint P[], int n)
void f2(widget w, Xrectangle *rp, Pixmap px)
```

If we adopt this organization, the functions *SelectionToServer* ( ), *SelectionFrom-Server* ( ), and *LoseSelection* ( ) can be declared static, so they are private to the module.

10.4.3.   Drag and Drop   Drag and drop is a user interface for transferring a selection from one application into another. When the user presses the selection button (usually the left button) over an already selected object, the cursor icon is replaced by a set of widgets that provide a visual representation of the selected object. The original icon is restored only when the button is released (the selection is dropped). As the cursor moves over different windows, the icon shape changes to indicate whether the window under the cursor is an acceptable drop site.

Implementing the drag and drop is quite complex, but the complexity is due to the user interface, which involves extensive visual feedback rather than to data transfer.

10.5.   CONCLUSIONS

The selection mechanism allows arbitrary data transfer between applications, provided a protocol for the data type is established. The protocol is implemented by the functions SelectionToServer ( ) and SelectionFromServer ( ), as shown in examples in Sec. 10.2.2, 10.3.1, and 10.3.2. Such applications can call high-level functions like those described in Sec. 10.4.2.

The selection mechanism involves a certain overhead because of the need to move data through the server. In general it should not be used to transfer data *within* an application. Suppose for example an application has different widgets that display images and transfer a set of pixels from Widget A to Widget B. Clearly the pixel array can be copied entirely within the client. Unfortunately the literature contains many examples of inappropriate selection use, including the case where a drag-and-drop mechanism is used to color shapes within an application.

Application designers should give serious considerations to editing multiple pictorial or graphic files within a single application by using different editing widgets for each file. Then data can be transferred between widgets without having to access the server. The price of such integration is a more complex program than a single editor file.

The application in Sec. 7.2.2 it involves such a dilemma. We could choose to use a text editor running separately from the drawing–editing program, then use the selection mechanism to transfer data back and forth. For example we can select a block of text in the text editor, so that when the application user selects a place in the drawing, the function XtGetSelectionValue ( ) is called to copy the selection instead of typing the text in place. To modify the text later, we select it in the drawing editor, then copy the selection to a text editor.

10.6. PROJECTS

1. Implement a selection mechanism for nonrectangular image parts. In particular the user should be able to select an image region by outlining it with a polygon. *Hint:* Two approaches are possible. In one we find the bounding rectangle of the polygon and use as selection data the image rectangle (as in Sec. 10.3.2) and the polygon (as in Sec.10.3.1). When the selection is copied in the requesting application, the entire rectangle is copied by using the polygon as a clip mask. In the other approach the polygon is scan-converted into a set of line segments, and each segment is then mapped into the corresponding pixel array. The selection consists of a sequence of pixel arrays, each with a header giving its position in the image and the number of pixels. The second method requires more complex implementation, but it results in a smaller amount of data in the selection.

2. Implement the program in Sec. 7.2.2 (Listing 7.2) by using the selection mechanism as suggested in Sec. 10.5. Compare the complexity and size of the two programs as well as the ease of use.

3. Modify the spy program in Sec. 2.5, so that instead of listing window properties, it copies its contents to a window of the spy application. This method allows pixmap transfers between applications.

11

Writing Widgets

11.1. INTRODUCTION

Writing a widget involves two major tasks: Creating an object with a particular functionality and making the object conform to Xt specifications. Chapter 11 focuses on the second task, since operations for drawing or event handling are essentially the same whether in a widget or an application.

The obvious question is what do we gain by conforming to Xt widget specifications? Two major gains involve taking advantage of the functionality offered by the resource mechanism and a uniform interface. To illustrate, we use a very simple widget class, a drawing widget, that is a subclass of Core with a few extra resources. If we need a widget to draw on, the Core class itself offers that facility. The program in Listing 11.1 shows part of program for displaying drawings using the Core widget class.

Listing 11.1. Program for Simple Displays

```
#include <X11/StringDefs.h>
#include <X11/Intrinsic.h>
void Scribble ();
main (arc, arv)
    char **arv;
{
    Widget toplevel, board;
    XtAppContext app;
    static XtActionsRec act[] = { "refresh", Scribble};
    toplevel = XtVaAppInitialize( &app, "Quick Test",
        (XrmOptionDescList)NULL, 0,
        &arc, arv, (String *)NULL, NULL);
    XtAppAddActions( app, act, XtNumber(act) );
    board = XtVaCreateManagedWidget("board", widgetClass,
            toplevel, XtNwidth, 200, XtNheight, 200, NULL);
    XtRealizeWidget(toplevel);
    XtAppMainLoop(app);
}
void Scribble (w, ep)
    Widget w;
    XEvent *ep;
{
    if (ep->type !=Expose) return;
}
```

The application consists of a window with one action procedure that can be specified in a resource file as:

```
z*board.translations: <Expose> : refresh()
```

Right now `Scribble()` does nothing, we must provide more code for drawing. But we already see something cumbersome: We must provide code and a resource file entry to handle Expose events, which seems superfluous. It should take no more than one statement to register `Scribble()` with the Intrinsics, so that it can be called in response to such events.

We next try to have `Scribble()` draw something. The new code is shown is Listing 11.2.

We must create a GC and ensure that the foreground is black. (This is not necessarily the default value.) In this program `Scribble()` draws only one line, but we can easily make it more general. We can add two members to the Core widget, an exposure callback, and a GC, which will make our program *and all future drawing programs* much simpler. We describe widget construction in Sec. 11.2, but Listing 11.3 shows the drawing program using the new widget.

The new program has 26 (nonempty) lines of code versus 34 in the previous program—a 23% reduction—but that is not the main benefit. We eliminated code

Listing 11.2. Action Procedure for Drawing

```
void Scribble (w, event)
    Widget w;
    XEvent *event;
{
    Display *Dpy = XtDisplay(w);
    Window win = XtWindow(w);
    static GC gc = 0;
    if (event->type != Expose) return;
    if (!gc) {
        XGCValuesvalues;
        unsigned long valuemask = GCForeground;
        values.foreground = BlackPixel (Dpy,
          DefaultScreen(Dpy));
        gc = XCreateGC( Dpy, DefaultRootWindow(Dpy),
          valuemask, & values);
    }
    XDrawLine(Dpy, win, gc, 10, 10, 180, 180);
}
```

Listing 11.3.   Program Using a Sketch Widget—File tsk.c

```c
#include <X11/StringDefs.h>
#include <X11/Intrinsic.h>
#include <Sketch.h>

void Scribble();

main(int arc, char **arv)
{
    Widget          toplevel, board;
    XtAppContext app;
    toplevel = XtAppInitialize (&app, "Test",
        (XrmOptionDescList)NULL, 0,
        &arc, arv, (String *)NULL, (ArgList)NULL, 0);
    board = XtVaCreateManagedWidget ("board",
        sketchWidgetClass, toplevel, XtNwidth, 200,
        XtNheight, 200, NULL);
    XtAddCallback (board, XtNredrawCallback, Scribble,
        NULL);
    XtRealizeWidget(toplevel);
    XtAppMainLoop(app);
}

void Scribble (Widget w)/*  we are not using the other
  callback arguments  */
{
    Display *Dpy = XtDisplay(w);
    Window win   = XtWindow (w);
    GC gc        = sketch_gc(w);

    XDrawLine(Dpy, win, gc, 10, 10, 180, 180);
}
```

for the action procedure and the GC; code not obviously relevant to the simple task at hand.

11.2.   ANATOMY OF A WIDGET

11.2.1.   Main Structures   Each widget has two structures: One is the same for all its instances (for the most part it holds pointers to functions); the other differs from instance to instance. The former is called the *class record* and the latter the *instance record.* In our case we have nothing useful to add to the class record—the callback and the GC go to the instance record, since these are likely to differ from instance to instance. The Xt convention for naming these structures is to append `ClassRec` and `Rec`, respectively, to the widget class name. If we call our new widget `Sketch`, the two parts are `SketchClassRec` and `SketchRec`.

Each widget inherits the members of its superclasses in each of the two parts, so if a widget has *N* superclasses, the class record and the instance record are each divided into *N + 1* parts. The parts are named like the structures by appending `ClassPart` and `Part` to the widget class name. In our example we have `SketchClassPart` and `SketchPart`. Listing 11.4 shows part of the *private* definition file `SketchP.h`. Because C does not allow empty structures, we include a member in the class part, even though we do not need it.

Listing 11.5 shows part of the *private* definition file `CommandP.h` of the Athena Command widget. Note: The order of the records is arbitrary. In `SketchP.H` the instance comes before the class; in `CommandP.H` it is the other way around. On the other hand the order of part declarations is important: New parts must be defined before full records, since these are used there. Also the declaration sequence inside each record corresponds to the widget hierarchy.

Listing 11.4. Widget Structure for the Sketch Widget

```
typedef struct {
     /*  ... various new members  ...  */
} SketchPart;

/*  Full Instance Record  */
typedef struct_SketchRec {
   CorePart core;
   SketchPart sketch;
} SketchRec;

typedef struct {
     /*  ... in this case only a place holder ...  */
} SketchClassPart;

/*  Full Class Record  */
typedef struct_SketchClassRec {
   CoreClassPart      core_class;
   SketchClassPart    sketch_class;
} SketchClassRec, *SketchWidgetClass;
```

11.5. Widget Structure for the Athena Command Widget

```
typedef struct _CommandClass {
   /*  a place holder  */
}CommandClassPart;

/*  Full class record declaration  */
typedef struct _CommandClassRec {
   CoreClassPart      core_class;
   SimpleClassPart    simple_class;
   LabelClassPart     label_class;
   CommandClassPart   command_class;
} CommandClassRec;

typedef struct {
   /*  ...  resources and private members  ...  */
} CommandPart;

/*  Full widget declaration  */
typedef struct _CommandRec {
   CorePart        core;
   SimplePart      simple;
   LabelPart       label;
   CommandPart     command;
} CommandRec;
```

A widget always has two definition files: The public file, whose name is the capitalized widget name (truncated if necessary to eight characters) with a .h appended (for example Sketch.h or Command.h); and the private file, whose name ends always with P.h (for example SketchP.h or CommandP.h). The latter contains structure definitions, which are normally hidden from application programs. (We give partial listings of two examples in Listings 11.4 and 11.5.) The former contains definitions needed by the application programs, such as resource names and types of convenience functions—in our case the following among others:

```
#define XtNredrawCallback "redrawCallback"
GC sketch_gc();
```

We provide complete listings later.

When writing code for a widget, we must assign values to class parts of superclasses as well as to the new class. This seems to be the most burdensome task of all, since superclasses may have many members that are not relevant to the functionality of the new widget.

Note: We *do not need* the superclass source to write code for a widget, only the private definition file. (The public definition file is always available.) On the other hand it is always helpful to look at the code of another widget for guidance. This model widget should be one with similar functionality.

11.2.2   Where Is What?   Before describing the widget itself, we consider where the different parts are and how these are accessed. When we call a function to construct a widget [for example `XtCreateWidget()`], we pass as argument to a point to the class record, then we receive a pointer to the instance record. For example we can create a sketch widget by the call:

```
extern SketchClassRec skc;
SketchRec  *sw = XtCreateWidget(  ...  , &skc,  ...  );
```

Things are not done this way in Xt because Xt does not encourage accessing individual class and instance members. (If we use C++, members can be declared `Private`, but we are working in C.) In particular in the widget source file (`sketch.c` in this case), we have the code:

```
SketchClassRec skc = {  ...  }
WidgetClass sketchWidgetClass = (WidgetClass)&skc;
```

In the public definition file (`Sketch.h` in this case), we have

```
extern Widget Class sketchWidgetClass;
```

Then the application code becomes

```
#include <Sketch.h>
SketchRec  *sw = XtCreateWidget(..., sketchWidgetClass,...);
```

This is more mnemonic than the original and avoids reference to the class record. (Note: With this approach the variable name used for the class record, `skc`, is not visible to applications, so it can be anything. The X encourages mnemonic names for widget writers as well, so the name `sketchClassRec` is the one actually used.)

The previous code for widget creation still allows private access to the instance record. The Xt has created the type `Widget` as a generic reference to an instance record, so the widget creation code is

```
Widget sw = XtCreateWidget (..., sketchWidgetClass, ...);
```

This is fine for applications, but not for the widget code itself, which must access individual instance members.

To deal with this problem, the public definition file `Sketch.h` also includes the following code:

```
typedef struct _SketchRec *SketchWidget;
```

Since we declare only a pointer to a structure, the C compiler need not know anything about the structure itself; therefore the definition is fine even in the absence of a private declaration file. We take advantage of this declaration inside the widget file `sketch.c` (which includes the private definition file). All functions are declared with arguments of the generic type `Widget`, but inside the functions we cast these arguments into the `SketchWidget` type, and then we can access the individual instance members, for example:

```
redraw(Widget w)
{
    SketchWidget sw = (SketchWidget)w;
    int width = sw->core.width;
    /*  ...  */
}
```

If we had written

```
redraw(Widget w)
{
    int width = w->core.width;
    /*  ...  */
}
```

the compiler would have complained.

11.2.3. Core Class Structure—Part 1   Since all widgets are subclasses of Core, we must familiarize ourselves with that structure. The definition files, `Core.h` and `CoreP.h`, are normally in the subdirectory `include/X11`. The widget program must initialize *all* parts of the class records—in our case both `core_class` (of type `CoreClassPart`) and `sketch_class` (of type `SketchClassPart`).

Members of instance records are initialized as needed. In particular the widget can safely ignore part of the instance record of its superclasses that has no bearing on it. Superclasses are assigned values by the Intrinsics. For example the core instance part has a member `window` that is given a value during realization of the widget. On the other we may wish to access the `width` and `height` members to assign nonzero default dimensions to our widget. We discuss how this is done in Sec. 11.3.2. For now we focus on the class part. Listing 11.6 (pp. 314–315) shows a possible initialization. Bold-faced values are always the same, as we explain later.

Comments in Listing 11.6 replicate the corresponding member of the structure definition. For example in `CoreP.h` there are the statements:

```
typedef struct_CoreClassPart {
   WidgetClass   superclass;
   String        class_name;
   /*  ...  */
} CoreClassPart;
```

Note: All but one structure member is from Core. The new widget has only one member, `extension`, that in this case serves only as a place holder; it is initialized to NULL. We now discuss core members individually.

The `superclass` is given the address of the class record of whatever the superclass is; it is used to access methods of that class. Here `widgeClassRec` refers to the Core class; for a composite widget, it is `compositeClassRec`, etc. The variable `widgetClassRec` is defined in the `CoreP.h` file. We do not use the methods (function) of the Core class in the sketch widget, so this assignment is not important here. We describe a widget in Sec. 11.5, where that member is used in a nontrivial way. This upward linking is the mechanism of inheritance: How a subclass obtains information about its superclass.

The role of the next two members, `class_name` and `widget_size`, is obvious as well as very important. When a widget is created, the Intrinsics have access only to the class record. Intrinsics use the `widget_size` member to allocate memory for the instance record.

The `class_initialize` is a procedure called by the Intrinsics before widgets in this class (in our case `Sketch`) are created. The `class_part_initialize` is similar, but it is also called before subclasses are created. Due to the simplicity of our widget, we do not need such initialization, so we assign both to NULL. The Intrinsics always check for null pointers before calling a procedure to avoid problems with such an assignment. The first procedure is useful when a new widget class introduces a new resource conversion type that must be registered with the Intrinsics. The second procedure is used in connection with inheritance.

The member `class_inited` should *always be assigned the value* FALSE. The Intrinsics change it to TRUE after initialization. The function `initialize()` is called to initialize the record of each *instance* of a particular widget class. As we pointed out previously the Intrinsics know only the size of the widget record, so its members must be accessed by functions provided by the widget writer. By assigning the value `Initialize` to this member, we promise to provide a function called `Initialize()`. In our case it is going to create the GC and provide default dimensions for the widget window, as described in Sec. 11.3.2. The `Initialize_hook` allows us to define a second initialization procedure. Since we can accommodate all initialization with one procedure, we assign it the value NULL. To avoid name space issues, `Initialize()` (and other functions in the right-hand column of Listing 11.6) should be declared static. Since the Intrinsics call such functions only through the widget record, for example, `w->core_class.initialize()`, there is no problem with the static declaration.

The function `realize()` is called by the Intrinsics to realize the widget, so it cannot be NULL. (Otherwise the widget never appears on the screen.) However we can assign a default procedure to the function through `XtInhereitRealize` value (defined in `CoreP.h`)

11.2.4. Core Class Structure—Part 2 The members `actions` and `num_actions` are used only if our widget has action procedures, namely, pairs of strings and function pointers, as described in Sec. 4.3.2. Since the `Sketch` widget class does not have such procedures, these members are given null values.

The next member, `resources`, is a pointer to an array of resource definitions as described in Sec. 3.3.2. It is essential for this to have a nontrivial value—there is little point in creating a widget without resources. Our assignment obligates us to define and initialize an array of type `XtResource` named `own_resources[]`. (The type `XtResourceList` is simply a pointer to the `XtResource` type.) The macro `XtNumber()` is used to compute the number of elements in an array and to assign it to `num_resources`.

The member `xrm_class` is used only by the Intrinsics, so it should *always be assigned the value* NULLQUARK.

If we set `compress_motion` to TRUE, consecutive motion events are compressed into one, which is what most widgets want. A drawing widget such as this is an exception to the rule. In a drawing widget we probably want to implement rubber banding, so we assign the value FALSE.

Exposure events often occur in groups, so it is wasteful to redraw the widget each time, therefore we assign the predefined value `XtExposeCompress-Multiple`. This is the case with most widgets. The same is true with the next member, `compress_enterleave`, which is normally given the value FALSE. The member `visible_interest` is usually given the value FALSE. Its purpose is to reduce unnecessary computation for displaying the widget. A detailed discussion of this is beyond our scope.

Listing 11.6. Initialization of Class Part—File sketch.c

```
/* ... */
#include "SketchP.h"
/* ... */
SketchClassRec sketchClassRec = {
/* Core class part */
/* WidgetClass        superclass              */  (WidgetClass) &widgetClassRec,
/* String             class_name              */  "Sketch",
/* Cardinal           widget_size             */  sizeof(SketchRec),
/* XtProc             class_initialize        */  NULL,
/* XtWidgetClassProc  class_part_initialize   */  NULL;
/* XtEnum             class_inited            */  FALSE,
/* XtInitProc         initialize              */  Initialize,
/* XtArgsProc         initialize_hook         */  NULL,
/* XtRealizeProc      realize                 */  XtInheritRealize,
/* XtActionList       actions                 */  NULL,
/* Cardinal           num_actions             */  0,
/* XtResourceList     resources               */  own_resources,
/* Cardinal           num_resources           */  XtNumber(own_resources),
/* XrmClass           xrm_class               */  NULLQUARK,
/* Boolean            compress_motion         */  FALSE,
/* XtEnum             compress_exposure       */  XtExposeCompressMultiple,
```

```
/*  Boolean              compress_enterleave   */  TRUE,
/*  Boolean              visible_interest      */  FALSE,
/*  XtWidgetProc         destroy               */  Destroy,
/*  XtWidgetProc         resize                */  Resize,
/*  XtExposeProc         expose                */  Redisplay,
/*  XtSetValuesFunc      set_values            */  SetValues,
/*  XtArgsFunc           set_values_hook       */  NULL,
/*  XtAlmostProc         set_values_almost     */  XtInheritSetValuesAlmost,
/*  XtArgsProc           get_values_hook       */  NULL;
/*  XtAcceptFocusProc    accept_focus          */  AcceptFocus,
/*  XtVersionType        version               */  XtVersion,
/*  XtPointer            callback_private      */  NULL;
/*  String               tm_table              */  NULL;
/*  XtGeometryHandler    query_geometry        */  NULL:
/*  XtStringProc         display_accelerator   */  NULL,
/*  XtPointer            extension             */  NULL,

/*  Sketch class part  */
/*  XtPointer            extension             */  NULL
};
```

The function destroy is called when a widget is destroyed. Our assignment obligates us to provide a function Destroy() to release memory or server resources that the widget was using. We also commit ourselves to providing two more functions, Resize(), to be called when widget dimensions are changed, and Redisplay(), to be called in response to expose events.

The member set_values is a function called in response to an XtSetValues call. The widget must perform any computations necessary to make the change in resources effective. For example if foreground color is a resource, we must change the GC. The widget may also refuse to change certain values, although this is not the case with the sketch widget. The assignment obligates us to provide a function SetValues(). The member set_values_ hook has a similar role; we think SetValues() can take care of all resource changes, so we give the value NULL to set_values_hook. The member set_values_almost mediates geometry requests, so the value XtInheritSetValuesAlmost is a reasonable choice for most widgets. The situation is similar with the XtInheritRealize function.

Since the member get_values_hook mediates the response to XtGet Values, we have no special problems; therefore we assign it a NULL value.

The member accept_focus points to a function that may be called by the Intrinsics to tell the widget that keyboard focus is available. In a drawing widget we want focus whenever we can obtain it, so we promise to provide the function AcceptFocus() to always return TRUE. This function comes into play if we invoke a pop-up menu over the drawing widget. When the menu pops down it may inform the drawing widget that focus is available. Such behavior depends on the widget set, but it does not hurt to provide for it.

The member version can assigned one of two values: XtVersion (as above) or XtVersionDontCare. The latter values indicates that recompilation is not needed for future versions of the Intrinsics. Clearly XtVersion is the safer choice of the two.

The callback_private is used only by the Intrinsics, so it should *always be initialized to* NULL. The tm_table refers to the default translation table. Since we have no action procedures, we do not need the table, hence the NULL value. The query_geometry is pertinent only to composite widgets, and display_ accelerator is pertinent only to command or menu button widgets, so we set both to NULL. We set the extension pointer to NULL.

In spite of the many assignments, most of these are routine, especially for relatively simple widgets. We made only one unusual assignment by requesting all motion events because of the nature of our widget. We summarize what we promised

- An array of type XtResource named own_resources to hold our resource specifications.

- Four functions with (in effect) no return: `Initialize()`,
  `Destroy()`, `Resize()`, and `Redisplay()`.
- Two functions with Boolean return: `AcceptFocus()` and
  `SetValues()`; the former could be a trivial function that returns always
  TRUE.

Implementing these promises is the real work, which we describe it in the Sec.
11.3. As indicated in Sec. 11.2.2, these functions (and the resource array) should be
declared static to avoid name conflicts. The Intrinsics never call them by name, only
through the widget class record.

11.3. SKETCH WIDGET IMPLEMENTATION

11.3.1   Definition Files   Listing 11.7 shows the public definition file of the
widget. Conditional definitions with the flag SKETCH_H allow us to include that
file more than once in programs without compiler complaints.

Listing 11.7. Public Definitions of the Sketch Widget—File `Sketch.h`

```
/*  Public Definition File of Sketch Widget  */
#ifndef SKETCH_H
#define SKETCH_H

#define XtNforeground "foreground"
#define XtCForeground "Foreground"

#define XtNredrawCallback "redrawCallback"
#define XtCRedrawCallback "RedrawCallback"

#define XtNuserData "userData"
#define XtCuserData "UserData"

extern WidgetClass sketchWidgetClass;

typedef struct  _SketchRec *SketchWidget;

#endif  /*  SKETCH_H  */

/*  convenience functions  */
GC sketch_gc();
GC pr_sketch_gc();
```

Listing 11.7 defines resource strings; the pointer to the class record, `sketchWidgetClass`; and a type, `SketchWidget`, which is a pointer to the instance record structure. Listing 11.7 also declares the type returned by the two convenience functions.

We use rather common names for the resources, which may be a source of problems. A resource is properly specified through both the widget path name and its own name. For example in an application named `doodle`, we may have a sketch widget named `canvas` that is the child of a container widget named `box`. We select blue for the foreground color, with the resource specification:

```
doodle.box.canvas.foreground: blue
```

The probability of conflict with another specification is extremely small. On the other hand the following specification begs for trouble:

```
*foreground: blue
```

Such wild-carding should be avoided except in internal fallback specifications. No matter how carefully we select resource names, there is no guarantee that we will avoid conflict.

We take a few moments here to describe widget instance creation. The function `XtVaCreateManagedWidget()` in Listing 11.3 takes a pointer to the class record `sketchWidgetClass` as argument. The only information about the instance record the widget creation function uses is its size (the third member, `widget_size`, in Listing 11.6). This information is used to allocate enough memory to hold a single instance of the widget. Then the Intrinsics call the pertinent initialization functions (seventh member, `initialize`, in Listing 11.6) to assign values to the instant record. In our example the Intrinsics call first the Core initialization function, then the Sketch initialization function. The creation function then returns a pointer to the instance record. (Because all pointers have the same size, we use a common type, `Widget`, for all widget types.) In short *the Intrinsics deal directly with members of the class record, but not with members of the instance record.*

Listing 11.8 shows the complete private definition file of the widget, part of which was shown in Listing 11.4. Listing 11.8 specifies the definition files included, full contents of the instance part, and a variable referring to the class record.

Besides the redraw callback and the public GC mentioned in Sec. 11.1, we added three other members: A foreground color, a private GC, and a pointer (`user_data`) on which to attach application-related data. We explain its use in Sec. 11.3.5. The term private is a misnomer, since it pertains to the GC: It is a read-only GC useful for drawing things under control of the widget only (for example

Listing 11.8. Private Definitions of the Sketch Widget—File
SketchP.h

```
/*  Private Definition File of Sketch Widget  */
#ifndef SKETCH_P_H
#define SKETCH_P_H

#include <X11/IntrinsicP.h>
#include <X11/CoreP.h>
#include "Sketch.h"

typedef struct {
   /*  Resource fields  */
   Pixel              foreground_pixel;
   XtCallbackList     redrawCallback;
   XtPointer          user_data;
   /*  Convenience Function fields  */
   GC    private_gc;
   GC    public_gc;
} SketchPart;

/*  Full Instance Record  */
typedef struct _SketchRec {
   CorePart     core;
   SketchPart   sketch;
} SketchRec;

typedef struct   {
   XtPointer    extension;
} SketchClassPart;

/*  Full Class Record  */
typedef struct _SketchClassRec  {
   CoreClassPart      core_class;
   SketchClassPart    sketch_class;
} SketchClassRec, *SketchWidgetClass;

extern SketchClassRec sketchClassRec;

#endif  /*  SKETCH_P_H  */
```

marking selections). It is not necessary to define a background member or dimensions, since these are part of the Core instance record.

In some cases it is clear which members to make internal and which to link with a resource (resource fields); in others it is somewhat arbitrary. Foreground color should obviously be a resource (users are likely to specify it in resource files). Making the redrawing function a callback lets us use the standard mechanism of the XtAddCallback() function. If we make the GC a resource, we must implement a mechanism for making it read only. The widget creates both GC at initialization time, and applications are not supposed to change them. Applications can change *members* of public_gc, but they cannot do that for private_gc. Having convenience functions automatically enforces the read-only rule.

The member user_data is a resource, but it can be accessed through a convenience function; for example:

```
XtPointer  *  sketch_hanger(sw)
       SketchWidget  sw;
{
       return (  &(sw->;sketch.user_data) );
}
```

A convenience function is faster than the resource mechanism, but application programmers would then have to deal with an unusual mechanism. Incidentally both Motif and OLIT primitive widgets use the resource mechanism for a similar (user data) member.

11.3.2.   Widget Source File   Listing 11.9 shows the source of the sketch widget. We do not repeat the class record initialization, since it is shown in Listing 11.6. We declare three resources in the same way as in Sec. 3.3.4, provide function declarations to initialize the class record, and initialize the global variable sketchWidgetClass, which points to the class record. This variable is used as the second argument of XtVaCreateManagedWidget(). We provide code for the functions. Note: Except for the convenience functions, all are declared static, so they cannot be used from other modules.

Since the appearance of the drawing widget is the responsibility of the application, all function code is quite simple. (In that sense a drawing widget is a good example for emphasizing conformance to Xt rules.)

The function AcceptFocus() is trivial. The function SetValues() receives information about changes in the resources. The old and new have resources values before and after the change, respectively. (We are not concerned with other arguments here.) If the foreground is changed, we update the GC, then return the value TRUE, which causes the Intrinsics to redisplay the widget. See Sec. 11.3.4 for some potential problems with this function.

Listing 11.9.   Sketch Widget Source File—File sketch.c

```
/*  Simple Sketch Widget Source File  */
#include <X11/Xos.h>
#include <X11/StringDefs.h>
#include <X11/Intrinsic.h>
#include <X11/Xatom.h>
#include "SketchP.h"

static XtResource own_resources[] = {

   {XtNforeground,  XtCForeground,
   XtRPixel,  sizeof(Pixel),
   XtOffsetOf(SketchRec, sketch.foreground_pixel),
   XtRString, "black" },

   {XtNredrawCallback, XtCRedrawCallback,
   XtRCallback, sizeof(XtCallbackList),
   XtOffset(SketchRec, sketch.redrawCallback),
   XtRCallback, (XtPointer) NULL },

   {XtNuserData, XtCuserData,
   XtRPointer, sizeof(XtPointer),
   XtOffsetOf(SketchRec, sketch.used_data),
   XtRImmediate, (XtPointer) NULL},
   };

static void Initialize(),Redisplay(), Destroy(), Resize();
static Boolean AcceptFocus(), SetValues();

SketchClassRec sketchClassRec = {
   /*  ... from Listing 11.6  ...  */
};
/*  Class record pointer, needed by applications  */
WidgetClass sketchWidgetClass =
   (WidgetClass) & sketchClassRec;

/*  Called when focus becomes available   */
static Boolean AcceptFocus (w, time_p)
   Widget w;
   Time  *time_p;
{
   return TRUE;
}
/*  Called any time Xt[Va]SetValues() is called  */
```

```
static Boolean SetValues(old, request, new, args,
num_args)
    Widget old, request, new;
    ArgList args;
    Cardinal  *num_args;
{
    SketchWidget oldsw = (SketchWidget)old;
    SketchWidget newsw = {SketchWidget)new;
    Boolean redisplay = FALSE;
    /*Compare old and new values  */
    if (oldsw->sketch.foreground_pixel
           !=newsw->sketch.foreground_pixel) {
       redisplay = TRUE;
       XSetForeground(XtDisplay(new),
          newsw->sketch.public_gc,
          newsw->sketch.foreground_pixel);
    }
    return redisplay;
}
static GC GetNormalGC(sw, kind  /*1 private, 0 public*/)
    SketchWidget sw;
{
    XGCValuesvalues;
    Display    *Dpy = XtDisplay(sw);
    static unsigned long valuemask = GCBackground |
      GCForeground | GCGraphicsExposures;
    values.foreground = sw->sketch.foreground_pixel;
    values.background = sw->core.background_pixel;
    values.graphics_exposures = False;
    if(kind) return XtGetGC( (Widget)sw, valuemask,
      &values);
    else return
       XCReateGC(Dpy, DefaultRootWindow(Dpy), valuemask,
          &values);
}
/* Called by the Intrinsic at Widget Creation Time   */
static void Initialize(request, new, args, num_args)
    Widget request, new;
    ArgList args;
    Cardinal *num_args;
{
    SketchWidget sw = (SketchWidget) new;
    sw->sketch.public_gc = GetNormalGC(sw, 0);
    sw->sketch.public_gc = GetNormalGC(sw, 1);
    if(sw-core.width <1) sw->core.width = 100;
```

```
      if(sw-core.height <1) sw->core.height = 100;
}
/*  Called when the widget is destroyed  */
static void Destroy (w)
   Widget w;
{
   SketchWidget sw = (SketchWidget)w;
   /*  free GC obtained through XtGetGC()  */
   XtReleaseGC(w, sw->sketch.private_gc);
   /*  free GC obtained through XCreateGC()  */
   XFreeGC(XtDisplay(w), sw->sketch.public_gc);
}
/*  Called when an Expose event occurs     */
static void Redisplay (w, ep, region)
   Widget  w;
   XEvent  *ep;
   Region  region;
{
   SketchWidget sw = (SketchWidget)w;
   XClearWindow(XtDisplay(sw), XtWindow(sw));
   if(XtHasCallbacks(
     (Widget)sw, XtNredrawCallback)==XtCallbackHasSome)
      XtCallCallbackList ((Widget)sw,
      sw->sketch.redrawCallback, NULL);
}
/*  Called SOMETIMES when either the widget OR A PARENT is
resized  */
static void Resize(w)
   Widget w;
{
   if( XtIsRealized(w)){
      XClearWindow(XtDisplay(w), XtWindow(w));
      Redisplay(w, (XEvent *)NULL, (Region)NULL);
   }
}
/*  Convenience Functions accessing the internal fields  */
GC sketch_gc(sw)
   SketchWidget sw;
{
   return sw->sketch.public_gc;
}
GC pr_sketch_gc(sw)
   SketchWidget sw;
{
   return sw->sketch.private_gc;
}
```

The Get NormalGC() is an internal function that provides a GC with foreground and background taken from resources and graphics exposures set to False (see Sec. 2.3.1 for the latter.) If the second argument is nonzero, it asks the Intrinsics for a read-only GC; otherwise it creates a read/write GC through an Xlib function call.

The function Initialize() ignores most of its arguments. It calls GetNormalGC() twice to create the two graphics contexts, then checks whether widget dimensions are initialized. If not, it assigns the value of 100 pixels to both of them: (The Core instance initialization procedure is called before the procedures of its subclasses.) Note: The foreground resource must be set during widget creation if it is going to affect the private GC. If it is set with a XtSetValues() call, it affects only the public GC. (See Sec. 11.3.4 for more on this topic.)

Implementing the remaining functions is straightforward. When an expose event occurs, for Intrinsics call the Redisplay() functions [w->core.expose()]. Whether the Resize() function is called depends on the parent of the widget, for example it may be called when the size is increased, but not when it is decreased.

Writing a new widget is fairly easy for simple widgets. Most of the effort lies in initializing the Core class record. We can increase the complexity of widget behavior with no more effort than implementing that behavior in an application.

11.3.3.   Adding Functionality to the Sketch Widget   Here we provide a rather frivolous example by adding a response to events in the sketch widget. In particular we want the display to be erased whenever the user presses a button and restored when the button is released. We do that by adding an event handler during initialization. Handler code is shown in Listing 11.10, where the modification of the initialization function are highlighted in the code fragment, with the original parts (from Listing 11.9) shown in normal type.

While this modification is not practically useful, it offers a template to develop an attractive feature for a drawing widget. Instead of the complex XEvent structure, we can offer application programs a simplified structure, such as the St_event of the Starter toolkit (see Sec. 2.5.2 and the Appendix). First we create a new callback list by adding a new member to the instance record:

```
XtCallbackList    userCallback
```

We define a respective resource with name, say, XtNuserCallback, with the following initialization:

```
{XtNuserCallback, XtCUserCallback,
XtRCallback, sizeof(XtCallbackList),
XtOffsetOf(SketchRec, sketch.userCallback),
XtRCallback, (XtPointer) NULL},
```

Listing 11.10. Additions to the Widget Source File—File sketch.

```
static void internal_handler(w, client_data, ep, disp)
   Widget w;
   XtPointer client_data;
   XEvent *ep;
   Boolean *disp;
{
   if(ep->type==ButtonPress) XClearWindow(XtDisplay(w),
     XtWindow(w));
   else if(ep->type==ButtonRelease)Redisplay(w,ep, NULL);
}
static void Initialize(request, new, args, num_args)
   Widget request, new;
   ArgList args;
   Cardinal *num_args;
{

   SketchWidget sw = (SketchWidget) new;
   sw->sketch.public_gc = GetNormalGC(sw, 0);
   sw->sketch.private_gc = GetNormalGC(sw, 1);
   if(sw->core.width <1) sw->core.width = 100;
   if(sw->core.height <1) sw->core.height= 100;
   XtAddEVentHandler(new,
       ButtonReleaseMask | ButtonPressMask |
       PointerMotionMask,
       Flase, internal_handler, NULL);
}
```

The internal handler computes the simplified structure, then passes it as *call_data* to a callback. In this case the function `internal_handler()` may take the form shown in Listing 11.11.

The function `simplify_event()` should also be part of the widget code, but since it is related to the widget functionality rather than following the rules that the Xt imposes on widgets, we do not discuss it here. (Basically it is a large switch statement that creates the corresponding simplified event for each event type.)

Applications programmers use simplified events by creating such a function as:

```
void simple_handler(Widget w, XtPointer client_data,
  XtPointer call_data)
{
   pEvent *ep = (pEvent *)call_data;
```

Listing 11.11.   Modification of the Widget Source File

```
void simplify_event();
typedef struct {
    /*  ...  */
} pEvent;
static void internal_handler(w,client_data, ep, disp)
        Widget w;
        XtPointer Client_data;
        XEvent *ep;
        Boolean *disp;
{
        pEvent *pp;
        simplify_event (ep, &pp);
        if(XtHasCallbacks(w, XtNuserCallback)==
          XtCallbackHasSome)
          XtCallCallbackList(w,
          ((SketchWidget)w)->sketch.userCallback, pp);
}
```

```
    switch(ep->kind) {
    }
}
```

then registering it as a callback:

```
XtAddCallback(mycanvas, XtNuserCallback, simple_handler,
  client_data);
```

11.3.4.   What Resources Should a Widget Have?   We gave very few resources to our drawing widget, which may seem surprising. We may think of such things as fonts, icon pixmaps, line styles, etc, as needed. Such items are indeed needed, but these should be considered to constitute the *state* of the widget rather than its resource set. For example a drawing widget may have a member that is the foreground (of Pixel type), but should differ from the resource member foreground_pixel. The value of foreground should be accessed and modified through convenience functions. We explain the reasons for such a design through an example.

Suppose we want to display a graph that contains curves in different colors. The redraw callback should contain code that sets color in the GC before drawing the respective curve. (Color values and curve points can be supplied as part of a

client structure.) We have various choice: One is to change the value of the foreground resource. Unfortunately, this causes a call to the SetValue() function in
Listing 11.9, which by returning TRUE causes another call to the redraw function,
and so forth. (We end up with an infinite sequence of calls to the redraw function.)

We can avoid such runaway behavior by returning FALSE from
SetValue(), but such a policy defies the purpose of that function. The correct
solution is to use resources only for parameters that remain constant or undergo
predictable changes during the lifetime of the widget instance. For example the
resource foreground_pixel should be used to specify the initial value. The
color of specific plots should be specified directly in the GC. We may still require
additional storage for temporary colors to allow such as operations as restore
previous color. For that we can use widget members that are not resources. However
instead of having individual members, we may prefer a more general mechanism, as
described in Sec. 11.3.5.

11.3.5.   Attaching User Data to a Widget   Suppose we want to use the
new widget to display not just a straight line, as in Listing 11.3, but a polygon. First
we define a structure that contains a pointer to the polygon vertices and their
number:

```
typedef struct {
    int n;
    XPoint    *P;
} my_polygon;
```

Assume we also have the declaration:

```
my_polygon A, B, C;
```

We can pass the polygons as client data to the Expose callback with a statement:

```
XtAddCallback(sketch_A,XtNredrawCallback, Scribble, &A);
```

Then Scribble() should include such code as:

```
my_polygon *point = (my_polygon *)client_data;
XDrawLines(Dpy, win, gc, point->P, point->n,
 CoordModeOrigin);
```

This works as long as we have no other need for the client data argument.
If we want to leave it available for other uses, we may attach the polygon structure
pointer to the widget user data. Listing 11.12 shows a utility function for doing this.

Listing 11.12. Attaching User Data to a Widget

```
Widget make_graph(Widget parent, char  *name, int n,
  Xpoint *poly)
{
  Widget local;
  my_polygon *dp;
  local = XtVaCreateManagedWidget(name, sketchWidgetClass,
    parent, XtNwidth, 200, XtNheight, 200, NULL);
  dp = (my_polygon *)malloc(size of(my_polygon));
  dp->n = n;
  dp->p = poly;
  XtVaSetValues(local, XtNuserData, (XtPointer)dp, NULL);
  XtAddCallback(local, XtNredrawCallback, Scribble, NULL);
  return local;
}

void Scribble(Widget w)
{
    Display *Dpy = XtDisplay(w);
    Window win = XtWindow(w);
    GC gc = sketch_gc(w);
    my_polygon *point;
    XtVaGetValues(w, XtNuserData, &point, NULL);
    XDrawLines(Dpy, win, gc, point->P, point->n,
      CoordModeOrigin);
}
```

We created in effect a new widget, one that displays polygons. If the polygon is to have a single color, we can select it through the foreground resource. However if we are going to use different colors, then we must use the approach discussed in Sec.11.3.4. In such a case we need a different structure. Listing 11.13 shows the definition of a type, collection, that can be used for that purpose and a redraw callback that extracts information from the widget user data.

11.4. CONCLUSIONS

Once the resource definition mechanism and the structure of core class methods are understood, writing noncomposite widgets differs little from writing

Listing 11.13.   Drawing Polygons in Many Colors

```
typedef struct {
    int n;
    XPoint *P;
    Pixel color;
} color_polygon;

#define MAX_NUMBER 128
typedef struct {
    int np;
    color_polygon *CP[MAX_NUMBER];
} collection;

void Scribble(Widget w)
{
    Display *Dpy = XtDisplay(w);
    Window win   = XtWindow(w);
    GC gc        = sketch_gc(w);
    register i;
    collection *group;
    Pixel default_color;

    XtVaGetValues(w, XtNuserData, &group, NULL);
    for(i=0; i<group->np, I++) {
        XSet Foreground(Dpy, gc, group->CP[i]->color);
        XDrawLines (Dpy, win, gc,
        group->CP[i]->P, group->CP[i]->n, CoordModeOrigin);
    }
    /*   restore default color   */
    XtVaGetValues(w, XtNforeground, &default_color, NULL);
    XSetForeground(Dpy, gc, default_color);
}
```

applications with the same functionality. The task is only slightly more complex for a composite widget.

The most serious design issue is to decide which parameter to make public (through resources or convenience functions) and which to keep private. The approach taken by Motif provides many public parameters (many widgets have over 50 resources). This provides flexibility at the expenses of confusion to nonexperienced application programmers.

A good strategy for writing a noncomposite new widget is to treat it initially as an application by using a drawing widget (such as the paper widget) and the user data resource (Sec. 11.3.5) for program parameters and state variables. The resulting widget prototype can be tested and revised before making it an Xt widget. In our experience it takes less than a day's work to convert a *well-written* widget prototype into an Xt widget.

In a composite widget the main work is to arrange the layout of its children; Chap. 12 shows an example.

Chapter 11 discusses in detail the class part initialization of the core widget. To write a new widget as a subclass of another class, we must consider initialization not only of the Core class part but also the class parts of all superclasses. The *P.h lists members of the class record, but it provides no suggestions for initialization. That record is usually quite small, so NULL values may suffice (see Project 2). On the other hand subclassing sometimes focuses on assigning a different function to a method of the superclass (see Project 4): in that case we may have to learn more about the superclass than what is in the *P.h file.

11.5.   PROJECTS

1.   The Starter toolkit function `set_handler()` takes as argument a function pointer, say, f, then whenever a mouse or keyboard event occurs, f is called with an argument pointer to the simplified event structure (described in Sec. 11.3.3). Implement this function using the `userCallback` mechanism of the sketch widget.

2.   The Motif toolkit has a primitive widget class, `XmPrimitive`, which is a direct subclass of `Core` with many additional resources, including foreground and simplified event information passed as part of `call_data`. Repeat the development of the sketch widget described in this chapter as a subclass of `XmPrimitive` rather than `Core`. What is the advantage of creating the sketch widget as a subclass of a Motif widget class?

     Hints: (1) Start by finding the file `Xm/PrimitiveP.h` that contains the description of the Primitive widget class: (2) Modify the `SketchP.h` file using Listing 11.5 as a model: (3) You can reuse most of the code for `sketch.c`, eliminate resources already contained in the Motif Primitive class; initialize the class part of Primitive (null or zero are fine for a first try); be sure to change the superclass from `widgetClassRec` to `xmPrimitiveClassRec` (otherwise you cannot access the resource of the superclass); and so forth.

3. Write an animated widget (as a subclass of Core or the Motif Primitive) by using time-outs. The time-out should be called from the initialization routine. You can use the code in Listing 5.15 inside the widget redraw and time-out functions, but you can also create more interesting animations. Provide a resource to specify the frequency of blinking.

4. Write a blinking text widget class as a subclass of a label class.

12

Examples of Widget Implementation

12.1. INTRODUCTION

Chapter 11 focuses on conforming to specifications of Xt; Chap. 12 is concerned with the appearance and behavior of widgets. As pointed out in Sect. 11.4, converting a well-written application into a widget is relatively straightforward. Nevertheless it is an important process, so we show a drawing procedure and an event handler for a nontrivial widget.

We describe a slider widget because it has a complex enough appearance and behavior to illustrate numerous concepts in X programming; it is also a Motif widget that suffers from poor design. The Motif slider widget is composite! It does not automatically provide hash marks, but instead it expects the application to provide them as children gadgets. This provides additional control over the shape of the hash marks at the expense of having a loop of calls to `XtVaCreateWidget()` in the program. It is a poor trade-off and a startling example of overkill in customization. The slider widget described in Sec. 12.2 provides hash marks and labels automatically.

Unless we want to create our own toolkit, we do not need to write a composite widget. All major toolkits have composite widgets, so we should be able to use one of them. If we write our own composite widget, we may have difficulty using it with children that are widgets from another toolkit. For example all Motif widgets have certain resources that are part of the `Primitive` Motif class. A widget may look for such a resource in its parent, and if its missing, it may not behave properly. (We observed such a problem in Motif version 1.2.3 and earlier. While it was fixed in version 1.2.4, there is no guarantee that such a problem will not recur under different circumstances.)

In short the only safe way to write composite widgets is to assume that their children are always from widget classes that we also wrote. With this caveat Sec. 12.3 describes how to convert the sketch widget into a composite widget. We call it a blackboard widget, since we can both draw on it and also pin other drawing widgets on it.

12.2. SLIDER WIDGET

12.2.1. Overall Organization   Figure 12.1 shows three instances of a slider widget; its description follows.

Let us assume that we have a program that draws the slider and handles the user interaction; we ask how to convert the program into a widget, so that we can use the resource mechanism. To draw the silder in Fig. 12.1, we need certain parameters illustrated in Fig. 12.2; its description follows (with the C variable names in parentheses):

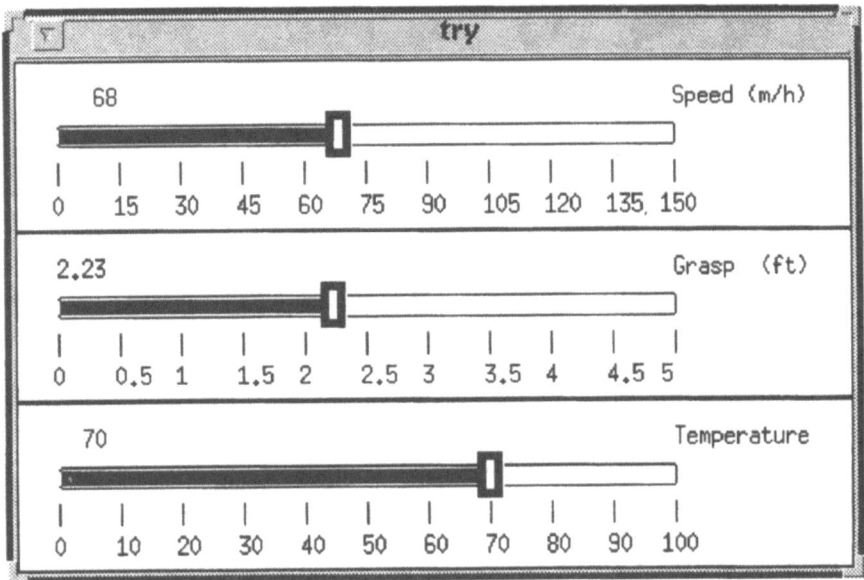

Figure 12.1. Appearance of the slider widget: Three instance that are part of an application called "try".

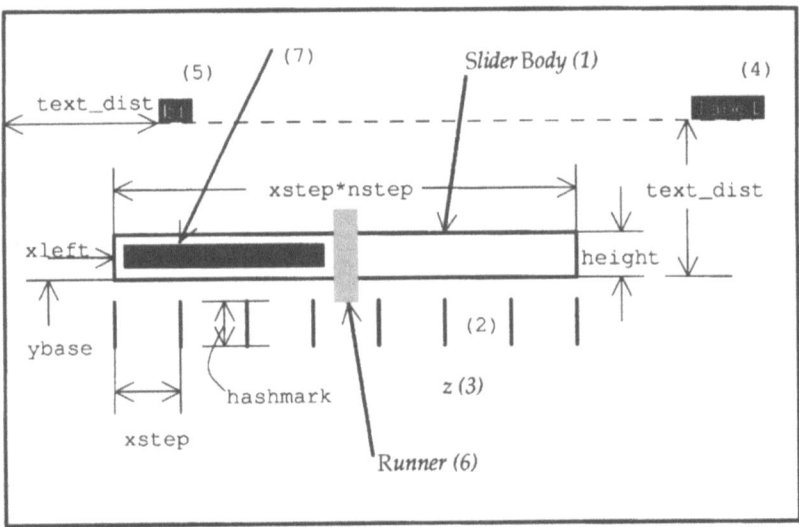

Figure 12.2. Definition of slider widget parameters. Numbers in parentheses refer to comments in the code listings. Labels in reverse video refer to strings that are parameters. Labels in constant width font refers to parameter names. Other labels are in italics.

- Leftmost and rightmost values of x for the slider body (*No. 1* in 12.2) (xleft and xright); also its vertical position (ybase) and height (height).
- Spacing (xstep) and number (nstep) of hash marks (*No. 2*).
- Foreground and background colors.
- Label placed to the right (label) and a buffer (bf[]) to hold the left label that denotes the selected value as well as the value itself (value) (*Nos. 4–5*).
- Position of two labels, in our example we use the same parameter, text_dist, to specify both horizontal and vertical positions.
- Place of the runner (*No. 6*) (x1) and its dimensions.

In addition we need a state variable for the event handler to indicate whether the runner has been grabbed (pick). Note: xright is not an independent parameter; it is computed as the sum of xleft and xstep*nstep. Other parameter choices are also possible; we can modify the design once we understand the process.

When we convert a program into a widget, we face a major decision: Which parameters should be resource fields in the widget structure and which internal fields. Listing 12.1 shows a possible definition of the structure.

We decided to keep most of the variables hidden. Clearly the label and the value should be resources because these are why we build a slider. We also add a user callback that is invoked when a value selection is made—it may be convenient for some applications (see examples below). The background color is available through core resources, so we add only the foreground color to the resources. We could assign a fixed range (for example 0–1, but instead we have a range resource for the upper value (the lower is always 0). Instead of a range we could provide upper and lower limits. The format string refers to the printf format in which the runner position is displayed; its default is %g.

We have the option of allowing the application to specify widget dimensions, but instead, we provide a scale resource that can be used to select sets of values. We could have omitted this altogether and computed parameters from the window dimensions. Either way we impose on the widget writer the obligation to compute sets of consistent parameters. Such a computation has nothing to do with X—it is simply planar geometry. A similar process can select a font on the basis of window dimensions, but we allow direct font selection in case the application or user wants to select a particular style. In this implementation the runner dimensions and shape are fixed.

Returning to Core class methods, we can dispense with the accept_focus method and assign the value NULL to it. On the other hand functions Initialize(), Set Values(), Redisplay(), and the internal event

Listing 12.1.   Record of a slider widget—File SliderP.h

```
typedef struct {
   /* Resource fields */
   Pixel              foreground_pixel;
   int                scale;
   XFontStruct        *font_used;
   String             label;
   float              value;
   float              range;
   String             format;
   XtCallbackList userCallback;
   /* Internal fields */
   GC gc;
   int x1, pick; /* state of the runner */
   char bf[16];
   int xleft, ybase, height, xstep, text_dist, hashmark;
   int nstep, xright;
   float scale_ratio;
} SliderPart;

/* Full Instance Record */
typedef struct _SliderRec {
   CorePart core;
   SliderPart slider;
} SliderRec;
```

handler are far more complex than in the case of the sketch widget. If the original slider program were written with static variables, the new program would have widget fields; for example `xleft` must be replaced by `sw->slider.xleft`. Such a replacement can be done mechanically through global substitutions.

Resource definitions are similar to those discussed earlier except for floating numbers. In this case initialization must be done indirectly, for example:

```
static float default_range = 100;

static XtResource own_resources[] = {
   /*...*/

   {XtNrange, XtCRange,
   XtRFloat, sizeof(float),
   XtOffsetOf(SliderRec, slider.range),
   XtRFloat, (XtPointer)(&default_range) },
```

```
/*...*/
};
```

A complete listing of resource definitions is given in Listing 12.6.

The same concern affects the callback design, for example:

```
void change_of_speed(w, client_data, call_data)
    Widget w;                                    /
    XtPointer client_data, call_data;
{
    float *xp = (float*)call_data;
    /*...*/
}
/*...*/
xtAddCallback(speed_slider, XtNuserCallback,
    change_of_speed, NULL);
```

There are various ways of using such a slider widget: To set a parameter that a later `XtVaGetValues()` extracts or to modify an ongoing process, such as game animation. Two of the sliders in Figure 12.1 control the player's movement speed and grasp (how close the cursor must be to a moving object to score a hit). In this case the user callback sets a parameter used by a game procedure. (Incidentally the game is fair when runners in the two sliders line up.)

We can add a covenience function that creates a slider widget with default parameters and a minimal application interface:

```
Widget make_slider (Widget parent, void (*usage)(double),
    char *label)
```

This function provides only the label and usage function. This arrangement assumes that a default callback (such as the one just listed) is provided. The usage function is called from inside the callback with the client data argument.

12.2.2. Slider Widget Implementation We now review some essential slider widget procedures. The slider can be displayed in three different sizes; the configuration is specified by a set of parameters given in Listing 12.2 together with the redraw function and parts of the initialization function. There is a lot of code, but it is not different from application code except that variables are stored in structures `sw->slider` and `sw->core` rather than in some other static location. The rest of the code has nothing to do with Xt widget policies, and it follows from material in Chap. 8.

Listing 12.3 shows the event handler and pertinent statements from the initialization procedure.

Again most of the code is independent of Xt widget policies. When a `ButtonRelease` event occurs, the handler processes it only if it is from Button 1.

Then it checks to see if the runner was grabbed before; if so, it performs the following operations: (1) Updates the displayed label, (2) changes the value of pick to indicate that the runner is no longer grabbed, and (3) invokes user callback.

If the mouse moves or a button is pressed, the mouse coordinates are saved in x and y, then a computation is made to find if the event occurred near the slider body. If not, the event is ignored. If the runner was not grabbed, a second computation is made to check whether the point (x, y) is near the runner. If not, the event is ignored, otherwise the label and runner position are updated.

We show how to provide additional means of handling the slider runner from the keyboard by using a translation table and action procedures in Listing 12.4. According to the table when the user presses the a (or A) key, the function Left_position() is called. Pressing the z (or Z) key invokes Right_position(). Each procedure redefines the value member, calls two functions that update other internal fields, then redraws the widget.

Finally we define proper entries for the class record of the slider widget in Listing 12.5. There is quite a bit more code in the widget, which is shown in Listings 12.6–12.8.

Listing 12.2.   Slider Appearance—File slider.c

```
/* Refer to Figure 12.2 for parameter illustration */
/* Object numbers refer also to the same figure. */

typedef struct {
    int xleft, ybase, height, xstep, text_dist, hashmark;
} slide_geometry;

static slide_geometry param[3]={
    {10, 40,  8, 20, 14,  6}, /* small */
    {20, 40, 10, 30, 20, 10}, /* medium */
    {20, 50, 20, 40, 25, 12}  /* large */
    };

/* Part of Initialize()*/
{
    SliderWidget sw = (SliderWidget) new;
    /*...*/
    sw->slider.xleft     = param[sw->slider.scale].xleft;
    sw->slider.ybase     = param[sw->slider.scale].ybase;
    sw->slider.height    = param[sw->slider.scale].height;
    sw->slider.xstep     = param[sw->slider.scale].xstep;
    sw->slider.text_dist =
                    param[sw->slider.scale].text_dist;
```

```
   sw->slider.hashmark  =
                    param[sw->slider.scale].hashmark;
   sw->slider.nstep     = 10;
   sw->slider.xright    =
     sw->slider.xstep*sw->slider.nstep+sw->slider.xleft;
   sw->slider.scale_ratio =
     sw->slider.range/(sw->slider.xright-sw->slider.xleft);
   sw->slider.x1 = value_to_pixels(sw);
   sprintf(sw->slider.bf, sw->slider.format,
     sw->slider.value);

   if (!sw->slider.font_used) {
      sw->slider.font_used = XQueryFont( Dpy,
      (Gcontext)XGContextFromGC(sw->slider.gc) );
   }
   else XSetFont(Dpy, sw->slider.gc,
       sw->slider.font_used->fid);

   sw->core.width = window_width(sw); /* must be computed
                                       after font */
   sw->core.height = 2*sw->slider.ybase;
   /*...*/
}

#define put_text(S, X, Y) XDrawString(XtDisplay(w), \
     XtWindow(w), sw->slider.gc, X, Y, S, strlen(S));

static void Redisplay(w, ep, region)
   Widget w;
   XEvent *ep;
   Region region;
{
   SliderWidget sw = (SliderWidget)w;
   register i, xx;
   static char rbf[16];
   float z, dz;

   /* Erase the old stuff and set the foreground for
   exclusive OR */
   XClearWindow(XtDisplay(w), XtWindow(w));
   XsetForeground(XtDisplay(w), sw->slider.gc,
      sw->slider.foreground_pixel^
        sw->core.background_pixel);
   XsetFunction(XtDisplay(w), sw->slider.gc, GXxor);
```

```
    /* Draw the body of the slider (Object No. 1) */
    XDrawRectangle (XtDisplay(w), XtWindow(w),
      sw->slider.gc,
        sw->slider.xleft,
          sw->slider.ybase-sw->slider.height,
        sw->slider.xstep*sw->slider.nstep,
          sw->slider.height);

    /* Draw the hash marks and their labels */
    dz = sw->slider.range/sw->slider.nstep;
    for (i=0, z=0; i<=sw->slider.nstep; i++, z+=dz) {
        /* Object No. 2 */
        xx = sw->slider.xleft + i*sw->slider.xstep;
        XDrawLine(XtDisplay(w), XtWindow(w),
            sw->slider.gc,
            xx,sw->slider.ybase + 8,
            xx, sw->slider.ybase + 8+sw->slider.hashmark);
        /* Object No. 3 */
        sprintf(rbf, "%g",z);
        put_text (rbf, i<10? xx-2: xx-6,
            sw->slider.ybase+32);
    }
    /* Draw the runner (Object No. 6) and the filled part */
    /* (Object No. 7) of the slider body */
    mark(w); /* In Listing 12.7 */

    /* Display the value selected and the label */
    /* Object No. 5 */
    put_text (sw->slider.bf,
          sw->slider.text_dist,
            sw->slider.ybase-sw->slider.text_dist);
    /* Object No. 4*/
    put_text (sw->slider.label,
          xx, sw->slider.ybase-sw->slider.text_dist);
}
```

Listing 12.3.   Slider Event Handling—File slider.c

```
static void my_handler (w, client_data, ep, disp)
    Widget w;
    XtPointer client_data;
    XEvent *ep;
```

```
    Boolean *disp;
{

    SliderWidget sw = (SliderWidget)w;
    int x, y, xyset = 0;

    switch (ep->type) {
    case ButtonRelease:
        /* This event is received even if it occurs
           outside the widget, provided the corresponding
           ButtonPress had occurred inside. */
        if((ep->xbutton).button != 1) return;
        /* We only do work if button 1 was released while */
        /* the runner has been moved. */
        if (sw->slider.pick) {
            update_label(w); /* update printout of runner
                                position */
            sprintf (sw->slider.bf, sw->slider.format,
                sw->slider.value);
            sw->slider.value = atof (sw->slider.bf);
            sw->slider.pick = 0;
            if(XtHasCallbacks(w,XtNuserCallback)==
                   XtCallbackHasSome)
               XtCallCallbackList (w,
                   sw->slider.userCallback,
                   (XtPointer)(&sw->slider.value));
        }
        break;
    case MotionNotify;
        if(ep->xmotion.state != Button1Mask) return;
        x = (ep->xmotion).x;
        y = (ep->xsmotion).y;
        xyset = 1;
        /* no break */
    case ButtonPress:
        if((ep->xbutton).button != 1) return;
        if(!xyset) {
            x = (ep->xbutton).x;
            y = (ep->xbutton).y;
        }
        /* Ignore event if it occurred outside the slider
           area */
        if(x<sw->slider.xleft || x>sw->slider.xright
            || y < sw->slider.height
```

```
       || y > sw->slider.ybase + 2*sw->slider.height)
          return;
       /* If the runner has not been picked up, pick it */
       /* only if the event occurred near it */
       if(!sw->slider.pick) {
          if(y > sw->slider.ybase - 2*sw->slider.height
          && y < sw->slider.ybase + sw->slider.height
          && x > sw->slider.x1-4 && x < sw->slider.x1+4)
             sw->slider.pick = 1;
          return;
       }
       else {
          update_label(w); /* update printout of runner
                             position */
          mark(w); /* erase runner */
          sw->slider.x1 = x;
          mark(w); /* redraw runner */
       }
       break;
    }
}
/* Part of Initialize()*/
{
    SliderWidget sw = (SliderWidget) new;
    /*...*/
    XtAddEventHandler(new,
       ButtonReleaseMask | ButtonPressMask |
       PointerMotionMask,
       False, my_handler, NULL);
}
```

Listing 12.4.   Event Handling from the Keyboard—File slider.c

```
/* Translation Table */

static char defTranslations[] =
   "<Key>a: left_position() \n\
    <Key>z: right_position()";

static void Left_position(), Right_position();

static XtActionsRec action[] = {
   {"left_position", Left_position},
```

```
   {"right_position", Right_position},
   };

/* Action Procedures */
static void Left_position(w)
   Widget w;
{
   SliderWidget sw = (SliderWidget)w;

   sw->slider.value = 0;
   value_to_pixels(sw); /* See Listing 12.7 */
   truncate_value(sw); /* See Listing 12.7 */
   Redisplay(w);
}

static void Right_position(w)
   Widget w;
{
   SliderWidget sw = (SliderWidget)w;

   sw->slider.value = sw->slider.range;
   value_to_pixels(sw); /* See Listing 12.7 */
   truncate_value(sw); /* See Listing 12.7 */
   Redisplay(w);
}
```

Listing 12.5.   Slider Class Record—File slider.c

```
/* The record is the same as for the sketch widget */
/* (Listing 11.6) except for the lines shown here. */
SliderClassRec sliderClassRec = {
/*... see Listing 11.6...*/
/*class_name*/    "Slider",
/*widget_size*/   sizeof(SliderRec),
/*... see Listing 11.6...*/
/*actions*/       action,
/*num_actions*/   2,
/*... see Listing 11.6...*/
/*accept_focus*/  NULL,
/*... see Listing 11.6...*/
/*tm_table*/      defTranslations,
/*... see Listing 11.6...*/
/* Slider class part */
```

```
/*extension*/      NULL
};
```

Listing 12.6.   Resource Definitions—File `slider.c`

```c
#include <X11/Xos.h>
#include <X11/StringDefs.h>
#include <X11/Intrinsic.h>
#include <X11/Xatom.h>
#include <X11/keysym.h>
#include "SliderP.h"
#include <math.h>

static float default_range = 100;
static float default_value = 50;

static XtResource own_resource[] = {

    {XtNforeground, XtCForeground,
    XtRPixel, sizeof(Pixel)
    XtOffsetOf(SliderRec, slider.foreground_pixel),
    XtRString, "black"},

    {XtNscale, XtCScale,
    XtRInt, sizeof(int),
    XtOffsetOf(SliderRec, slider.scale),
    XtRImmediate, (XtPointer) MEDIUM_SLIDER },

    {XtNfont, XtCFont,
    XtRFontStruct, sizeof(XFontStruct *),
    XtOffsetOf(SliderRec, slider.font_used),
    XtRImmediate, (XtPointer) NULL},

    {XtNlabel, XtCLabel,
    XtRString, sizeof(String),
    XtOffsetOf(SliderRec, slider.label),
    XtRString, (XtPointer) NULL},

    {XtNvalue, XtCValue,
    XtRFloat, sizeof(float),
    XtOffsetOf(SliderRec, slider.value),
    XtRFloat, (XtPointer) (&default_value) },
```

```
{XtNrange, XtCRange,
XtRFloat, sizeof(float),
XtOffsetOf(sliderRec, slider.range),
XtRFloat, (XtPointer)(&default_range) },

{XtNformat, XtCFormat,
XtRString, sizeof(String),
XtoffsetOf(SliderRec, slider.format),
XtRString, "%g"},

{XtNuserCallback, XtCUserCallback,
XtRCallback, sizeof(XtCallbackList),
XtOffsetOf(SliderRec, slider.userCallback),
XtRCallback, (XtPointer) NULL},
};
```

Listing 12.7. Assorted Slider Widget Code—File slider.c

```
static GC GetNormalGC(sw)
    SliderWidget sw;
{
    XGCValuesvalues;
    Display *Dpy = XtDisplay(sw);
    static unsigned long valuemask =
        GCBackground | GCForeground | GCGraphicsExposures;

    values.foreground = sw->slider.foreground_pixel;
    values.background = sw->core.background_pixel;
    values.graphics_exposures = False;

    return XCreateGC( Dpy, DefaultRootWindow(Dpy),
        valuemask,&values);
}
/* Convert value to pixel location and vice versa */
static float pixels_to_value(sw)
    SliderWidget sw;
{
    float tmp = sw->slider.scale_ratio*
        (sw->slider.x1-sw->slider.xleft);
    sw->slider.value = tmp > sw->slider.range?
        sw->slider.range: tmp < 0? 0: tmp;
    return sw->slider.value;
}
```

```
static int value_to_pixels(sw)
   SliderWidget sw;
{
   int tmp = sw->slider.xleft +
         sw->slider.value/sw->slider.scale_ratio + 0.5;
   sw->slider.x1 = tmp > sw->slider.xright?
     sw->slider.xright:
         tmp < sw->slider.xleft? sw->slider.xleft: tmp;
   return sw->slider.x1;
}
/* Compute Label length */
static int window_width(sw)
   SliderWidget sw;
{
   return sw->slider.xright + 20 +
     XTextWidth(sw->slider.font_used,
         sw->slider.label, strlen(sw->slider.label));
}
/* Mark Runner */
static void mark(w)
   Widget w;
{
   SliderWidget sw = (SliderWidget)w;

   XSetLineAttributes(XtDisplay(w), sw->slider.gc,
       4, LineSolid, CapButt, JoinMiter);
   XDrawRectangle(XtDisplay(w), XtWindow(w),
       sw->slider.gc,
       sw->slider.x1-4,
       sw->slider.ybase-sw->slider.height-4,
       8, sw->slider.height+8);
   XSetLineAttributes(XtDisplay(w), sw->slider.gc,
       1, LineSolid, CapButt, JoinMiter);

   XDrawLine (XtDisplay(w), XtWindow(w), sw->slider.gc,
       sw->slider.x1-6,
       sw->slider.ybase-sw->slider.height,
       sw->slider.x1+6,
       sw->slider.ybase-sw->slider.height);
   XDrawLine(XtDisplay(w), XtWindow(w), sw->slider.gc,
       sw->slider.x1-6, sw->slider.ybase,
       sw->slider.x1+6, sw->slider.ybase);

   XFillRectangle(XtDisplay(w), XtWindow(w),
     sw->slider.gc,
```

```
        sw->slider.xleft,
        sw->slider.ybase-sw->slider.height+2,
        abs(sw->slider.x1-sw->slider.xleft-6),
        sw->slider.height-3);
}

static void update_label(w)
    Widget w;
{
    SliderWidget sw = (SliderWidget)w;

    /* first erase old label */
    put_text (sw->slider.bf,
        sw->slider.text_dist,
        sw->slider.ybase - sw->slider.text_dist);
    pixels_to_value(sw);
    sprintf(sw->slider.bf, sw->slider.format,
      sw->slider.value);
    put_text (sw->slider.bf,
        sw->slider.text_dist,
        sw->slider.ybase - sw->slider.text_dist);
}
static void truncate_value(sw)
    SliderWidget sw;
{
    sprintf(sw->slider.bf, sw->slider.format,
      sw->slider.value);
    sw->slider.value = atof(sw->slider.bf);
}
```

Listing 12.8.   Other Major Functions—File slider.c

```
static void Initialize(request, new, args, num_args)
    Widget request, new;
    ArgList args;
    Cardinal *num_args;
{
    Display *Dpy = XtDisplay(new);
    SliderWidget sw = (SliderWidget) new;

    sw->slider.gc = GetNormalGC(sw);
    if(sw->slider.scale < SMALL_SLIDER
    || sw->slider.scale > LARGE_SLIDER)
```

```
            sw->slider.scale = MEDIUM_SLIDER;

    /*...code from Listings 12.2 and 12.3...*/
}
static void Destroy(w)
    Widget w;
{
    SliderWidget sw = (SliderWidget)w;
    XtReleaseGC(w, sw->slider.gc);
}
static Boolean SetValues(old, request, new, args,
  num_args)
    Widget old, request, new;
    ArgList args;
    Cardinal *num_args;
{
    SliderWidget oldsw = {SliderWidget)old;
    SliderWidget newsw = (SliderWidget)new;
    SliderWidget requestsw = (SliderWidget)request;
    Boolean redisplay = FALSE;
    Display *Dpy = XtDisplay(new);

    /* Compare old and new values */
#define NE(field) (oldsw->field ! = newsw->field)
    if (NE(slider.foreground_pixel)) {
        redisplay = TRUE;
        XSetForeground(Dpy, newsw->slider.gc,
            newsw->slider.foreground_pixel);
    }
    if(NE(slider.font_used)) {
        redisplay = TRUE;
        XSetFont (Dpy, newsw->slider.gc,
          newsw->slider.font_used->fid);
    }
    if(NE(slider.value)) {
        redisplay = TRUE;
        value_to_pixels(newsw); /* recomputed runner
                                    location */
    }
    if (NE(slider.label)) {
        redisplay = TRUE;
        newsw->core.width = window_width(newsw);
    }
```

```
#undef NE
    return redisplay
}
```

12.3.   COMPOSITE WIDGET

12.3.1.   Definition Files and Class Record Initialization   Listing 12.9
shows the private definition file BBoardP.h of the blackboard widget; differences
from SketchP.h in Listing 11.8 are highlighted. To make things more
interesting, we allow for a variety of resizing policies selected with two new
resource fields, rigid and float_children. To support these policies, we
add two internal fields, old_width and old_height. The resource field
homogeneous controls the class of widgets that the blackboard widget is allowed
to have as children.

Public definitions are the same as in Listing 11.7, with the addition of string
definitions for names of three new resources: XtNrigid, XtNfloatChildren,
and XtNhomogeneous. Definitions of the first resource in the source file of the
widget are

```
{XtNrigid, XtCRigid,
XtRBoolean, sizeof(Boolean),
XtOffsetOf(BBoardRec, bboard.rigid),
XtRImmediate, (XtPointer) TRUE},
```

Listing 12.9.   Widget Structure for BlackBoard Widget—**File BBoardP.h**

```
/* Private Definition File of BBoard Widget */
#ifndef BBOARD_HP_H
#define BBOARD_HP_H

#include <X11/IntrinsicP.h>
#include <X11/CoreP.h>
#include <X11/CompositeP.h>
#include "BBoard.h"

typedef struct {
    /* Resource fields */
    Pixel           foreground_pixel;
    Boolean         rigid;
    Boolean         float_children;
    Boolean         homogeneous;
```

```
    XtCallbackList redrawCallback;
    XtPointer      user_data;
    /* Convenience Function fields */
    GC             private_gc;
    GC             public_gc;
    /* Internal fields */
    Dimension old_width, old_height;/*to be used by resize*/
} BBoardPart;

/* Full Instance Record */
typedef struct _BBoardRec {
    CorePart        core;
    CompositePart  composite;
    BBoardPart      bboard;
} BBoardRec;

typedef struct {
    XtPointer extension;
} BBoardClassPart;

/* Full Class Record */
typedef struct _BBoardClassRec {
    CoreClassPart core_class;
    CompositeClassPart composite_class;
    BBoardClassPart bboard_class;
} BBoardClassRec, *BBoardWidgetClass;

extern BBoardClassRec bboardClassRec;

#endif /* BBOARD_HP_H */
```

The other two are similar (also initialized to TRUE). Listing 12.10 is the initialization of the class part; it mainly lists initializations that differ from those in Listing 11.6. Note: The superclass field now points to the composite class record rather than the core class record.

Listing 12.10.   Initialization of Class Part—File bboard.c

```
static void InsertChild(), DeleteChild();
static XtGeometryResult GeometryManager();

BBoardClassRec bboardClassRec = {
```

```
/* Core class part */
{
   /*superclass*/    (WidgetClass) &compositeClassRec,
   /*class_name*/    "BBoard",
   /*...same as in Listing 11.6...*/
 /* Composite class part */
 {
   /* geometry_manager */ GeometryManager,
   /* change_managed */       NULL,
   /* insert_child */      InsertChild,
   /* delete_child */      DeleteChild,
   /* extension */            NULL,
 },
 /* BBoard class part */
 {
   /*extension*/ NULL
 }
};
```

12.3.2. **Widget Source File**   Initialization of class records requires us to supply three functions that we describe here. Geometry manager is a function called by the widget any time the geometry of one of its children must be changed; a possible implementation is given in Listing 12.11. The first argument in this function is the *child* widget whose geometry is being changed. In this case we insist that children always grant the requested change.

The second function (which is not provided in our example) is called when one of the children becomes managed. This is important for a widget that changes its layout when a child becomes managed, but in our case we decided to have the parent layout independent from the child layout. Thus we are left with the last two functions in Listing 12.12.

The function `InsertChild()` is called by the Intrinsics when a managed widget is created with a parent of the blackboard class, its argument is the child widget. We choose not to accept children that are not widgets, since we do not want to worry about event handling for children that are gadgets. Also if the homogeneous resource field is TRUE, we refuse to accept children that are not of the same class as the parent. (This is certainly too strict a requirement; we can require the child to be only a subclass of the parent class or both parent and child to be subclasses of a third class.) The `bboardWidgetClass` is defined (in the same way as `sketchWidgetClass` in Listing 11.9) as a pointer to the class record `bboardClassRec` in Listing 12.10.

Listing 12.11.   Blackboard Widget Source File (Part)—File bboard.c

```
static XtGeometryResult GeometryManager (w, desired,
  allowed)
    Widget w;
    XtWidgetGeometry *desired, *allowed;
{
    if(desired->request_mode & CWX) x->core.x = desired->x;
    if(desired->request_mode & CWY) w->core.y = desired->y;
    if(desired->requst_mode & CWWidth)
      w->core.width = desired->width;
    if(desired->request_mode & CWHeight)
      w->core.height = desired->height;
    if(desired->request_mode & CWBorderWidth)
          w->core.border_width = desired->border_width;

    return XtGeometryYes;
}
```

Listing 12.12.   BlackBoard Widget Source File (Part)—File bboard.c

```
static void InsertChild(w)
    Widget w;
{
    BBoardWidget sw = (BBoardWidget)XtParent(w);
    if(!XtIsWidget(w)) {
       /* issue warning */
       return;
    }
    if (sw->bboard.homogeneous && XtClass(w) !=
      bboardWidgetClass) {
       /* issue warning */
       return;
    }
    (*((CompositeWidgetClass)
      (bboardWidgetClass->core_class.superclass))->
       composite_class.insert_child)(w);
}
static void DeleteChild(w)
    Widget w;
{
```

```
(*((CompositeWidgetClass)
  (bboardWidgetClass->core_class.superclass))->
    composite_class.delete_child)(w);
}
```

The last statement of the function `InsertChild()` invokes the composite class method for actually inserting the child. It has a complex structure, which we explain by using intermediate variables. The following expression refers to the item in the fifth line in Listing 12.10 (the superclass pointer):

```
(bboardWidgetClass->core_class.superclass)
```

Its value is the address of the composite class records, so we can assign it to a variable by the statement:

```
CompositeWidgetClass f = (CompositeWidgetClass)
  (bboardWidgetClass->core_class.superclass);
```

The casting avoids complaints from the compiler. Substituting `f` into the last statement of `InsertChild()`, we have [after replacing (f) by f]:

```
(*f->composite_class.insert_child)(w);
```

The expression `f->composite_class.insert_child` refers to a member of the class record of the composite class, the method `insert_child`. Since this is a function pointer declared by the equivalent of `void (*insert_child)();`, we must add `(*...)` around the expression before we can call the function. The interpretation of the expression in the `DeleteChild()` is identical to the preceding explanation.

Such cumbersome expressions are due to the lack of inheritance in C language. The implementation of the composite widget has functions that actually insert and delete children, so we wish to call them from a subclass. In a language that supports inheritance (C++ for example), we call the superclass method directly. Here we must perform a new initialization of the class record, then call the original method from within the new function.

12.3.3. Adding Functionality to the Blackboard Widget   When a widget is resized, it is normally redrawn, so there is nothing to do unless we want to rearrange the display. The code in Listing 12.13 shows an implementation of `Resize()` that lets us change the layout of children.

Listing 12.13.   BlackBoard Widget Source File (Part)—File bboard.c

```
static void Resize(w)
    Widget w;
{
    BboardWidget sw = (BBoardWidget)w;
    int nk;
    Widget *kids, *wp;
    float sx, sy;
    register i;
    Position x, y;
    Dimension ww, wh;

    if(!sw->bboard.float_children) return;
    nk = sw->composite.num_children;
    if(nk < 1) return;
    kids = sw->composite.children;

    sx = (float)sw->core.width/sw->bboard.old_width;
    sy = (float)sw->core.height/sw->bboard.old_height;
    sw->bboard.old_width = sw->core.width;
    sw->bboard.old_height = sw->core.height;

    for (i=0, wp=kids; i<nk; i++, wp++) {
        XtVaGetValues(*wp, XtNx, &x, XtNy,&y,
            XtNwidth, &ww, XtNheight, &wh, NULL);
        x *= sx; y *= sy;
        XtVaSetValues(*wp, XtNx, x, XtNy, y, NULL);
        if (XtClass(*wp) == bboardWidgetClass) {
            BBoardWidget stw = (BBoardWidget) (*wp);
            if (!stw->bboard.rigid) {
                ww *=sx; wh *=sy;
                XtVaSetValues(*wp, XtNwidth, ww, XtNheight,
                    wh, NULL);
            }
        }
    }
}
```

If the resource field float_children is false, the widget does not change its appearance after resizing, so the function returns immediately. It does the same if it has no children. (These actions assume that whatever is drawn, is generated by an expose callback.) If the widget has children that are allowed to float, then it computes two scale factors (in the x and y directions) and saves those dimensions to be used to calculate scale factors in the next resizing.

Next the function enters a loop to find the position and dimensions of each child. All children are relocated, so they keep the same relative position as before. If a child is of the blackboard class and its resource field `rigid` is false, then it is also resized to keep the same relative dimensions with respect to its parent window.

We can use the blackboard widget to diplay a tree (for example the widget tree calculated in Sec. 5.13). Each time we display only a node and its children (starting from the root). Each node is a blackboard widget, when we click on a node, say, *A*, we create a pop-up window that displays *A* and its children.

12.3.4.   Resizing and Moving Children to a Composite Widget   In most applications the user can resize and move only the top window; internal windows must be resized indirectly. However there is no fundamental reason why this has to be so. We need to provide only an event handler for the purpose; this can be either in the application or the widget. We describe here geometry transformations required in response to such an event. Let *x* and *y* be coordinates of the point to which we want to move a child widget. If these are with respect to the parent widget, then we can use them directly; if they are not, then these must be transformed accordingly. The function `XtTranslateCoords()` translates coordinates with respect to the root window. By using it twice, we ensure accomplishing the correct transformation. The following code implements the process:

```
Position x_root, y_root, x0_root, y0_root;
/*...*/
XtTranslateCoords(w, x, y, &x_root, &y_root);
/* x_root, y_root are with respect the root window */
XtTranslateCoords(XtParent(w), 0, 0, &x0_root,&y0_root);
/* x0_root, y0_root are coordinates of the parent */
/* origin with respect the root window */
XtVaSetValues(w, XtNx, x_root - x0_root, XtNy,
  y_root - y_root, NULL);
```

There is some advantage in having the event inside the child widget, because we can derive the widget identity from the event structure.

12.4.   CONCLUSIONS

When writing a widget we must be aware of the two types of code involved: The code to interface with Xt structures and the Intrinsics and the code that gives functionality to the widget. In general the former presents a lesser challenge, especially after we write our first widget; most of this code does not change much from widget to widget. The latter is no different than application code.

12.5. PROJECTS

1. Implement the slider widget so that scale and font are selected on the basis of window width and height. Be sure to impose upper and lower limits on both dimensions.
2. Add a resource to control the precision of the return of the slider value, for example integer, integer that is a multiple of 10, decimal number with two digits, etc. Precision should also be reflected in the display.
3. Add entries in the translation table of the slider widget to move the runner exactly on the nearest hashmark.
4. Use the blackboard and sketch widget to create a simple menu panel.

Appendix

Software

A.1. OVERVIEW

The Starter toolkit was originally developed as an education tool to allow graduate and undergraduate students to write graphics or image-processing programs easily without being overwhelmed by X Window System complexity. It has been used for such a purpose since 1993. From the beginning the goal was not to provide a complete toolkit but to support only the most common operations used in graphics and image processing. It was assumed that if students needed to use parts of X not covered by the Starter toolkit, they could access them by writing Xlib or Xt code. The Starter toolkit offers hooks for such extensions, and the name starter was deliberately chosen to emphasize this feature of the toolkit.

The need to support extensions was one reason that we did not use a toolkit such as *Tk*. Another reason for creating one more toolkit was our commitment to the C (or C++) language. In significant parts of our work, the graphics interface was used only during development and debugging, and the final code was stripped of all window-system-related parts.

We eventually found that the Starter toolkit was useful not only for avoiding the complexity of the X Window System but also as a supplement when the major part of a program was in Xlib (as in the spy program in Listing 2.2). However such usage conflicts with the original intention. Initially names were kept as simple as possible, but once mixed with significant amounts of Xlib and Xt code, an identifying prefix was desirable. Another problem was that the original version support selection menus in terms of peer objects of a major toolkit, such as Motif (the particular toolkit was determined at compilation time). When the Starter toolkit was linked to a program that had its own ideas about selection menus, there were problems. This led to a *stripped-down* version of the toolkit with macros that redefine names by adding the prefix St_.

Having two versions of a library (even if one is in essence a subset of the other) does not seem to be a good solution, but another centrifugal force becomes apparent at the same time. As PCs became increasingly popular in both the laboratory and the classroom it was necessary to provide tools to simplify programming in the Microsoft Windows environment. Kevin Hunter, who was the teaching assistant in the undergraduate graphics course, with the help of other students ported a large part of the Starter application toolkit to the *win32* process inferface (API) for Windows '95 and Windows NT. Clearly the PC and X Starter toolkits must differ in how they hook with the main window system; thus the spell was broken, and we had to include functions that were different in each version.

The version of the Starter toolkit included with the code in this book is minimal and of course includes all the hooks for X.

A.2. DATA TYPES USED IN THE STARTER TOOLKIT

St_event

Type defined as

```
typedef struct {
    int x, y;      /* location of the cursor */
    int kind;      /* what kind of event occurred */
    char key;      /* what key was struck on the keyboard, if
                      any */
    long origin; /* where it comes from (widget) */
    long time;     /* time of the event in milliseconds */
} pEvent;
#define St_event pEvent
```

The possible values for kind are declared in the file Starter.h, which can be found in starter/include.

A.3. FUNCTIONS

This section documents Starter toolkit functions used in program examples in this text.

St_arguments(int arc, char **arv)	Pass the arguments of the command line to the Intrinsics. Used when an application uses Starter toolkit functions to create its main window.
int St_back_color (char *cname)	Set the background color to the given name (e.g., red, orange, etc.); returns 0 if the color is successfully set, otherwise it returns −1.
void St_clear_screen (int x, int y, int W, int H)	If any argument is negative, the entire drawing window is erased; otherwise only a rectangle with upper left corner coordinates x, y and dimensions W and H is erased.
void St_collect_text (St_event *p)	Event handler for collecting strings of characters typed on the window; see also St_init_text(), St_set_string_use(), and St_get_string().

**void St_draw_area
(PaperWidget w)**

Copy the display pointer, window, and GC associated with w to the static variables of the module containing Starter toolkit drawing functions such as St_put_line() and St_fore_color().

**void St_draw_window (void
(*f) (), void (*g) (St_event *),
intw, inth, char *s)**

Argument f is a pointer to a drawing function, as in vis_window (); g is the event handler, w and h are the width and height of the window, respectively; and s is the window label.

**void St_fill_rectangle (int x,
int y, int W, int H)**

Display a filled rectangle with upper left corner coordinates x, y and dimensions W and H.

int St_for_color(char*cname)

Set the foreground color to the given name (e.g., red, orange, etc.); returns 0 if the color is successfully set; otherwise it returns -1.

**void St_get_default_args
(Display **dpp, Window *wp,
GC *gcp)**

Return the values of the first three arguments of Xlib functions needed to draw on windows created by the Starter toolkit.

**void St_get_string
(St_event *p)**

Event handler that, in response to a button press, places a prompt at the cursor location and then displays typed text there. It calls St_init_text () and St_collect_text ().

**int St_init_text (int x,
int y, int k).**

Initialize text collection *when the event handler is* collect_text (). Characters typed on the keyboard appear in the application window, starting at the location with coordinates x, y. If k is nonzero pressing the return key terminates text entry. Otherwise the user must press the escape key to terminate text entry; see also set_string_use ().

int St_make_color_cursor (unsigned char iconbits [], int hx, int hy, char *color, char *mask_color)	Create a 16×16 cursor icon using the array `iconbits`. Arguments `hx` and `hy` are coordinates of the cursor hot spot, the point whose coordinates are returned by the event handler. The upper left corner of the icon is 0, 0. The last two arguments must be character strings specifying colors of the cursor and its mask. Function returns an integer used to reference the cursor from the applications program. Function returns a negative index when not enough memory is left to create the structure. The mask is automatically created.
void St_put_line (int x1, int y1, int x2, int y2)	Display a straight line segment joining a pair of points with coordinates `x1`, `y1`, and `x2`, `y2`, respectively.
void St_put_text(char*text, put x, put y).	Display the string `text` so that it starts at `x`, and its baseline is at `y`; it returns the width of the displayed text in pixels. *Warning*: The string should not contain new line characters.
void St_set_foregr (long c)	Set the foreground color to the value `c`.
void St_set_redraw (void (*f) ())	Argument `f` is the name of a function that normally takes no arguments; it should be called whenever it is necessary to redraw a window. *Advanced Use*: In reality, the Intrinsics call `f` with the widget when an expose event occurred as its argument. Applications that deal with multiple windows may find this feature useful.
void St_set_string_use (void (*f) (char *))	Used when the eventg handler is `St_collect_text ()`. After the user terminates text entry, the function `f` is called with the entered text as its argument.
Cursor St_true_cursor (int c)	Return the Cursor XID, given the return of the `St_make_color_cursor ()` function.

void St_use_replace_mode()	Set the drawing mode to replacement. (The old value is replaced by the new.)
void St_use_xor_mode()	Set the drawing mode to exclusive OR. (The value in the refresh memory is formed by the bitwise exclusive OR of the old and the new values.)
void St_vis_window (void (*f)(), int w, int h)	Create a window with width w and height h or default values if arguments are unreasonable. When the window is ready, call f() to create the display contents. The function f() is also called whenever the window must be redrawn in response to display changes; for example if the window is obscured by another, then becomes visible.
void St_xflush()	Flush the graphics instructions to the server. Normally drawing instructions are buffered until there are events in the server queue. Calling this function causes immediate execution.

A.4. RESOURCES AND CONVENIENCE FUNCTION OF PAPER CLASS WIDGETS

Paper class widgets can be created by specifying paperWidgetClass. This class inherits all Core class resources, and it has the following additional resources (in alphabetical order):

- **XtNfont** (type XFontStruct *): Font to be used for text display; default is the default server font.
- **XtNforeground** (type Pixel): Foreground color; default is black.
- **XtNredrawCallback** (type XtCallbackList): Expose event callback; function pointer passed to St_vis_window () or St_draw_window as first argument is *not* this callback. Starter toolkit has an internal callback that does some preliminary work, then calls that function; default is NULL.
- **XtNrigid** (type Boolean): Used internally by the Starter toolkit to establish constraints that do not allow the user to resize the widget window; default is True.

- **XtNuserCallback** (type `XtCallbackList`): Callback in response to keyboard and mouse events. A pointer to a simplified event structure of type `St_event` is passed as *call data*. This is *not* the same as the function passed as second argument to `St_draw_window`. Starter toolkit has an internal callback that calls the function with the pointer as the only argument; default is NULL.
- **XtNuserData** (type `XtPointer`): Place to hang data; default is NULL.
- **XtNvisual** (type `Visual *`): Server visual; a read-only resource to be used with color map and raster image functions.

In addition there are three convenience functions:

- **GC paper_gc (Widget w)** : Return the read/write graphic context.
- **GC pr_paper_gc (Widget w)** : Return the read-only graphic context.
- **XtPointer *paper_hanger (Widget w)** : Return a pointer to the location used to store user data. Note: Before calling any of the drawing functions, the function `St_draw_area()` must be called.

REFERENCES

[AS90]   P. J. Asente and R. R. Swick, *X Window System Toolkit*. Digital
           Press/Butterworth–Heinemann, Newton, MA, 1990.

[JR94]   E. F. Johnson and K. Reichard, *Advanced X Window Applications
           Programming* M&T Books, MIS:Press, Inc., New York, 1994.

[Ki95]   P. E. Kimball, *The X Toolkit Cookbook*, Prentice Hall, Englewood Cliffs,
           NJ, 1995.

[Kr96]   M. J. Kirkland, *OpenGL Programming for the X Window System*.
           Addison-Wesley, Reading, MA, 1996.

[MvR96]   J. D. Murray and W. vanRyper, *Graphics File Formats*, 2d ed. O'Reilly,
           Sebastopol, CA, 1996.

[Ny92]   A. Nye (ed.). *Xlib Reference Manual*, vol. 2, 3d ed. O'Reilly, Sebastopol.
           CA, 1992.

[Ou94]   J. K. Ousterhout, *Tcl and the Tk Toolkit*, Addison-Wesley, Reading, MA,
           1994.

[Pa96]   T. Pavlidis, *Interactive Computer Graphics in X* PWS Publishing,
           Boston, 1996.

[Pi83]   Rob Pike, "Graphics in Overlapping Bitmap Layers", *ACM Transactions
           on Graphics* **2**, No. 2, 135 (April 1983).

[SG92]   R. W. Scheifler and J. Gettys, *X Window System*, 3d ed. Digital Press,
           Burlington, MA, 1992.

Index